INDIVIDUALISED MATHEMATICS

Developed by the School Ma[illegible]ct in association with the Nation[illegible]

REVISION

The right of the University of Cambridge to print and sell all manner of books was granted by Henry VIII in 1534. The University has printed and published continuously since 1584.

CAMBRIDGE UNIVERSITY PRESS

Cambridge
London New York New Rochelle
Melbourne Sydney

Published by the Press Syndicate of the University of Cambridge
The Pitt Building, Trumpington Street, Cambridge CB2 1RP
32 East 57th Street, New York, NY 10022, USA
10 Stamford Road, Oakleigh, Melbourne 3166, Australia

First published 1985

Printed in Great Britain at the University Press, Cambridge

British Library cataloguing in publication data
Individualised mathematics.
Revision
1. Mathematics – 1961–
I. School Mathematics Project II. National
Extension College
510 QA39.2

ISBN 0 521 31850 5

The School Mathematics Project

When the SMP was founded in 1961, its main objective was to devise radically new secondary school mathematics courses to reflect, more adequately than did the traditional syllabuses, the up-to-date nature and usages of mathematics. The first texts produced embodied new courses for O-level and A-level, and SMP GCE examinations were set up, available to schools through any of the GCE examining boards.

Since its beginning the SMP has continued to develop new materials and approaches to the teaching of mathematics. Further series of texts have been produced to meet new needs, and the original books are revised or replaced in the light of changing circumstances and experience in the classroom.

The SMP A-level course is now covered by *Revised Advanced Mathematics Books 1, 2* and *3*. Five shorter texts cover the material of the various sections of the A-level examination SMP Further Mathematics. The SMP Additional Mathematics syllabus has been revised and a new text replaces the original two books at this level.

The six Units of *SMP 7–13*, designed for pupils in that age-range, provide a course which is widely used in primary schools, middle schools and the first two years of secondary schools. A useful preliminary to Unit 1 of *SMP 7–13* is *Pointers*, a booklet for teachers which offers suggestions for mathematical activities with young children.

There is now a range of SMP materials for the eleven to sixteen age-range. The SMP O-level course is covered by *Books 1, 2* and *New Books 3, 4, 5. Books A–G* and *X, Y, Z,* together with the booklets of the *SMP Calculator Series*, also cover the O-level course, while *Books A–H* provide a CSE course for which most CSE boards offer a suitable examination.

SMP 11–16, designed to cater for about the top 85% of the ability range, is the newest SMP secondary school course, providing varied materials which facilitate the provision of a differentiated curriculum to match the varying abilities of pupils. Publication of this course began in 1983 and will be complete in 1988.

Teacher's Guides accompany all these series.

The SMP has produced many other texts, and teachers are encouraged to obtain each year from Cambridge University Press, The Edinburgh Building, Shaftesbury Road, Cambridge CB2 2RU, the full list of SMP publications currently available. In the same way, help and advice may always be sought by teachers from the Executive Director at the SMP Office, Westfield College, Kidderpore Avenue, London NW3 7ST. SMP syllabuses and other information may be obtained from the same address.

The SMP is continually evaluating old work and preparing for new. The effectiveness of the SMP's work depends, as it always has done, on the comments and reactions received from a wide variety of teachers – and also from pupils – using SMP materials. Readers of the texts can, therefore, send their comments to the SMP in the knowledge that they will be valued and carefully studied.

The authors of the original books on whose work this series is based are named in *The School Mathematics Project: The First Ten Years*, published by the Cambridge University Press.

SMP Individualised Mathematics has been produced by a team consisting of

Judy Bonsall	G. Merlane
G. S. Howlett	L. Savins
M. K. Leach	D. R. Skinner
J. L. Lloyd	J. V. Tyson

John Lloyd led the work on the series until his death in 1977, and the final editing has been carried out by Derek Skinner. Many others have helped with advice and criticism, particularly those students who worked through the material in draft form.

Contents

Preface		*page* vii
Introduction		ix
How to use this book		xii
Consolidation 1		1
1.1	Numbers and graphs	1
1.2	Geometry	4
1.3	Matrices	8
1.4	Algebra	11
	Answers	14
Consolidation 2		25
2.1	Number bases and trigonometry	25
2.2	Statistics and probability	28
2.3	Algebraic structure	31
2.4	Equations, orderings and formulas	33
2.5	Transformations	36
	Answers	41
Consolidation 3		56
3.1	Trigonometry and statistics	56
3.2	More transformations	60
3.3	Geometry	64
3.4	Algebra	68
3.5	Using a calculator	71
	Answers	74

Consolidation 4 90
4.1 Plane geometry 90
4.2 Algebra 94
4.3 Three-dimensional geometry 97
4.4 Probability 101
Answers 103

Consolidation 5 117
5.1 Linear programming 117
5.2 Growth and decay 119
5.3 Matrices and topology 122
5.4 Three-dimensional geometry 126
Answers 131

Preface

SMP Individualised Mathematics is based upon the content of *SMP Books 1–5* and *Books A–G, X, Y, Z*, covering the syllabus for the O-level SMP Mathematics.

There are two main distinguishing features of the series. First, the material is presented in a programmed form and the books are thus suitable for use in individualised learning, where self-assessment and clear explanation play a major role. The carefully structured development of each topic makes the books suitable for use by students working alone with minimum tuition, in schools, technical colleges, colleges of further education and on courses organised by the National Extension College.

Secondly, instead of the spiral development of the SMP texts, *SMP Individualised Mathematics* presents the mathematics by topics. Each book, apart from the one devoted to revision, presents the work on a particular theme. Hence the books will prove useful to pupils who have missed work through absence from class, to students coming from abroad, and to pupils transferring to a different school. The style and arrangement of these books should make them very suitable for use by pupils in the sixth form who are working to improve their earlier performance at CSE or O-level. The books will also be useful for revision and consolidation.

Although written with the SMP O-level course in mind, *SMP Individualised Mathematics*, like other SMP texts, can be used to prepare for other O-level examinations based on similar syllabuses.

The titles in this series are as follows:

Computation and Graphs
Probability and Statistics
Algebra 1: Language and Structure
Algebra 2: Equations, Formulas and Graphs
Further Algebra and Computation
Matrix Algebra and Isometric Transformations
Further Matrices and Transformations
Geometry 1: Symmetry and Trigonometry
Geometry 2: Shapes and Similarity
Geometry 3: Three Dimensions
Revision

Introduction

The ten teaching books and *Revision* contain a total of 49 chapters;a possible teaching/learning sequence is listed on pages x, xi . The five chapters of *Revision* are based on this sequence, so that each may be used at the appropriate stage.

For example, Chapter 1 is a revision (or 'consolidation') unit based on the first eleven units (Number to Functions) in the sequence. Thus Chapter 1 of this book fits into place after these eleven units, and hence it is Unit 12 in the sequence.

Chapter 2 of *Revision* (Consolidation 2) is Unit 23 in the sequence, and covers the work of Units 13 to 22; Chapter 3 is Unit 33 covering the work of Units 24 to 32; Chapter 4 is Unit 42 covering the work of Units 34 to 41; and Chapter 5 is Unit 49 covering the work of Units 43 to 48.

A teaching sequence

The list on pages x, xi gives a suggested sequence for studying all the material in the SMP Individualised Mathematics series. The column headed 'source' shows the book in which a particular unit is to be found. The list of codes for the books is given underneath. (The numbering has been chosen purely to follow the order in which the titles are printed in the Preface to each book; there is no other significance in the order.)

I	*Computation and Graphs*
II	*Probability and Statistics*
III	*Algebra 1: Language and Structure*
IV	*Algebra 2: Equations, Formulas and Graphs*
V	*Further Algebra and Computation*
VI	*Matrix Algebra and Isometric Transformations*
VII	*Further Matrices and Transformations*
VIII	*Geometry 1: Symmetry and Trigonometry*
IX	*Geometry 2: Shapes and Similarity*
X	*Geometry 3: Three Dimensions*
XI	*Revision*

Unit	*Title*	*Source*
1	Number	Book I Chapter 1
2	Angles, coordinates and tessellations	Book VIII Chapter 1
3	Extending the number system	Book I Chapter 2
4	Symmetry	Book VIII Chapter 2
5	Graphs	Book I Chapter 3
6	Vectors	Book VIII Chapter 3
7	Information matrices	Book VI Chapter 1
8	Set language	Book III Chapter 1
9	Matrix algebra	Book VI Chapter 2
10	Relations	Book III Chapter 2
11	Functions	Book III Chapter 3
12	Consolidation 1	Book XI Chapter 1
13	Reflection	Book VI Chapter 3
14	Combining sets and combining functions	Book III Chapter 4
15	Number bases	Book I Chapter 4
16	Trigonometry: the sine and cosine functions	Book VIII Chapter 4
17	Rotation	Book VI Chapter 4
18	Mathematical structure	Book III Chapter 5
19	Equations and orderings	Book IV Chapter 1
20	(Elementary) statistics	Book II Chapter 1
21	Formulas	Book IV Chapter 2
22	(Elementary) probability	Book II Chapter 2
23	Consolidation 2	Book XI Chapter 2
24	Trigonometry: the tangent function and Pythagoras' theorem	Book VIII Chapter 5
25	Enlargement and stretching	Book VII Chapter 1
26	Similarity	Book IX Chapter 1
27	Gradients	Book IV Chapter 3
28	Shearing	Book VII Chapter 2
29	Triangles and quadrilaterals	Book IX Chapter 2
30	Further statistics	Book II Chapter 3
31	Quadratic expressions	Book V Chapter 1
32	The calculator and flow diagrams	Book V Chapter 2
33	Consolidation 3	Book XI Chapter 3
34	Polyhedra	Book X Chapter 1
35	Area	Book IX Chapter 3
36	Transformations combined	Book VII Chapter 3
37	Circles	Book IX Chapter 4
38	Further probability	Book II Chapter 4
39	Drawings, plans and elevations	Book X Chapter 2
40	Proportion	Book V Chapter 3
41	Cylinders, cones and spheres	Book X Chapter 3
42	Consolidation 4	Book XI Chapter 4

43	Further work with matrices	Book VII Chapter 4
44	Linear programming	Book IV Chapter 4
45	The Earth as a sphere	Book X Chapter 4
46	Growth and decay	Book V Chapter 4
47	Topology	Book VII Chapter 5
48	Angles and loci in three dimensions	Book X Chapter 5
49	Consolidation 5	Book XI Chapter 5

How to use this book

Each chapter of this book covers approximately ten chapters (units) of the 'teaching' books, and begins with a list showing where these units may be found (book and chapter reference).

The principal aim is to provide a number of questions that test the topics dealt with in these units. As a result, the 'teaching' material is necessarily brief.

Hence each section of a chapter covers two or three units; and after each section heading there is another reference to where these units may be found. This is followed by the 'text' of that section: a summary of the teaching material in each of the relevant units. (These summaries are often very similar to the summaries towards the end of each of the original chapters.) Finally, the main part of each section is an exercise containing questions on this material.

As in the 'teaching' books, the answers to all these exercises are grouped together at the end of the chapter. However, in this book no 'flags' are used. It is suggested that each exercise should be worked through in one sitting, if possible, and then the answers checked. Of course, if this is not possible, or is inconvenient, you can always stop at the end of any question and check your work up to that point!

As explained in the Introduction, if you are working through the complete course, then each chapter should be tackled at the appropriate stage of the course. Otherwise, each chapter – or indeed each section – may be used independently for revision practice whenever required.

Consolidation 1

This chapter covers the first eleven units of the course.
These units are to be found in the following books:
Computation and Graphs (Chapters 1, 2 and 3);
Algebra 1: Language and Structure (Chapters 1, 2 and 3);
Matrix Algebra and Isometric Transformations (Chapters 1 and 2);
Geometry 1: Symmetry and Trigonometry (Chapters 1, 2 and 3).

1.1 Numbers and graphs (Chapters 1, 2 and 3 of *Computation and Graphs*)

Chapter 1

The integers are the numbers . . . $^-3$ $^-2$ $^-1$ 0 1 2 3 4 5 6 . . .
Even numbers are . . . $^-4$ $^-2$ 0 2 4 6 8 . . .
Odd numbers are . . . $^-3$ $^-1$ 1 3 5 7 9 . . .
Prime numbers are 2 3 5 7 11 13 17 . . .
Rectangle numbers are 4 6 8 9 10 12 14 15 . . .
Square numbers are 1 4 9 16 25 36 . . .
Cube numbers are 1 8 27 64 125 . . .
Triangle numbers are 1 3 6 10 15 21 28 . . .
Factors and prime factors.
The order of applying the operations +, −, ×, ÷, square, square root.
Calculations with negative numbers

$4 + {}^-2 = 2$; $4 - {}^-2 = 6$; $4 \times {}^-2 = {}^-8$; ${}^-4 \times {}^-2 = {}^+8$

The meaning and the use of the ordering symbols $<$ and $>$.
Indices and the index laws

$a^m \times a^n = a^{(m+n)}$, $a^0 = 1$,
$a^m \div a^n = a^{(m-n)}$, $a^{-m} = \dfrac{1}{a^m}$,
$(a^m)^n = a^{mn}$.

Scientific notation (standard index form):

$345.67 = 3.4567 \times 10^2$.

Chapter 2

A rational number is the ratio of two integers. Fractions are rational numbers.
Addition, subtraction, multiplication and division of fractions.

Division of a number into a given ratio
(36 in the ratio 2:3:4 is 8, 12, 16).
Addition, subtraction, multiplication and division of decimals.
Percentages
16% of £42.00 = $\frac{16}{100}$ × £42.00 = £6.72,
45 cm as a percentage of 3 m (i.e. 300 cm) = $\frac{45}{300}$ × 100% = 15%,
If 8% of a total mass is 60 g, then the total mass = $\frac{60}{8}$ × 100 g = 750 g.
Accuracy; significant figures; decimal places.
Changing fractions into decimals, and vice-versa.
The use of three-figure tables (logarithms, reciprocals, squares and square roots).
Pythagoras' theorem
(in a right-angled triangle $a^2 + b^2 = h^2$).

Chapter 3

The purpose of a graph.
The axes of a graph should be graduated and labelled. The units should be stated.
The independent variable (often labelled x) is plotted across the page.
A straight-line graph is called a linear graph.
The gradient of a linear graph is constant.
Algebraic graphs illustrate relations of the form

$$y = \text{function}\,(x).$$

Straight-line graphs correspond to equations of the form

$$y = ax + b.$$

Exercise A

(A calculator should not be used in this exercise except in question 20.)

1 List the numbers between 60 and 100 that are
(a) prime (b) squares (c) cubes.

2 Write down the next four triangle numbers after 36.

3 (a) Write down all the (proper) factors of the number 126.
(b) Which of these are prime factors?
(c) Express the number 126 as the product of prime factors.

4 Evaluate the following.
(a) $6 + 3 \times 2$ (b) $6 \times 3 + 2$ (c) $6 \times (3 + 2)$
(d) $6 + (3 \times 2)$ (e) $(6 \times 3) + 2$ (f) $(6 + 3) \times 2$

5 Evaluate the following.
(a) $12 + {}^-4$ (b) $12 - {}^-4$ (c) $12 \times {}^-4$ (d) ${}^-12 + 4$
(e) ${}^-12 + {}^-4$ (f) ${}^-12 - {}^-4$ (g) $12 \div {}^-4$ (h) ${}^-12 \div {}^-4$

6 Evaluate the following.
(a) $3^2 + 4^2$ (b) $(3 + 4)^2$ (c) $(3 \times 5)^2$
(d) $\sqrt{(25 + 144)}$ (e) $\sqrt{25} + \sqrt{144}$ (f) $\sqrt{(4 \times 49)}$

7 Which of the following are true?

(a) $6 > 3$ (b) $6 > {}^{-}3$ (c) ${}^{-}6 > 3$ (d) ${}^{-}6 > {}^{-}3$ (e) $3 < {}^{-}6$ (f) ${}^{-}3 < {}^{-}6$

8 Simplify the following.

(a) $a^5 \times a^7$ (b) $a^5 \times b^7$ (c) b^9/b^3
(d) $(c^4)^3$ (e) $p^5 \times p^{-6}$ (f) x^3/x^{-2}

9 $p = 64$, $q = 256$, $r = 16\,384$.
Express the numbers p, q and r as powers of 2. Hence state a relation between p, q and r.

10 Evaluate the following as fractions.

(a) 2^{-3} (b) $(\frac{2}{3})^{-4}$

11 Express the following numbers in standard form (scientific notation).

(a) 326.7 (b) 0.002 05 (c) 5 000 000 (d) 0.001

12 Write the following as single numbers.

(a) 2.73×10^3 (b) 9.03×10^{-2} (c) 1.732×10^1

13 Evaluate the following, giving the answers in standard form.

(a) $(17.2 \times 10^2) \times (0.04 \times 10^3)$ (b) $(5.6 \times 10^3) \times (4.5 \times 10^{-2})$
(c) $(2.4 \times 10^{-4}) \times (8.5 \times 10^2)$

14 Evaluate the following, giving the answers as single numbers.

(a) $\frac{3}{5} + \frac{1}{8}$ (b) $\frac{1}{4} + \frac{3}{20}$ (c) $3\frac{1}{4} + 9\frac{5}{6}$
(d) $\frac{4}{9} - \frac{1}{6}$ (e) $2\frac{1}{4} - \frac{5}{8}$ (f) $10\frac{1}{6} - 9\frac{5}{8}$
(g) $8 \times \frac{2}{3}$ (h) $9 \times \frac{1}{6}$ (i) $\frac{2}{5} \times 20$ (j) $\frac{1}{12} \times 132$
(k) $\frac{3}{4} \times \frac{5}{6}$ (l) $\frac{2}{5} \times \frac{10}{13}$ (m) $\frac{10}{21} \times \frac{14}{15}$ (n) $3\frac{3}{4} \times 5\frac{1}{3}$
(o) $\frac{3}{4} \div 3$ (p) $\frac{3}{5} \div 4$ (q) $\frac{4}{5} \div 5$ (r) $10 \div \frac{1}{4}$
(s) $6 \div 2\frac{1}{2}$ (t) $\frac{3}{4} \div \frac{5}{6}$ (u) $\frac{2}{5} \div \frac{10}{13}$ (v) $3\frac{3}{4} \div 4\frac{2}{7}$

15 (a) Divide 72 in the ratio 2:3:7.
(b) Divide 100 in the ratio 1:2:3:4.

16 Evaluate the following.

(a) $95.4 + 0.055 + 6.78$ (b) $16.4 - 37.88 + 25.6$ (c) 13.2×0.45
(d) $180.84 \div 13.2$ (e) $0.031\,837 \div 79$

17 Evaluate the following.

(a) 12% of £34.50 (b) 7.5% of 400 m (c) 0.8% of 6000 people

18 (a) Express 28 g as a percentage of 800 g.
(b) Express £740 as a percentage of £500.
(c) Given that 12.6 is 36% of a certain number x, find the value of x.

19 (a) Express the number 12.0498 as a number correct to three decimal places, and as a number correct to three significant figures.
(b) Express $\frac{3}{16}$ as an exact decimal.
(c) Express 0.016 as a fraction in its lowest terms.

20 Use tables or a calculator to find the values of the following (correct to three significant figures where necessary):

(a) the reciprocals of 2.4, 16.8 and 0.005;
(b) the squares of 17, 378 and 0.008;
(c) the square roots of 676, 1000 and 0.900.

21 Illustrate the following information graphically.

(a) Age of tree (years)	5	8	12	15	20	30	40	50
Circumference of trunk (cm)	30	50	75	120	150	200	240	250

(b) Date in July	2	5	9	12	16	19	23	26	30
Maximum temperature (°C)	15	18	19	20	18	17	19	23	24

22 Draw the graphs of the following for values of x from 0 to 6.

(a) $y = 2x - 5$ (b) $x + 2y = 12$ (c) $y = \frac{x^2 + 4}{10}$

1.2 Geometry (Chapters 1, 2 and 3 of *Geometry 1: Symmetry and Trigonometry*)

Chapter 1

Angles are measured in turns, right-angles, degrees and radians.
For a polygon of n sides the sum of the interior angles is $(n - 2) \times 180°$, and the sum of the exterior angles is 360°.
In a regular polygon all the sides are equal and all the angles are equal.
Bearings are measured in degrees, turning clockwise from North.
The cartesian coordinates of a point are its (x, y) coordinates.
The polar coordinates of a point are its (r, θ) coordinates; where r is the distance from the pole, and θ is the angle with the initial line Ox.
Tessellations are patterns made by repeating one or more shapes so that they fill the plane without overlapping or leaving any gaps.

Chapter 2

Symmetry in two and three dimensions involves lines, axes, and planes of symmetry, and ideas of rotational symmetry of order n.
A shape (in two dimensions) has line symmetry if one half reflects into the other half. The mirror-line is the line of symmetry.
A solid (in three dimensions) has a plane of symmetry if one half reflects into the other half. The plane of symmetry is the mirror.
A shape (or a solid) has rotational symmetry of order n about an axis of symmetry if it coincides with itself n times when rotated through one turn.
(For 'true' rotational symmetry, $n > 1$.)
For a shape in two dimensions the axis is perpendicular to the plane of the shape. The centre of symmetry is the point where the axis meets the shape.
A regular polygon with n sides has n lines of symmetry, and rotational symmetry of order n.

Vectors can be used to represent anything that can be written in component form.
Various ways of writing vectors are **a**, **AB**, $\underset{\sim}{AB}$, $\begin{bmatrix} ^-4 \\ 3 \end{bmatrix}$.

Two vectors may (usually) be added, or subtracted, by adding or subtracting their components.

A vector may be multiplied by a scalar (a single number).

(But note that the two statements above do not apply to vectors whose components are different kinds of units: for example, distance and direction.)

Two vectors are geometrically equal (or equivalent) if they represent the same displacement; i.e. have the same components.

If **AB** = **CD** then *AB* is equal to *CD* in length, and *AB* is parallel to *CD*.

Translation: a shape (or solid) is translated if every point of it is displaced by the same vector.

Exercise B

1 Find the sizes of the lettered angles in Figure 1.

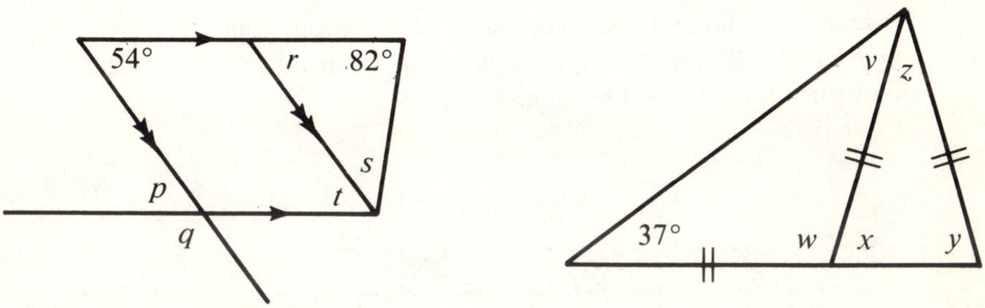

(a) (b) Figure 1

2 (a) Calculate the sum of the interior angles of a polygon with 15 sides.
(b) What is the sum of the external angles of this polygon?
(c) If this polygon is regular, find the size of an interior angle.

3 (a) The sum of the interior angles of a polygon is 1260°. How many sides does it have?
(b) The sum of the exterior angles of a polygon is 360°. How many sides does it have?
(c) The interior angle of a regular polygon is 160°. How many sides does it have?

4 (a) Write down the cartesian coordinates of the lettered points in Figure 2.
(b) Write down the polar coordinates of the points *A*, *B*, *D*, *E*, *G* and *H* in Figure 2. (You may assume that angle *DOE* is 37°.)
(c) Write down the following bearings.
A from *O* *B* from *A* *C* from *D* *D* from *C*
E from *O* *F* from *G* *G* from *O* *H* from *O*.

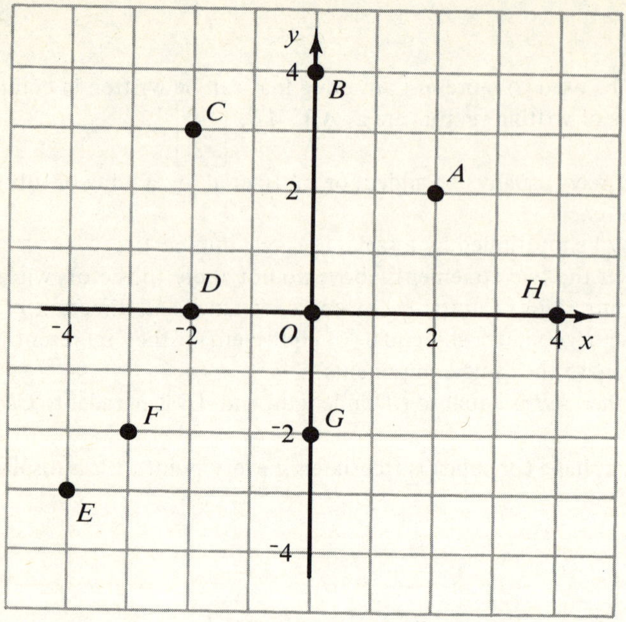

Figure 2

5 (a) Which of the following regular polygons will tessellate?
Triangle, quadrilateral, pentagon, hexagon, octagon, dodecagon

(b) Copy the tessellation started in Figure 3, and continue it on the right by adding about three more Hs and seven more Ts.

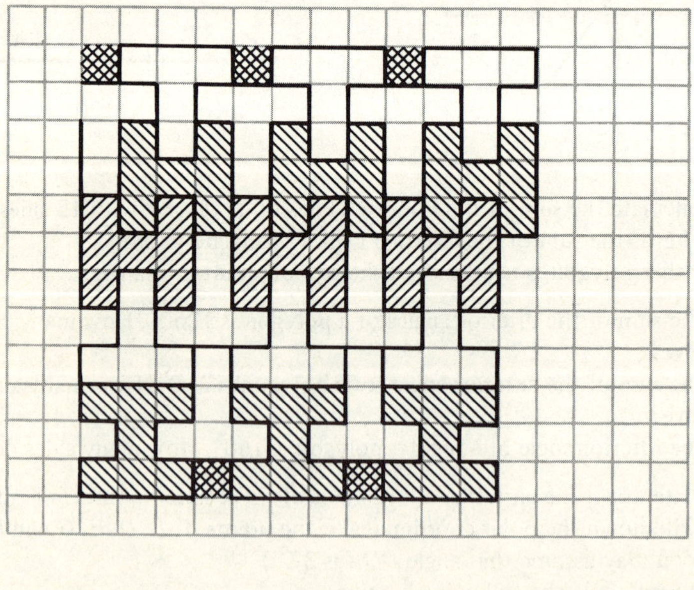

Figure 3

6 Describe the symmetry of the shapes shown in Figure 4.

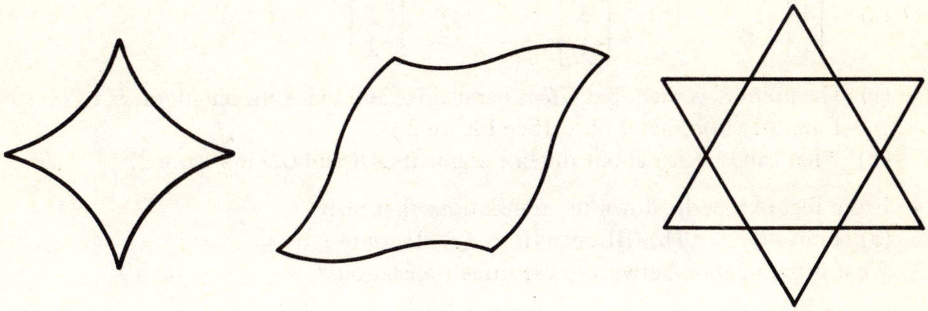

(a) (b) (c) Figure 4

7 (a) Draw a quadrilateral that has one line of symmetry and no rotational symmetry.
(b) Draw a shape that has rotational symmetry of order 4, but no lines of symmetry.

8 Sketch a regular octagon, and mark on your sketch the lines of symmetry and the centre of rotational symmetry. What is the order of rotational symmetry of this octagon?

9 Describe the symmetries of each of the solids shown in Figure 5.

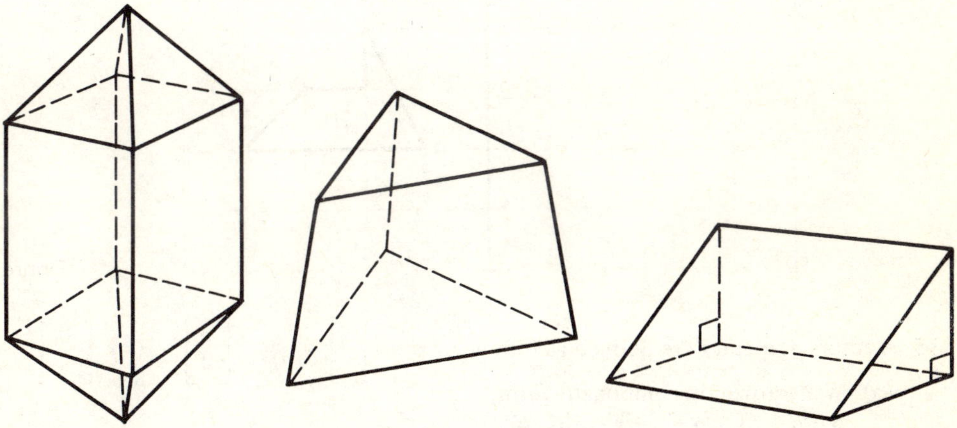

(a) (b) (c) Figure 5

10 (a) An aircraft flies at a speed of 400 km/hour on a bearing of 123°. Find, by scale drawing, how far north and how far east of its starting point it is after one hour.
(b) A second aircraft leaves at the same time, and flies due west at a speed of 200 km/hour. Find, by scale drawing, the distance and bearing of the second aircraft from the first after they have both been flying for one hour.

11 (a) From Figure 2 write down the position vectors (in cartesian component form) for the points A, B, D, F and H.
(b) Write down similarly the displacement vectors for the journeys **AB, CF, DE, GH, HE.**

12 Copy Figure 2 (mark only the points C, D, F and G), join up the quadrilateral $CDFG$, and draw the image of $CDFG$ under the following translations.

(a) $\begin{bmatrix} 4 \\ 1 \end{bmatrix}$ (b) $\begin{bmatrix} 3 \\ -1 \end{bmatrix}$ (c) $\begin{bmatrix} -2 \\ -2 \end{bmatrix}$

13 (a) The point K is such that GK is parallel to, and twice the length of, HA. Find the coordinates of K. (See Figure 2.)

(b) What can you say about the line segments AB and GD in Figure 2?

14 From Figure 6, write down the translations that map

(a) I onto II, (b) III onto II, (c) III onto I.

What is the relation between these three translations?

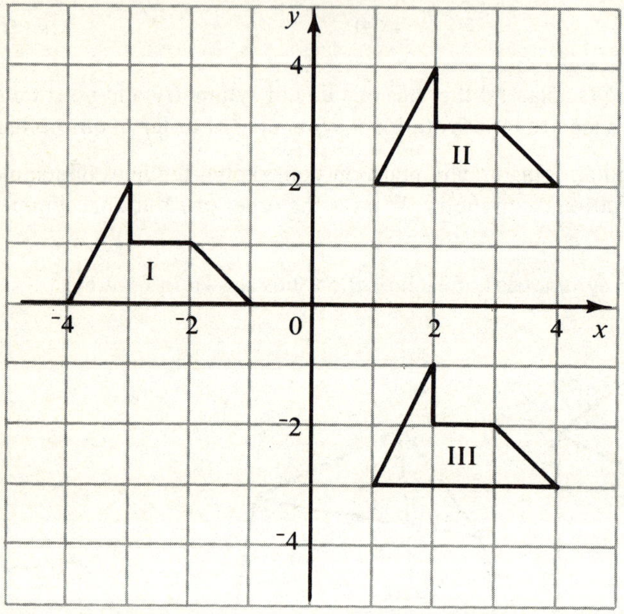

Figure 6

15 Vectors **p**, **q** and **r** are defined as follows: $\mathbf{p} = \begin{bmatrix} 3 \\ 1 \end{bmatrix}$, $\mathbf{q} = \begin{bmatrix} 3 \\ -4 \end{bmatrix}$, $\mathbf{r} = \begin{bmatrix} 0 \\ -5 \end{bmatrix}$.

(a) Write down, in component form,

$\mathbf{p} + \mathbf{q}$, $3\mathbf{r}$, $\mathbf{p} + \mathbf{q} + \mathbf{r}$, $5\mathbf{q} - 4\mathbf{r}$.

(b) What combination of **p**, **q** and **r** will give the zero vector?

1.3 Matrices (Chapters 1 and 2 of *Matrix Algebra and Isometric Transformations*)

Chapter 1

A matrix is a rectangular array of numbers (the elements or members).
Bold capital letters, such as **A**, **M**, etc., are used to denote matrices.
A matrix of order (shape) 3×4 has 3 rows and 4 columns.

A row matrix has only one row; a column matrix has only one column.
A square matrix has the same number of rows and columns.
An information matrix contains numerical information relating the elements of a domain (sometimes listed at the side of the matrix) and the elements of a range (listed along the top of the matrix).
A route matrix shows the number of routes between the towns in a network of roads.
A directed network has one or more 'one-way' roads.
The directed route matrix for such a network is square but not symmetrical.
A 'two-stage route' between two towns passes through just one intermediate town.
Incidence matrices show relations between any two of towns, roads and regions.
The usual incidence matrices are **R** the incidence of towns on roads;
S the incidence of roads on regions;
T the incidence of towns on regions.

Chapter 2

Two matrices are compatible for (i.e. may be combined by) addition and subtraction if they are of the same order.
In addition (or subtraction) of two matrices, the corresponding elements are added (or subtracted).
A matrix may be multiplied by a single number (a scalar). When this is done, every element is multiplied by the scalar.
Two matrices are compatible for matrix multiplication when they follow the 'Domino rule': the number of columns in the first matrix is equal to the number of rows in the second matrix. (For example, a $3 \times m$ matrix may be multiplied by a $n \times 5$ matrix only if $m = n$. The result is a 3×5 matrix whatever the value of m.) (Matrix multiplication is a little complicated, and may need revision!)
Matrix multiplication is associative; but in general it is **not** commutative.

Under addition and subtraction the identity is a zero matrix (all elements zero).
Under multiplication the identity is a unit square matrix: e.g. $\begin{bmatrix} 1 & 0 & 0 & \dots & 0 \\ 0 & 1 & 0 & \dots & 0 \\ \vdots & & & \ddots & \\ 0 & 0 & 0 & \dots & 1 \end{bmatrix}$

The determinant of the 2×2 matrix $\begin{bmatrix} a & b \\ c & d \end{bmatrix}$ is $D = ad - bc$.
If $D = 0$, the matrix is 'singular'.
Provided it is non-singular, the inverse of this matrix is $\begin{bmatrix} \frac{d}{D} & \frac{^-b}{D} \\ \frac{^-c}{D} & \frac{a}{D} \end{bmatrix}$.
The mnemonic 'RC' (row first; column second) is helpful in work with matrices.

Exercise C

1 Express the following information in a 2×4 matrix **N**.
In Book F, Chapter 1 has 22 pages and 22 diagrams; Chapter 2 has 20 pages and 1 diagram; Chapter 3 has 25 pages and 49 diagrams; and Chapter 4 has 23 pages and 39 diagrams.

2 Express the following information in a 2 × 3 matrix **T**.
On Saturday 18 cars, 3 coaches and 9 lorries used a ferry; on Sunday 24 cars, 13 coaches, but no lorries used the ferry.

3 (a) Pre-multiply each of **N** and **T** by the row matrix $\begin{bmatrix} 1 & 1 \end{bmatrix}$.
Which of these answers 'make sense'?

(b) Which of the matrices **N** and **T** can be post-multiplied by the column matrix $\begin{bmatrix} 1 \\ 1 \\ 1 \end{bmatrix}$?
What information is given by the result?

4 Write down the route matrices for the networks shown in Figure 7.

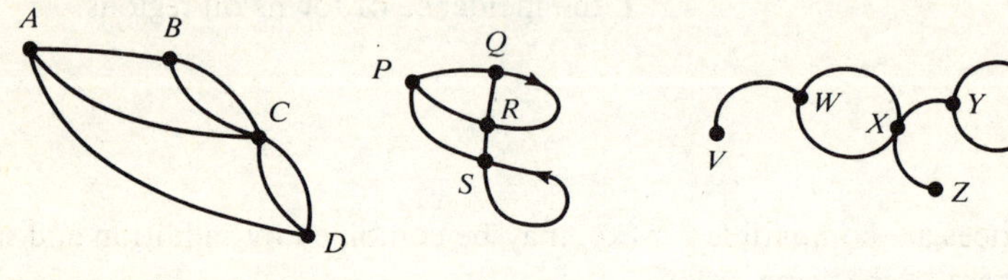

Figure 7

5 Draw networks corresponding to the following matrices.

(a)
$$\text{from}\;\begin{matrix} P \\ Q \\ R \\ S \end{matrix}\overset{\displaystyle\text{to}\atop\displaystyle P\;\;Q\;\;R\;\;S}{\begin{bmatrix} 2 & 0 & 1 & 0 \\ 0 & 0 & 2 & 0 \\ 1 & 2 & 0 & 1 \\ 0 & 0 & 1 & 0 \end{bmatrix}}$$

(b)
$$\text{from}\;\begin{matrix} X \\ Y \\ Z \end{matrix}\overset{\displaystyle\text{to}\atop\displaystyle X\;\;Y\;\;Z}{\begin{bmatrix} 1 & 1 & 1 \\ 0 & 0 & 1 \\ 1 & 0 & 1 \end{bmatrix}}$$

6 Evaluate or construct the two-stage matrices for the networks described in question 5.

7 For the first part of question 6 list or describe all the two-stage routes that start and finish at (a) P; (b) R.

8 In Figure 8, capital letters $(A, B, \ldots)$ denote towns, lower case letters $(p, q, \ldots)$ denote regions, and numbers $(1, 2, \ldots)$ denote roads.
For each network, construct the incidence matrix **T** to show the incidence of towns on regions, and the incidence matrix **V** to show the incidence of regions on roads.

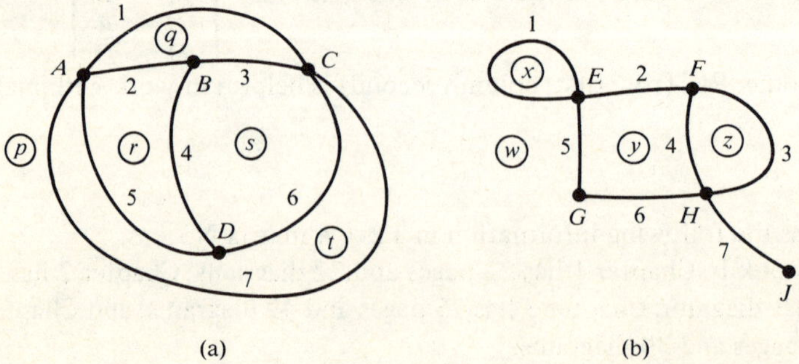

Figure 8

9 For each part of question 8 evaluate the product **TV**.

10 Where possible, evaluate the following.

(a) $\begin{bmatrix} 2 & 1 & ^{-}3 \\ 1 & 2 & 4 \end{bmatrix} + \begin{bmatrix} ^{-}1 & ^{-}2 & 3 \\ 0 & ^{-}4 & ^{-}1 \end{bmatrix}$ (b) $\begin{bmatrix} 5 & 0 & 6 \\ 2 & ^{-}3 & ^{-}4 \end{bmatrix} - \begin{bmatrix} 2 & ^{-}1 & 0 \\ 1 & 0 & ^{-}3 \\ 0 & 4 & ^{-}2 \end{bmatrix}$

(c) $\begin{bmatrix} 5 & 6 \\ 0 & ^{-}3 \\ 3 & 5 \end{bmatrix} + \begin{bmatrix} 1 & 2 & 3 \\ ^{-}7 & ^{-}3 & ^{-}1 \\ 8 & 1 & ^{-}5 \end{bmatrix}$ (d) $\begin{bmatrix} 1 & 6 \\ 0 & 5 \\ 6 & ^{-}3 \end{bmatrix} - \begin{bmatrix} 6 & ^{-}1 \\ ^{-}4 & ^{-}4 \\ 5 & 2 \end{bmatrix}$

11 Evaluate the following.

(a) $3 \times \begin{bmatrix} 2 & ^{-}5 & ^{-}3 \\ 0 & 6 & ^{-}4 \end{bmatrix}$ (b) $^{-}4 \times \begin{bmatrix} ^{-}2 & 5 \\ 2 & ^{-}4 \\ 3 & ^{-}1 \end{bmatrix}$

12 Write down the expressions for, and evaluate, the determinants of the following matrices.

(a) $\begin{bmatrix} 5 & 3 \\ 3 & 2 \end{bmatrix}$ (b) $\begin{bmatrix} 6 & ^{-}4 \\ ^{-}3 & 2 \end{bmatrix}$ (c) $\begin{bmatrix} ^{-}4 & 3 \\ ^{-}5 & 4 \end{bmatrix}$

13 Where possible, find the inverses of the matrices listed in question 12.

1.4 Algebra (Chapters 1, 2 and 3 of *Algebra 1: Language and Structure*)

Chapter 1

The following symbols are used in set notation: ℰ, ∈, ⊂, ⊃, ′, ∉, ⊄, ⊅.
A Venn diagram shows the relation between several sets and a universal set.
A set is a collection of elements (or members) that are all different.
A set is denoted by a capital letter.
Sets may be defined by listing the elements (in any order) or by using a 'set-builder': a description or formula identifying the elements.
If all the elements of set A are also members of set B, then A is a subset of B.
(A proper subset of A contains at least one, but not all, of the elements of A.)
A universal set for a given situation is a set containing **all** the elements that we wish to consider in that particular situation.
The complement of a set contains all the elements of the universal set that are not in the original set.

Chapter 2

A relation is a connection (or mapping) between the members of two sets; or among the members of one set.
A relation can be shown by an arrow diagram or a mapping diagram; by a description giving the object in terms of the image; or by a mathematical statement giving the image in terms of the object.

The object set, or domain, is the set with which we start.
The set with which we end is the image set, or the range.
A mapping connects the members of the domain onto the members of the range.
If the arrows in a mapping diagram are reversed, the inverse relation is obtained.
Relations may be one-to-one; one-to-many; many-to-one; or many-to-many.
In a self-inverse relation the inverse relation is the same as the original.

Chapter 3

A function is a relation in which every member of the domain has a unique image. (In other words a function is either a one-to-one or a many-to-one relation.)
Function notation: $x \to 5x + 2$ or $f: x \to 5x + 2$ or $f(x) = 5x + 2$.
The letters f, g and h are often used to denote functions.
A composite function is built up (or composed) from two simpler functions. Its composition can be shown in a flow diagram.
The inverse of a function 'undoes' the effect of the function.
The inverse of a one-to-one relation is still a function; but the inverse of a many-to-one relation is not a function.
The inverse of the function f is denoted by f^{-1}.
In self-inverse functions the inverse is identical to the original.
$x \to k - x$ and $x \to \frac{k}{x}$ $(x \neq 0)$ are self-inverse functions.

Exercise D

1 List the members of the following sets.
(a) The planets of the Solar System.
(b) Prime numbers between 40 and 60.
(c) The last twelve letters of the alphabet.
(d) Integral values of x such that $2x > 15$ and $3x + 1 < 40$.

2 Describe these sets.
(a) $\{12, 14, 16, 18\}$ (b) {Belfast, Cardiff, Edinburgh, London}
(c) $\{b, f, j, p, v\}$ (d) $\{21, 28, 35, 42, \ldots\}$

3 For the universal set & = {integers from 25 to 36 inclusive}
the sets P, Q and R are defined as follows.
P = {rectangle numbers}, Q = {multiples of 3}, $R = \{27, 28, 29, 30\}$.
(a) List the members of &, P and Q.
(b) Define & in the form $\{x : \ldots\}$.
(c) Deduce the value(s) of x if $x \in P$ and $x \in R$.

4 For the sets listed in question 3 put the appropriate symbol in place of the star (*) in the following.
(a) $29 * P$ but $29 * R$ (b) $P * Q$ and $Q * P$ (c) $P' * Q'$ but $Q' * P'$

5 (a) List all the proper subsets of the set R defined in question 3.
(b) For the universal set & and the set R defined in question 3 list the members of R'.

6 Draw a Venn diagram to illustrate the sets defined in question 3.

7 A mapping is set up between a domain (object set) D and a range (image set) R, where

$$D = \{x : 1 < x < 7, x \text{ an integer}\} \text{ and } R = \{y : 20 < y < 31, y \text{ an integer}\}.$$

Draw mapping (arrow) diagrams to show the following relations.

(a) $x \rightarrow 2x + 20$ (b) $4x + 13 < y$ (c) 'x is a factor of y'

8 Give a verbal description (x is . . .) and the mathematical expression ($x \rightarrow$ . . .) for the following mappings.

(a) x y

$2 \rightarrow {}^-1$
$4 \rightarrow 3$
$6 \rightarrow 7$
$8 \rightarrow 11$

(b) x y

$2 \rightarrow 0.04$
$4 \rightarrow 0.16$
$6 \rightarrow 0.36$
$8 \rightarrow 0.64$

(c) x y

$2 \rightarrow 150$
$4 \rightarrow 75$
$6 \rightarrow 50$
$8 \rightarrow 37.5$

9 For each part of question 8 write down
the image of 10 under the relation;
the type of relation (many-to-one, etc.);
the inverse relation.

10 Which of the following are functions for the given domain?
(a) $x \rightarrow 1 - 3x$ (x is a rational number)
(b) $x \rightarrow 1 - 3x$ (x is an integer)
(c) $x \rightarrow$ country of birth of x (inhabitants of Europe)

11 For which of the relations in question 10 is the inverse of the relation a function?

12 The function f is 'multiply by 2 and subtract 5', and the function g is 'subtract from 4'.
(a) Express f, g and fg in the form $f : x \rightarrow \ldots$.
(b) Evaluate the following: $f(4)$, $g(4)$, $fg(4)$, $gf(4)$.
(c) Express $f^{-1}, g^{-1}, (fg)^{-1}$ and $f^{-1}g^{-1}$ in the form $k : x \rightarrow \ldots$.
(d) Evaluate $f^{-1}(4)$, $g^{-1}(4)$, $(fg)^{-1}(4)$ and $f^{-1}g^{-1}(4)$.

13 For the functions defined in question 12 draw the flow diagram for gf, and use it to find the value of $gf(4)$.

14 Describe in words and express in the form $f^{-1} : x \rightarrow \ldots$ the inverses of the following.
(a) 'multiply by $\frac{1}{2}$'
(b) 'add 3 and then square'
(c) 'square and then add 3'
(d) 'subtract from 100'

Answers

Exercise A

1 (a) 61, 67, 71, 73, 79, 83, 89, 97
(b) 64 ($= 8^2$), 81($= 9^2$) The number 100 should not be included as the question asks for numbers n such that $60 < n < 100$.
(c) 64 ($= 4^3$)

2 The triangle numbers are obtained from the sequence $t_{n+1} = t_n + n + 1$.
36 is the 8th triangle number; hence the next four are
$36 + 9 = 45$, $45 + 10 = 55$, $55 + 11 = 66$, $66 + 12 = 78$.

3 (a) 126 may be factorised as $2 \times 63, 3 \times 42, 6 \times 21, 7 \times 18$, or 9×14.
The proper factors (i.e. excluding 1 and 126) are 2, 3, 6, 7, 9, 14, 18, 21, 42, 63.
(b) The prime factors of 126 are 2, 3, and 7.
(c) The (unique) prime factorisation of 126 is $2 \times 3 \times 3 \times 7$ (or $2 \times 3^2 \times 7$).

4 (a) 12 (b) 20 (c) 30 (d) 12 (e) 20 (f) 18

5 (a) 8 (b) 16 (c) $^-48$ (d) $^-8$ (e) $^-16$ (f) $^-8$ (g) $^-3$ (h) $^+3$

6 (a) $9 + 16 = 25$ (b) $7^2 = 49$ (c) $15^2 = 225$ (or $3^2 \times 5^2 = 9 \times 25 = 225$)
(d) $\sqrt{169} = 13$ (e) $5 + 12 = 17$ (f) $\sqrt{196} = 14$ (or $\sqrt{4} \times \sqrt{49} = 2 \times 7 = 14$)

7 (a) and (b) are true, the remainder are false.

8 (a) a^{12} (b) $a^5 b^7$ (c) b^6
(d) c^{12} (e) p^{-1} (f) x^5

9 (a) $p = 2^6, q = 2^8, r = 2^{14}$; $pq = r$

10 (a) $\frac{1}{2^3} = \frac{1}{8}$ (b) $(\frac{3}{2})^4 = \frac{3^4}{2^4} = \frac{81}{16} = 5\frac{1}{16}$

11 (a) 3.267×10^2 (b) 2.05×10^{-3} (c) 5×10^6 (d) 1×10^{-3}

12 (a) 2730 (b) 0.0903 (c) 17.32

13 (a) 6.88×10^4 (b) 2.52×10^2 (c) 2.04×10^{-1}

14 (a) $\frac{29}{40}$ (b) $\frac{8}{20} = \frac{2}{5}$ (c) $12\frac{13}{12} = 13\frac{1}{12}$ (d) $\frac{5}{18}$
(e) $1\frac{10}{8} - \frac{5}{8} = 1\frac{5}{8}$ (f) $9\frac{28}{24} - 9\frac{15}{24} = \frac{13}{24}$
(g) $\frac{16}{3} = 5\frac{1}{3}$ (h) $\frac{9}{6} = 1\frac{1}{2}$ (i) $\frac{40}{5} = 8$ (j) $\frac{132}{12} = 11$
(k) $\frac{15}{24}$ (l) $\frac{2}{1} \times \frac{2}{13} = \frac{4}{13}$ (m) $\frac{2}{3} \times \frac{2}{3} = \frac{4}{9}$
(n) $\frac{15}{4} \times \frac{16}{3} = \frac{5}{1} \times \frac{4}{1} = 20$ (o) $\frac{3}{4} \times \frac{1}{3} = \frac{1}{4}$ (p) $\frac{3}{5} \times \frac{1}{4} = \frac{3}{20}$
(q) $\frac{4}{5} \times \frac{1}{5} = \frac{4}{25}$ (r) $\frac{10}{1} \times \frac{4}{1} = 40$
(s) $\frac{6}{1} \div \frac{5}{2} = \frac{6}{1} \times \frac{2}{5} = \frac{12}{5} = 2\frac{2}{5}$ (t) $\frac{3}{4} \times \frac{6}{5} = \frac{3}{2} \times \frac{3}{5} = \frac{9}{10}$
(u) $\frac{2}{5} \times \frac{13}{10} = \frac{1}{5} \times \frac{13}{5} = \frac{13}{25}$
(v) $\frac{15}{4} \div \frac{30}{7} = \frac{15}{4} \times \frac{7}{30} = \frac{1}{4} \times \frac{7}{2} = \frac{7}{8}$

15 (a) 12, 18, 42 (A ratio of 2:3:7 gives a total of 12 parts. Hence 1 part is $\frac{72}{12} = 6$.)
(b) 10, 20, 30, 40 ($1 + 2 + 3 + 4 = 10$ parts. Hence 1 part $= \frac{100}{10} = 10$.)

16 (a) 102.235 (b) 4.12 (c) 5.94 (d) 13.7 (e) 0.000 403

17 (a) £4.14 (b) 30 m (c) 48 people

18 (a) 3.5% (b) 148% (c) 1% = 12.6/36 = 0.35; hence $x = 35$

19 (a) 12.050, 12.0 (b) 0.1875 (c) $\frac{16}{1000} = \frac{2}{125}$

20 (a) 0.417, 0.0595, 200 (b) 289, 143 000, 0.000 064
(c) 26, 31.6, 0.949

21 See Figure A.

(a)

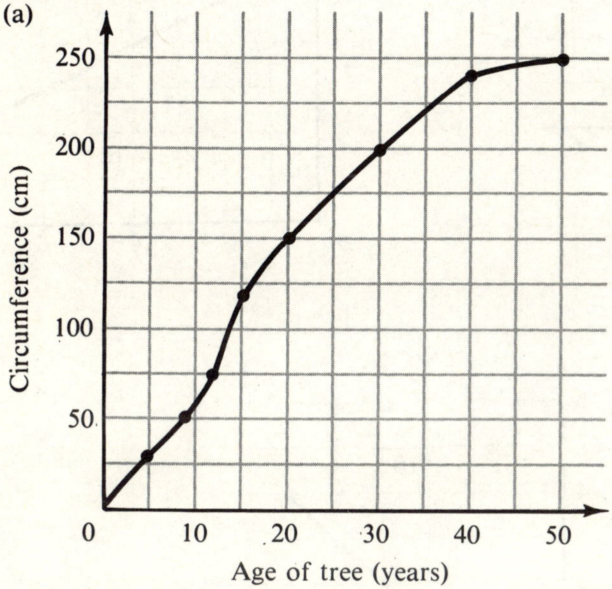

(b)

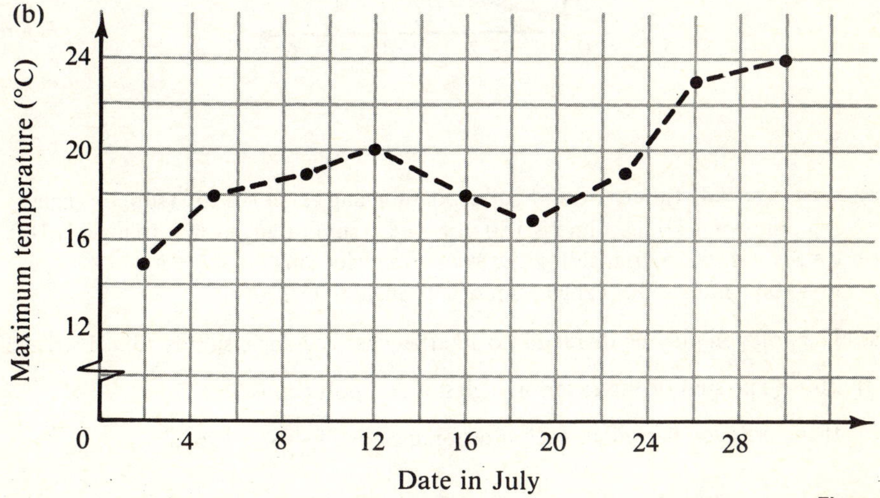

Figure A

22 (a) $y = 2x - 5$

x	0	3	6
y	$^-5$	1	7

(b) $x + 2y = 12$

x	0	3	6
y	6	4.5	3

(c) $y = \dfrac{(x^2 + 4)}{10}$

x	0	2	4	6
y	0.4	0.8	2.0	4.0

See Figure B.

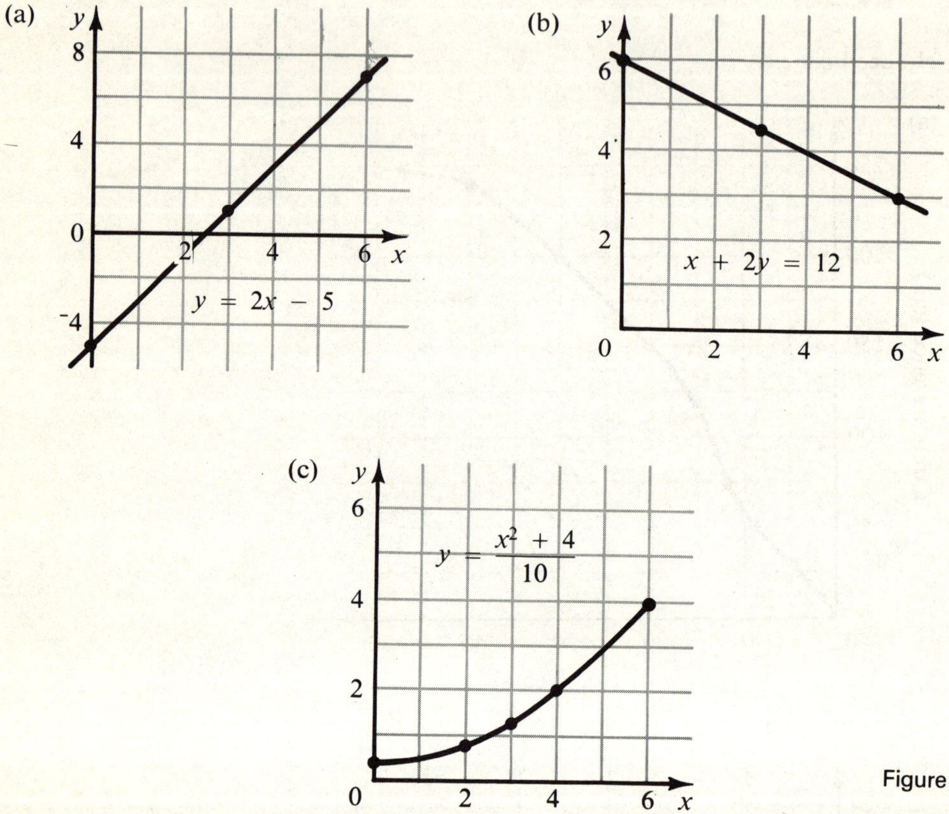

Figure B

Exercise B

1 (a) $p = r = t = 54^\circ$ (alternate and corresponding angles), $q = 126^\circ$ (sum of angles at a point on a straight line is 180°), $s = 44^\circ$ (sum of angles in a triangle is 180°)

(b) $v = 37^\circ$ (isosceles triangle), $y = x = 74^\circ$ (exterior angle $= 37^\circ + v$), $w = 106^\circ$ and $z = 32^\circ$ (angle sum of a triangle is 180°)

2 (a) The polygon may be divided into 13 triangles. The angle sum is $13 \times 180^\circ = 2340^\circ$.

(b) 360° (The sum of the exterior angles of any polygon is 360°.)

(c) If the polygon is regular, each interior angle is $\dfrac{2340^\circ}{15} = 156^\circ$.

(or: each exterior angle $= \dfrac{360^\circ}{15} = 24^\circ$; each interior angle is $180^\circ - 24^\circ = 156^\circ$)

3 (a) The polygon can be divided into 1260/180 (= 7) triangles. Hence the polygon has a total of 9 sides.
(b) Impossible to say, as the sum of the exterior angles of **any** polygon is 360°.
(c) The exterior angle is 20°, and so the number of sides is $360^\circ/20^\circ = 18$.

4 (a) $A(2, 2), B(0, 4), C(^-2, 3), D(^-2, 0), E(^-4, ^-3), F(^-3, ^-2), G(0, ^-2), H(4, 0)$
(b) $A(2\sqrt{2}, 45^\circ), B(4, 90^\circ), D(2, 180^\circ), E(5, 217^\circ), G(2, 270^\circ), H(4, 0^\circ)$
(c) The bearing of A from O is 45°; of B from A is 315°; of C from D is 0°; of D from C is 180°; of E from O is 233°; of F from G is 270°; of G from O is 180°; and of H from O is 090°.

5 (a) All triangles and quadrilaterals will tessellate, and so will regular hexagons.
(b) See Figure C.

Figure C

6 See Figure D.

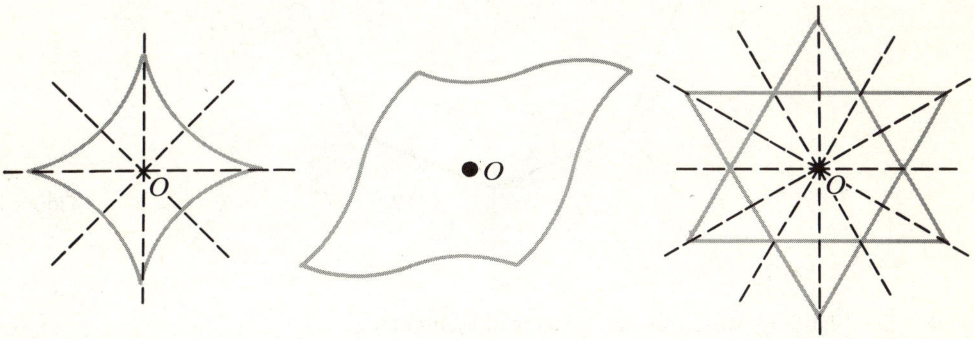

(a) (b) (c) Figure D

(a) has four lines of symmetry, and rotational symmetry of order 4 about the point O;
(b) has rotational symmetry (only) of order 2 about the point O;
(c) has six lines of symmetry and rotational symmetry of order 6 about the point O.

7 See Figure E for some possibilities.
In (a) the quadrilateral must be a kite, an arrowhead, or a 'crossed' quadrilateral.
There are many possibilities for (b).

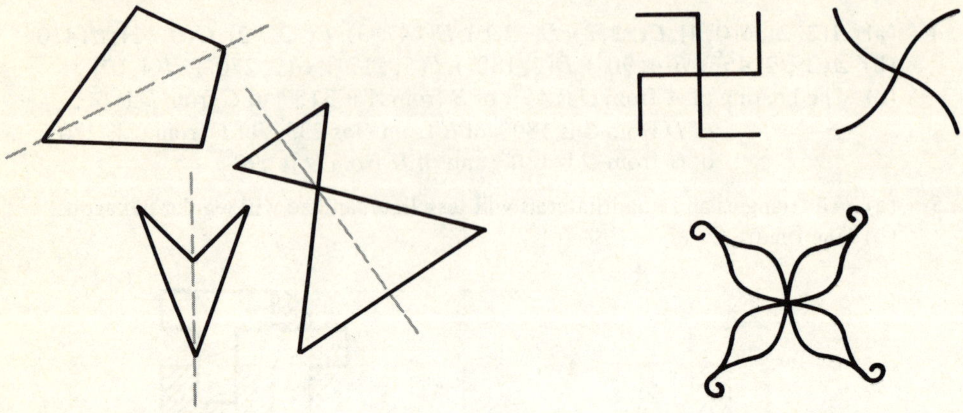

(a) (b) Figure E

8 See Figure F. A regular octagon has rotational symmetry of order 8.

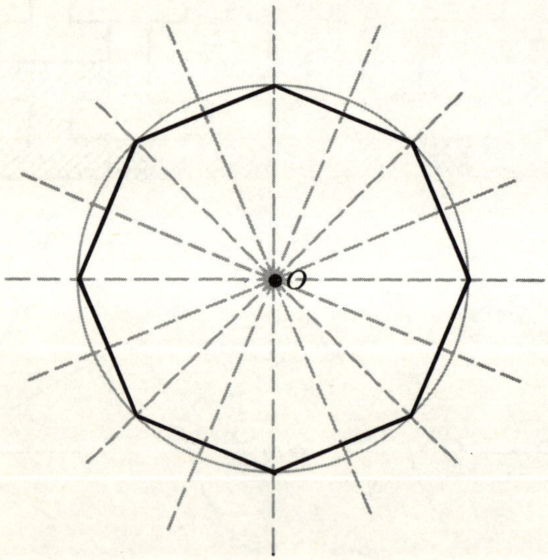

Figure F

9 See Figure G, which shows the axes of symmetry.
Each pair of axes of symmetry defines a plane of symmetry.

(a) There is one vertical axis of symmetry, about which the solid has rotational symmetry of order 4; and four horizontal axes of symmetry, about each of which the solid has rotational symmetry of order 2.
There are four vertical planes, and one horizontal plane, of symmetry.

(b) There is one vertical axis of symmetry (about which the solid has rotational symmetry of order 3); and three vertical planes of symmetry.

(c) There is one vertical plane of symmetry, and one diagonal plane of symmetry. There is one axis of symmetry (of rotational order 2), formed by the intersection of the two planes of symmetry.
(These results are easier to see if the solid is rotated as in Figure G(d).)

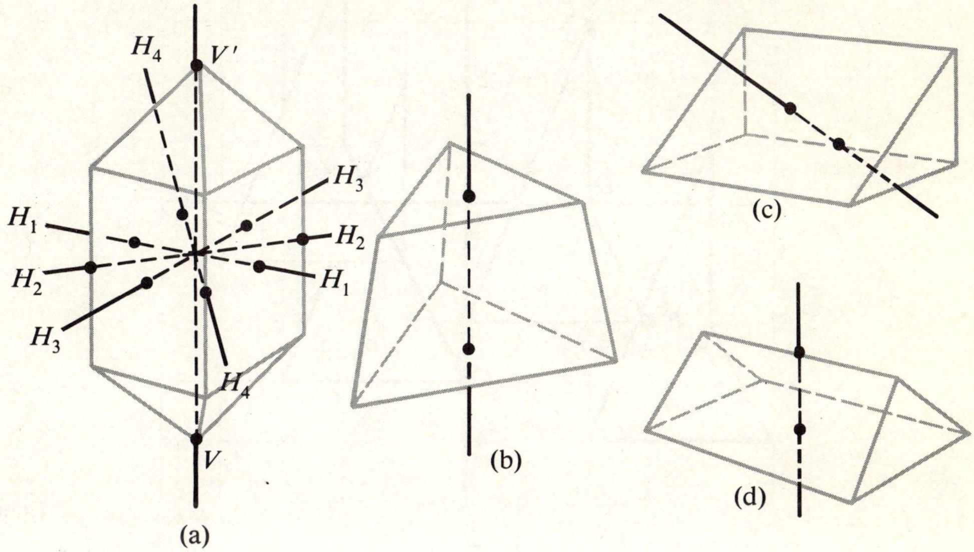

10 See Figure H.

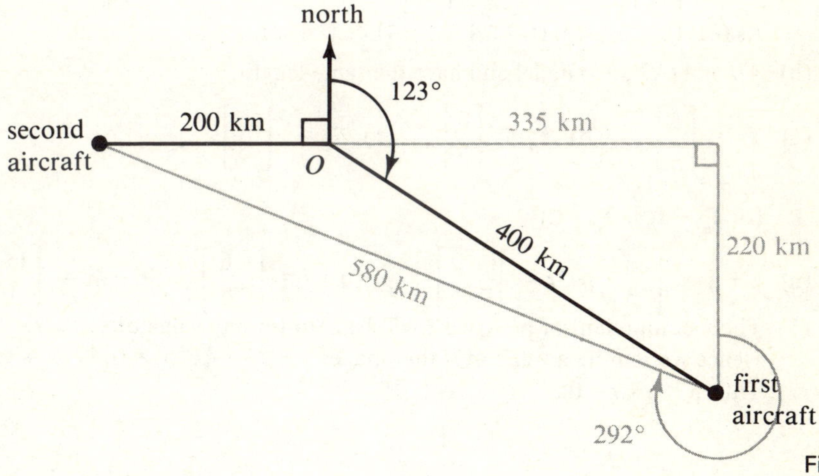

Figure H

The first aircraft is ⁻220 km north (i.e. 220 km south) and 335 km east of O. The second aircraft is 580 km away from the first aircraft on a bearing of 292°. (Distances are correct to the nearest 5 km.)

11 (a) **OA** = $\begin{bmatrix} 2 \\ 2 \end{bmatrix}$ **OB** = $\begin{bmatrix} 0 \\ 4 \end{bmatrix}$ **OD** = $\begin{bmatrix} -2 \\ 0 \end{bmatrix}$ **OF** = $\begin{bmatrix} -3 \\ -2 \end{bmatrix}$ **OH** = $\begin{bmatrix} 4 \\ 0 \end{bmatrix}$

(b) **AB** = $\begin{bmatrix} -2 \\ 2 \end{bmatrix}$ **CF** = $\begin{bmatrix} -1 \\ -5 \end{bmatrix}$ **DE** = $\begin{bmatrix} -2 \\ -3 \end{bmatrix}$ **GH** = $\begin{bmatrix} 4 \\ 2 \end{bmatrix}$ **HE** = $\begin{bmatrix} -8 \\ -3 \end{bmatrix}$

12 See Figure I.

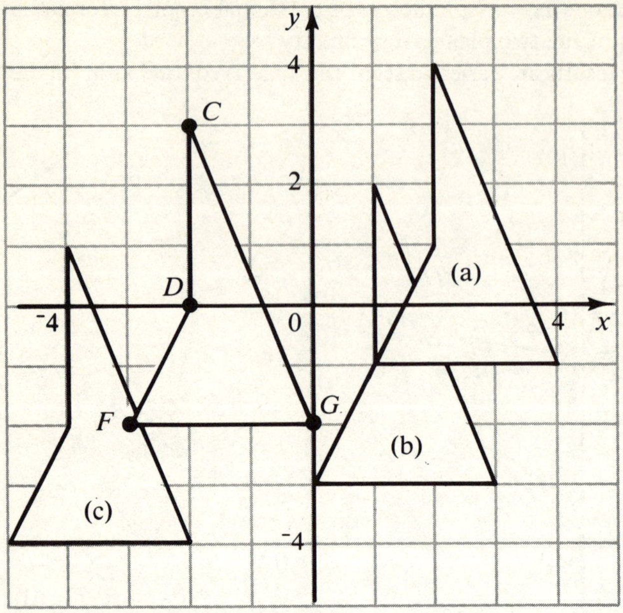

Figure I

13 (a) $\mathbf{HA} = \begin{bmatrix} {}^{-}2 \\ 2 \end{bmatrix}$, hence $\mathbf{GK} = \begin{bmatrix} {}^{-}4 \\ 4 \end{bmatrix}$.

As G is $(0, {}^{-}2)$, K is $(0 + {}^{-}4, {}^{-}2 + 4)$ or $({}^{-}4, 2)$.

(b) AB and GD are parallel and have the same length.

14 (a) $\mathbf{T}_a = \begin{bmatrix} 5 \\ 2 \end{bmatrix}$ (b) $\mathbf{T}_b = \begin{bmatrix} 0 \\ 5 \end{bmatrix}$ (c) $\mathbf{T}_c = \begin{bmatrix} {}^{-}5 \\ 3 \end{bmatrix}$

$\mathbf{T}_c + \mathbf{T}_a = \mathbf{T}_b$

(or $\mathbf{T}_a - \mathbf{T}_b + \mathbf{T}_c = \mathbf{0}$)

15 (a) $\mathbf{p} + \mathbf{q} = \begin{bmatrix} 6 \\ -3 \end{bmatrix}$, $3\mathbf{r} = \begin{bmatrix} 0 \\ -15 \end{bmatrix}$, $\mathbf{p} + \mathbf{q} + \mathbf{r} = \begin{bmatrix} 6 \\ -8 \end{bmatrix}$, $5\mathbf{q} - 4\mathbf{r} = \begin{bmatrix} 15 \\ 0 \end{bmatrix}$

(b) The x-component of $\mathbf{p} - \mathbf{q} + k\mathbf{r}$ will be zero for any value of k.
Hence we require a value of k that makes $1 - {}^{-}4 + k({}^{-}5) = 0$; i.e. $k = 1$.
Thus $\mathbf{p} - \mathbf{q} + \mathbf{r} = \mathbf{0}$.

Exercise C

1

$\mathbf{N} =$

	Chapter 1	Chapter 2	Chapter 3	Chapter 4
pages	22	20	25	23
diagrams	22	1	49	39

2

$\mathbf{T} =$

	cars	coaches	lorries
Saturday	18	3	9
Sunday	24	13	0

3 (a) $[1 \quad 1]\,\mathbf{N} = [44 \quad 21 \quad 74 \quad 62]$ This is not very meaningful.

$[1 \quad 1]\,\mathbf{T} = [42 \quad 16 \quad 9]$

This gives the total number of each type of vehicle using the ferry over the weekend.

(b) **N cannot be multiplied by the column matrix as it is not compatible.** **(N has four columns, whereas the column vector has only three rows.)**

$\mathbf{T}\begin{bmatrix}1\\1\\1\end{bmatrix} = \begin{bmatrix}30\\37\end{bmatrix}$ A total of 30 vehicles used the ferry on Saturday. A total of 37 vehicles used the ferry on Sunday.

4 (a)
$$\begin{array}{c|cccc} & A & B & C & D \\ \hline A & 0 & 1 & 1 & 1 \\ B & 1 & 0 & 2 & 0 \\ C & 1 & 2 & 0 & 2 \\ D & 1 & 0 & 2 & 0 \end{array}$$

(b)
$$\begin{array}{c|cccc} & P & Q & R & S \\ \hline P & 0 & 1 & 1 & 1 \\ Q & 1 & 0 & 2 & 0 \\ R & 1 & 1 & 0 & 1 \\ S & 1 & 0 & 1 & 1 \end{array}$$

(c)
$$\begin{array}{c|ccccc} & V & W & X & Y & Z \\ \hline V & 0 & 1 & 0 & 0 & 0 \\ W & 1 & 0 & 2 & 0 & 0 \\ X & 0 & 2 & 0 & 1 & 1 \\ Y & 0 & 0 & 1 & 2 & 0 \\ Z & 0 & 0 & 1 & 0 & 0 \end{array}$$

5 See Figure J.

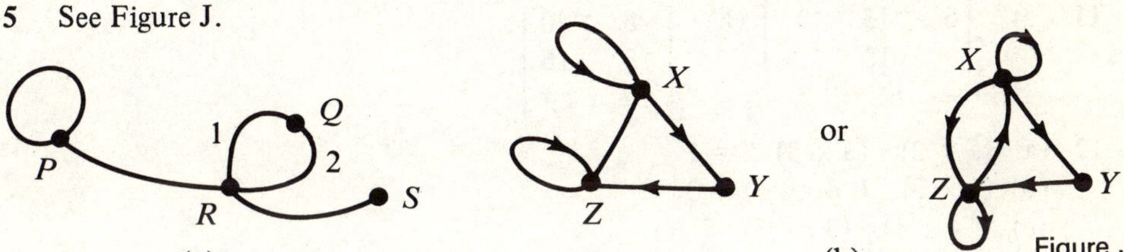

Figure J

6 (a)
$$\begin{array}{c|cccc} & P & Q & R & S \\ \hline P & 5 & 2 & 2 & 1 \\ Q & 2 & 4 & 0 & 2 \\ R & 2 & 0 & 6 & 0 \\ S & 1 & 2 & 0 & 1 \end{array}$$

(b)
$$\begin{array}{c|ccc} & X & Y & Z \\ \hline X & 2 & 1 & 3 \\ Y & 1 & 0 & 1 \\ Z & 2 & 1 & 2 \end{array}$$

7 (a) There are four routes that involve going round the loop twice (clockwise + clockwise, clockwise + anti-clockwise, anti-clockwise + clockwise, anti-clockwise + anti-clockwise) and one other route, P to R to P.

(b) There are four routes R to Q to R (road 1 + road 1, road 1 + road 2, road 2 + road 1, road 2 + road 2) and two other routes, R to P to R, and R to S to R.

8 (a)
$$\mathbf{T} = \begin{array}{c|ccccc} & p & q & r & s & t \\ \hline A & 1 & 1 & 1 & 0 & 1 \\ B & 0 & 1 & 1 & 1 & 0 \\ C & 1 & 1 & 0 & 1 & 1 \\ D & 1 & 0 & 1 & 1 & 1 \end{array} \qquad \mathbf{V} = \begin{array}{c|ccccccc} & 1 & 2 & 3 & 4 & 5 & 6 & 7 \\ \hline p & 1 & 0 & 0 & 0 & 0 & 0 & 1 \\ q & 1 & 1 & 1 & 0 & 0 & 0 & 0 \\ r & 0 & 1 & 0 & 1 & 1 & 0 & 0 \\ s & 0 & 0 & 1 & 1 & 0 & 1 & 0 \\ t & 0 & 0 & 0 & 0 & 1 & 1 & 1 \end{array}$$

(b)
$$\mathbf{T} = \begin{array}{c|cccc} & w & x & y & z \\ \hline E & 2 & 1 & 1 & 0 \\ F & 1 & 0 & 1 & 1 \\ G & 1 & 0 & 1 & 0 \\ H & 2 & 0 & 1 & 1 \\ J & 1 & 0 & 0 & 0 \end{array} \qquad \mathbf{V} = \begin{array}{c|ccccccc} & 1 & 2 & 3 & 4 & 5 & 6 & 7 \\ \hline w & 1 & 1 & 1 & 0 & 1 & 1 & 2 \\ x & 1 & 0 & 0 & 0 & 0 & 0 & 0 \\ y & 0 & 1 & 0 & 1 & 1 & 1 & 0 \\ z & 0 & 0 & 1 & 1 & 0 & 0 & 0 \end{array}$$

9 (a)

$$\mathbf{TV} = \begin{array}{c} \\ A \\ B \\ C \\ D \end{array} \begin{array}{c} \begin{array}{ccccccc} \mathit{1} & \mathit{2} & \mathit{3} & \mathit{4} & \mathit{5} & \mathit{6} & \mathit{7} \end{array} \\ \begin{bmatrix} 2 & 2 & 1 & 1 & 2 & 1 & 2 \\ 1 & 2 & 2 & 2 & 1 & 1 & 0 \\ 2 & 1 & 2 & 1 & 1 & 2 & 2 \\ 1 & 1 & 1 & 2 & 2 & 2 & 2 \end{bmatrix} \end{array}$$

(b)

$$\mathbf{TV} = \begin{array}{c} \\ E \\ F \\ G \\ H \\ J \end{array} \begin{array}{c} \begin{array}{ccccccc} \mathit{1} & \mathit{2} & \mathit{3} & \mathit{4} & \mathit{5} & \mathit{6} & \mathit{7} \end{array} \\ \begin{bmatrix} 3 & 3 & 2 & 1 & 3 & 3 & 4 \\ 1 & 2 & 2 & 2 & 2 & 2 & 2 \\ 1 & 2 & 1 & 1 & 2 & 2 & 2 \\ 2 & 3 & 3 & 2 & 3 & 3 & 4 \\ 1 & 1 & 1 & 0 & 1 & 1 & 2 \end{bmatrix} \end{array}$$

The product **TV** states the number of ways that one can leave a particular town and join a particular road, by crossing just one region.

A '2' usually means that you can join a road from either side. Higher values occur in (b) for towns E and H since for each of these towns there are two ways onto region w.

10 (a) $\begin{bmatrix} 1 & -1 & 0 \\ 1 & -2 & 3 \end{bmatrix}$ (d) $\begin{bmatrix} -5 & 7 \\ 4 & 9 \\ 1 & -5 \end{bmatrix}$

(b) and (c) are not possible as, in each case, the two matrices are not of the same order.

11 (a) $\begin{bmatrix} 6 & -15 & -9 \\ 0 & 18 & -12 \end{bmatrix}$ (b) $\begin{bmatrix} 8 & -20 \\ -8 & 16 \\ -12 & 4 \end{bmatrix}$

12 (a) $(5 \times 2) - (3 \times 3) = 1$
(b) $(6 \times 2) - (-4 \times -3) = 0$
(c) $(-4 \times 4) - (3 \times -5) = -1$

13 (a) $\begin{bmatrix} 2 & -3 \\ -3 & 5 \end{bmatrix}$ (b) not possible, as the determinant is zero. (c) $\frac{1}{-1}\begin{bmatrix} 4 & -3 \\ 5 & -4 \end{bmatrix} = \begin{bmatrix} -4 & 3 \\ -5 & 4 \end{bmatrix}$

(Notice that (c) is self-inverse.)

Exercise D

1 (a) {Mercury, Venus, Earth, Mars, (Asteroids), Jupiter, Saturn, Uranus, Neptune, Pluto}
(b) {41, 43, 47, 53, 59}
(c) {O, P, Q, R, S, T, U, V, W, X, Y, Z}
(d) {8, 9, 10, 11, 12}

2 (a) The even integers (or multiples of 2) between 12 and 18 inclusive.
(or . . . between 11 and 18 . . . or 11 and 19 or 12 and 18 or 12 and 19)
(b) Capitals of the four countries that make up the United Kingdom.
(c) The first consonant after each vowel of the alphabet.
(d) Multiples of 7 greater than 20 (or 19, 18, . . . , 14).
(Or multiples of 7 equal or greater than 21.)

3 (a) $\mathscr{E} = \{25, 26, 27, 28, 29, 30, 31, 32, 33, 34, 35, 36\}$
$P = \{25, 26, 27, 28, 30, 32, 33, 34, 35, 36\}$ $Q = \{27, 30, 33, 36\}$
(b) $\mathscr{E} = \{x : 25 \leqslant x \leqslant 36, x \text{ an integer}\}$ or $\{x : 24 < x < 37, x \text{ an integer}\}$
(c) $x = 27, 28$ or 30

4 (a) $29 \notin P$ but $29 \in R$
(b) $P \supset Q$ and $Q \subset P$
(c) $P' \subset Q'$ but $Q' \not\subset P'$ (or $P' \not\supset Q'$ but $Q' \supset P'$)

5 (a) $\{27, 28, 29\}$, $\{27, 28, 30\}$, $\{27, 29, 30\}$, $\{28, 29, 30\}$, $\{27, 28\}$, $\{27, 29\}$, $\{27, 30\}$, $\{28, 29\}$, $\{28, 30\}$, $\{29, 30\}$, $\{27\}$, $\{28\}$, $\{29\}$, $\{30\}$
(b) $\{25, 26, 31, 32, 33, 34, 35, 36\}$

6 See Figure K.

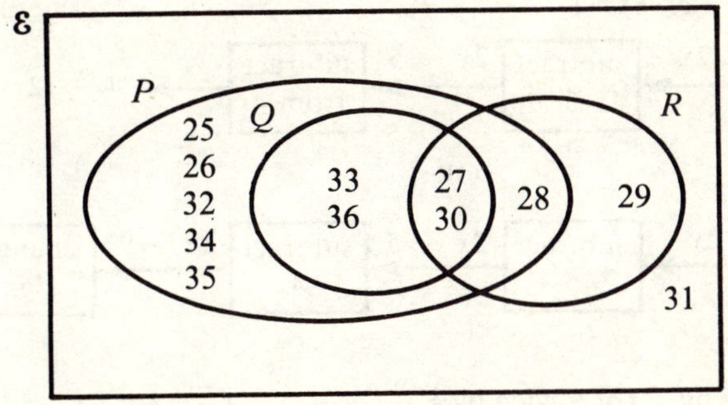

Figure K

7 See Figure L.

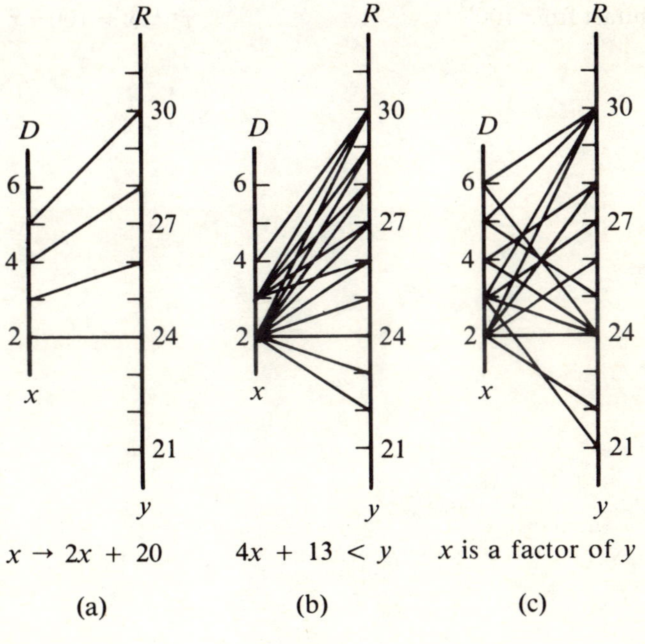

Figure L

8 (a) 'half of $(y + 5)$' $x \to 2x - 5$
(b) 'the square root of $100y$' $x \to x^2/100$ (or $0.01x^2$)
(c) '300 divided by y' $x \to 300/x$

9 (a) The image of 10 is 15; one-to-one; $x \to (x + 5)/2$, i.e. $\frac{x+5}{2}$
(b) The image of 10 is 1; many-to-one; $x \to \pm\sqrt{(100x)}$
(c) The image of 10 is 30; one-to-one; $x \to 300/x$

10 All of these are functions.

11 The inverses of (a) and (b) are functions.

12 (a) $f: x \rightarrow 2x - 5$ $g: x \rightarrow 4 - x$ $fg: x \rightarrow 2(4 - x) - 5 = 3 - 2x$

(b) $f(4) = 3$, $g(4) = 0$, $fg(4) = {}^{-}5$, $gf(4) = 1$

(c) $f^{-1}: x \rightarrow (x + 5)/2$, $g^{-1}: x \rightarrow 4 - x$,

$(fg)^{-1}: x \rightarrow (3 - x)/2$, $f^{-1}g^{-1}: x \rightarrow (9 - x)/2$

(d) 4.5, 0, $^{-}0.5$, 2.5

13 See Figure M. $gf(4) = 1$

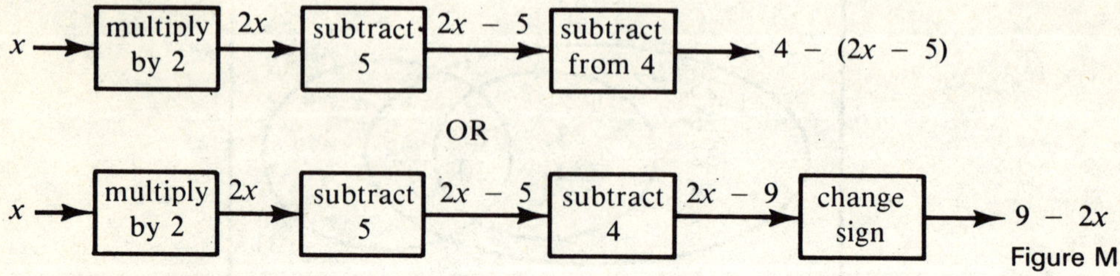

Figure M

14 (a) 'multiply by 2' (or 'divide by $\frac{1}{2}$') $f^{-1}: x \rightarrow 2x$

(b) 'take the square root, and then subtract 3' $f^{-1}: x \rightarrow \pm\sqrt{x} - 3$

(c) 'subtract 3, and then take the square root' $f^{-1}: x \rightarrow \pm\sqrt{(x - 3)}$

(d) 'subtract from 100' $f^{-1}: x \rightarrow 100 - x$

Consolidation 2

This chapter covers Units 13 to 22 of the course.
These units are to be found in the following books:
Computation and Graphs (Chapter 4);
Probability and Statistics (Chapters 1 and 2);
Algebra 1: Language and Structure (Chapters 4 and 5);
Algebra 2: Equations, Formulas and Graphs (Chapters 1 and 2);
Matrix Algebra and Isometric Transformations (Chapters 3 and 4);
Geometry 1: Symmetry and Trigonometry (Chapter 4).

2.1 Number bases and trigonometry (Chapter 4 of *Computation and Graphs* and Chapter 4 of *Geometry 1: Symmetry and Trigonometry*)

Number bases

'Everyday' arithmetic uses decimal or denary arithmetic ('arithmetic base ten') using the ten symbols 0, 1, 2, 3, 4, 5, 6, 7, 8 and 9.
Binary arithmetic (arithmetic base two) uses only the two digits 0 and 1.
Octal arithmetic (base eight) uses the eight digits 0, 1, 2, 3, 4, 5, 6 and 7.
Duo-decimal arithmetic (base twelve) uses twelve digits. Two new digits are needed: *t* (for ten) and *e* (for eleven) are often used.
Hex(adecimal) arithmetic using a base of sixteen is used in computer programming. The numbers ten to fifteen are usually written as A, B, C, D, E, F.
Changing bases: If $(\ldots)_{10}$ is a decimal number and $(\ldots)_{16}$ is a hex number,

$$27C_{16} = (2 \times 256 + 7 \times 16 + 12)_{10} = 636_{10}$$
$$678_{10} = (2 \times 256 + 166)_{10} = (2 \times 256 + 10 \times 16 + 6)_{10} = 2A6_{16}$$

Trigonometry

Trigonometry provides a method of calculating results that might otherwise be obtained by scale drawing.
In a right-angled triangle the sine relation connects the hypotenuse, one side, and the angle opposite that side.
The 'sine picture' is shown in Figure 1.

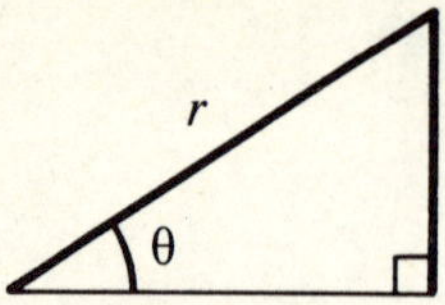

Figure 1

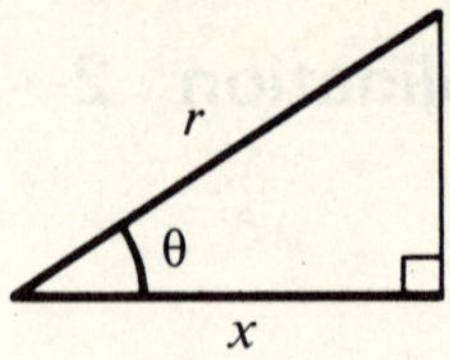

Figure 2

$y = r \sin\theta \quad \sin\theta = y/r$ $\quad\quad$ $x = r\cos\theta \quad \cos\theta = x/r$

The cosine relation connects the hypotenuse, one side, and the angle adjacent (next) to that side.

The 'cosine picture' is shown in Figure 2.

For angles greater than 90°, the graphs of the sine and cosine functions show the connections with the functions of the acute angles.

Sines and cosines are used in problems involving right-angled triangles when the hypotenuse is either given or has to be calculated.

Exercise A

1 (a) Change the following numbers in base eight into denary (base ten) numbers.
15, 27, 77, 100, 123

(b) Change the following hex numbers (base sixteen) into denary numbers. (A = ten, etc.)
39, 4F, C5, FF, 100

2 Change the denary numbers 9, 15, 32, 63 and 100 into
(a) octal numbers, (b) hex numbers.

3 Express the number 121_n as a denary number for $n = 3, 4, 5, 6, 7, 8$ and 9. Does 121_n represent a square number for every value of n?

4 Given that all the numbers in this question are octal (base eight), work out the following, leaving your answers as octal numbers.
(a) $537 + 444$ (b) $537 - 444$ (c) $1000 - 456$ (d) 302×41
(e) $16567 \div 23$

5 Given that all the numbers in this question are duo-decimal (base twelve), work out the following, leaving your answers as duo-decimal numbers.
(a) $30e + 5t9$ (b) $ete - 678$ (c) $100 - te$ (d) $2e5 \times t$
(e) $29t93 \div e$

6 (a) Make an accurate copy of Figure 3, and measure the lengths of PR and QR.
(b) Calculate the lengths of PR and QR correct to three significant figures.

7 An aircraft flies 240 km on a bearing of 080° and then 410 km on a bearing of 148°. Find by scale drawing
(a) how far east, and how far north, it travels on each stage;
(b) the total distance travelled north and east;
(c) how far the aircraft is from its starting point.

8 Find the answers to question 7 by calculation.

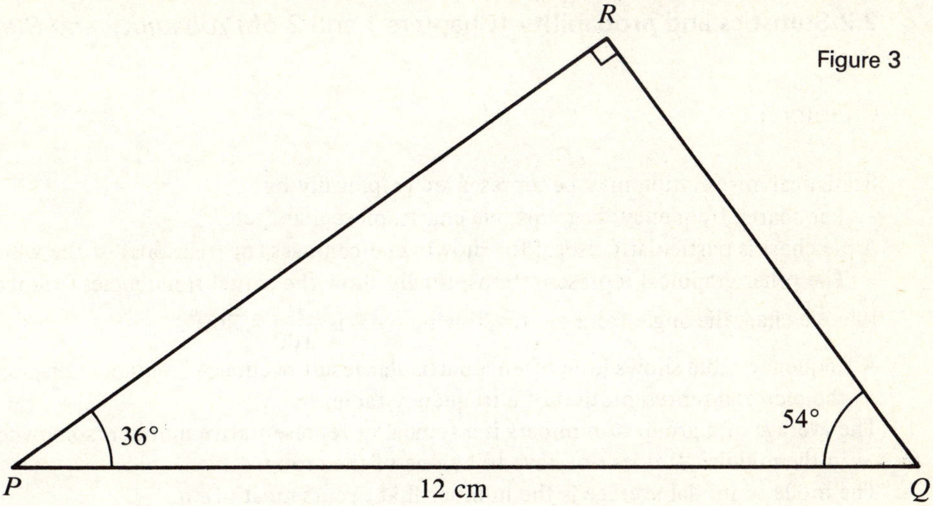

Figure 3

9 Calculate, correct to three significant figures, the value of x for each part of Figure 4.

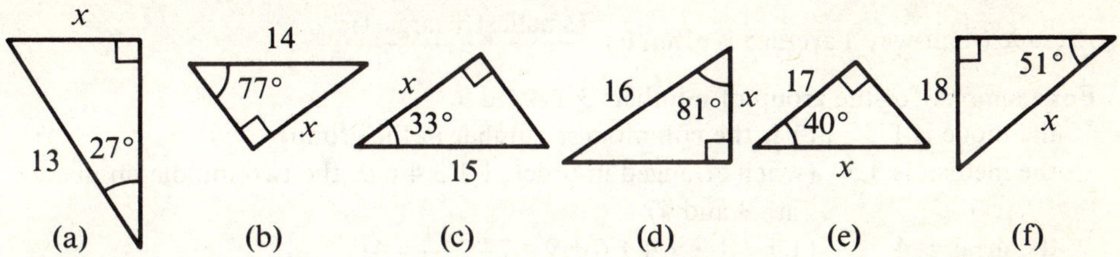

Figure 4

10 Calculate, correct to three significant figures, the value of y for each part of Figure 5.

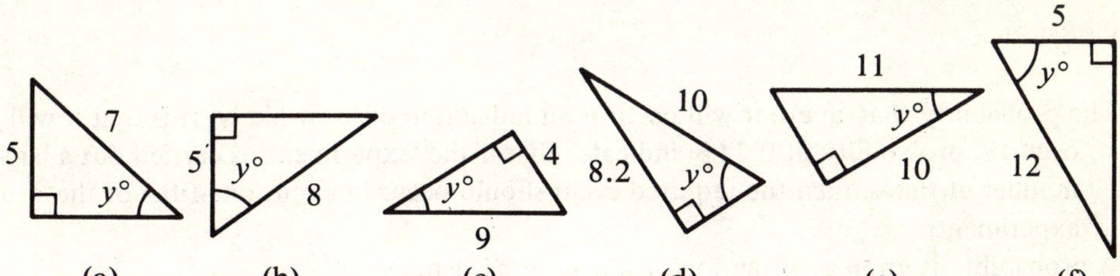

Figure 5

11 Write down the values of the following correct to three significant figures.
(a) $\sin 220°$, $\sin 330°$, $\sin 440°$
(b) $\cos 220°$, $\cos 330°$, $\cos 440°$

12 Find the value or values of x (correct to the nearest whole number) between 200 and 400, for which
(a) $\sin x° = 0.250$; (b) $\sin x° = {}^{-}0.250$; (c) $\cos x° = 0.600$;
(d) $\cos x° = {}^{-}0.600$.

2.2 Statistics and probability (Chapters 1 and 2 of *Probability and Statistics*)

Chapter 1

Statistical information may be represented graphically by bar charts, frequency diagrams, pie charts, pictograms, etc.

A pie chart is particularly useful for showing percentages (or fractions) of the whole. The other graphical representations usually show the actual frequencies (numbers).

In a pie chart the angle for a sector showing $p\%$ is $\dfrac{p}{100} \times 360°$.

A frequency table shows how often a particular result occurs. A frequency diagram is the pictorial representation of a frequency table.

The average of a group of numbers is a typical or representative number 'somewhere in the middle'. It does not have to be one of the group.

The mode or modal average is the number that occurs most often.

The median (average) is the number in the middle (or half-way between the two middle numbers) when the group is arranged in order of size.

The mean (average) is obtained by adding up all the results, and then dividing by the number of results.

A crude ('half-way') average is given by $\dfrac{(\text{smallest} + \text{largest})}{2}$.

For example: for the group of numbers 3 1 4 1 6 9

the mode is 1 (1 is the commonest number in the group)

the median is 3.5 (when arranged in order, 1 1 3 4 6 9, the two middle numbers are 3 and 4)

the mean is 4 $(1 + 1 + 3 + 4 + 6 + 9 = 24; \dfrac{24}{6} = 4)$

the 'half-way' average is $\dfrac{(1+9)}{2} = 5$.

A sensible degree of accuracy should be used in quoting an average.

Chapter 2

The probability that an event will occur is an indication of 'how likely' it is that it will occur. A probability of 0.2 ($\frac{1}{5}$) indicates that if the 'experiment' is carried out a large number of times, then the required event should occur in about one-fifth of the experiments.

A probability is given as a fraction, decimal, or percentage, p.

$p = 0$ represents 'impossible', and $p = 1$ (or 100%) represents 'certain'.

The possibility space of an 'experiment' is the set of all the equally likely possible outcomes. For a 'two-stage' experiment these outcomes can be shown on a possibility-space diagram.

Exercise B

1 Figure 6 shows diagrammatically the answers of a class of children to the question 'How many pets do you have?'
(There were no brothers or sisters in the class.)

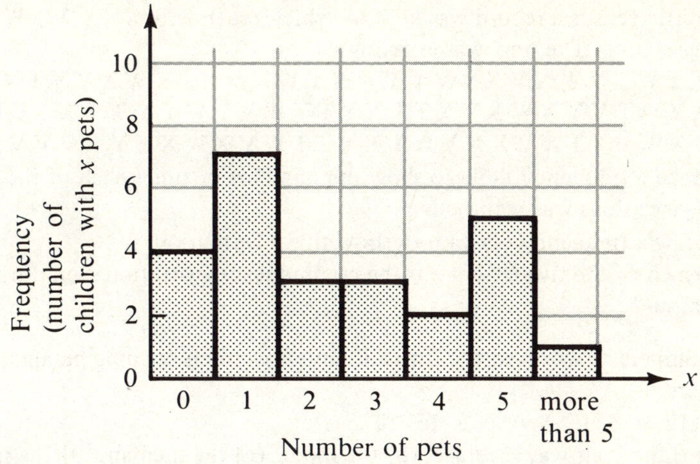

(a) How many children have no pets?
(b) How many children have more than four pets?
(c) How many children are there in the class altogether?
(d) What is the total number of pets that they have between them?
(e) What is the mode, or modal number of pets (i.e. the number given most often in answer to the question)?
(f) What is the median number of pets (i.e. the number of pets of the 'middle' child)?
(g) What is the mean (average) number of pets per child?

2 Illustrate the information below (a) on a bar chart; (b) on a pie chart.
Votes cast at a local election:

Mr C	3440	Dr S	2195
Mrs L	5621	Mr X	1437
Mr M	980		

3 The pie chart in Figure 7 shows the relative production of tin at four mines.

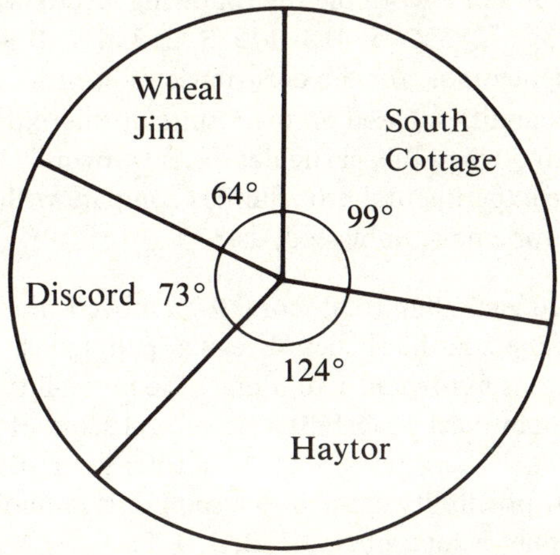

Figure 7

(a) What percentage of the total production was mined at South Cottage mine?
(b) If the total output was 34 650 tonnes calculate the output from Haytor mine.

4 In a traffic census a record was kept of vehicles seen with a 'T', 'V', 'W', 'X' or 'Y' registration. The 'log' was as follows.

W X Y Y W T V W X V X V V Y Y W X Y W X V X T Y W X Y V T V T T W V
X Y X Y W T V Y X W X V X T T X Y T Y W V Y W Y Y W T X T V W X Y W
T X Y X W Y Y T X V X X V W Y X Y T T W V X W X Y Y X V V V X W

(a) Make a frequency table to show the numbers of times each of the five registrations was recorded.
(b) Draw a frequency diagram to show this information.
(c) Which of the five letters was the commonest registration seen during the census?

5 The numbers of words in the thirteen sentences of an opening paragraph of a book are

8 13 12 9 8 15 8 4 8 9 13 18 5 .

Find (a) the 'half-way' average, (b) the mode, (c) the median, (d) the mean.

6 State the median for each of the following groups of numbers.
(a) 2 3 3 6
(b) 2 3 3 6 7
(c) 2 3 3 6 7 10
(d) 2 3 3 6 7 10 13

7 Calculate the mean number of rooms per house from the following frequency table.

Number of rooms (R)	2	3	4	5	6	7	8	9	10
Frequency (number of houses with R rooms)	2	12	17	34	65	58	31	8	5

8 From an ordinary pack of 52 playing cards (with a total of 12 picture cards) a card is chosen at random. State the probabilities (as fractions) that it is
(a) a heart but not a picture card;
(b) a black picture card;
(c) a red queen?

9 In twenty-five throws of a worn die the following results were obtained.

2 6 3 5 4 3 1 2 3 2 5 4 3 1 5 3 2 3 4 6 3 4 1 2 3

(a) Make a frequency table for the occurrence of each score.
(b) State the probabilities, based on the results of this experiment, for each of the scores 1 to 6 when this particular die is thrown.
(c) How do these experimental probabilities compare with the expected probabilities for a new, unbiassed, die?

10 For a certain board game the 'total score' for a move is the sum of the scores on two unbiassed spinners in the shapes of regular pentagons.
(a) If each spinner is numbered 1 to 5 draw the possibility space for the total score.
What is the theoretical probability of: a total score of six;
a total score of more than six?
(b) Draw the new possibility space if one spinner is renumbered 1, 2, 2, 3, 5 and the other spinner is renumbered 1, 2, 3, 3, 5.
What is the theoretical probability now of: a total score of six;
a total score of more than six?

2.3 Algebraic structure (Chapters 4 and 5 of *Algebra 1: Language and Structure*)

Chapter 4

The intersection of two sets A and B is the set of elements that belong to both the sets. It is written $A \cap B$.

The union of two sets A and B is the set of elements that belong to A, or B, or both. It is written $A \cup B$.

Two sets that do not intersect are said to be disjoint.

The empty set is the set that contains no elements. It is denoted by $\emptyset$.

For example: if $A = \{2, 3, 5, 8\}$; $B = \{2, 3, 5, 7\}$; and $C = \{4, 6, 8\}$

then $A \cap B = \{2, 3, 5\}$ (intersection),

$A \cup B = \{2, 3, 5, 7, 8\}$ (union), and

$B \cap C = \emptyset$ (B and C are disjoint).

A Venn diagram may show *either* the actual elements, *or* the **number** of elements, in each region. The context should make it clear what is shown.

$n(A)$ means the number of elements in the set A. In the example above

$n(A) = 4$; $n(A \cap B) = 3$; $n(A \cup B) = 5$; $n(B \cap C) = 0$.

A simple function involves one operation only. A composite function is composed from several simple functions applied in succession.

If the composite function h is formed from f and g by applying f first and g second, then h is written as $h = gf$.

An inverse flow diagram uses the inverse of each operation (box); and applies them in the reverse order.

For example; for $f: x \to 3(x - 4)$

the flow diagram is x → [subtract 4] → [multiply by 3] → $f(x)$;

and the inverse flow diagram is

x → [divide by 3] → [add 4] → $f^{-1}(x)$.

Chapter 5

Elements are the 'things' (bits and pieces, objects) used in mathematics.

Examples of elements are: numbers, sets, matrices, transformations, functions.

A binary operation is a method (rule) for combining two elements.

For example: addition of two integers; multiplication of two matrices; combination of two functions; intersection of two sets; etc.

Operations such as 'square' are unary as they operate on one element only.

A relation (for example, $=, >, \cap$) expresses a connection between two elements.

An operation $*$ on a set S is commutative if

$a * b = b * a$ for all a and b belonging to S.

An operation $*$ on S is associative if

$(a * b) * c = a * (b * c)$ for all a, b and c belonging to S.

The identity element e of a set S under the operation $*$ obeys the law

$a * e = e * a = a$ for all a belonging to S.

(Not all combinations of S and $*$ have an identity.)
For integers under addition the identity is 0 (the zero element).
For integers under multiplication the identity is 1 (the unit element).

The inverse of an element a of a set S is the element b of S which is such that $a * b = b * a = e$ (where e is the identity of S under the operation $*$).
The inverse of a is written as a^{-1}.

A set S is closed under the operation $*$ if $a * b$ belongs to S for all a and b belonging to S.

Multiplication is distributive over addition (on, for example, the set of real numbers) because $a \times (b + c) = a \times b + a \times c$, for all a, b, c belonging to S.

Exercise C

1 For a universal set $\mathscr{E} = \{\text{integers from 10 to 25 inclusive}\}$ the sets P, Q, R and S are defined as follows.
$P = \{\text{prime numbers}\}$, $Q = \{\text{multiples of 3}\}$, $R = \{\text{odd numbers}\}$,
$S = \{\text{multiples of 2}\}$
(a) List the members of P, Q, R and S; and draw a Venn diagram to show these sets.
(Enter the actual members of the sets on your diagram.)
(b) Describe the relation between P and Q and express this relation in set notation.
(c) Describe the relation between P and R and express this relation in set notation.
(d) List the members of the union of Q and R.
(e) List the members of the intersection of Q and S.
(f) What is the relation between R and S?
(g) Describe, and define in set notation, the set $\{25\}$.
(h) State the values of the following.
$n(P), n(Q \cup R), n(R \cap S), n(S \cap Q)$
(i) Draw a Venn diagram showing the *number of elements* in each region.

2 The village of Midian has 60 inhabitants and three organisations: the Women's Institute (WI), the Gardening Association (GA), and the Tennis Club (TC).

A quarter of the inhabitants belong to all three organisations, a quarter to just two organisations, a quarter to one organisation only, and the remainder to none. Two-thirds of the village belong to the GA, one-half to the WI, and one-third to the TC. 27 members of the GA belong to the WI and 18 members of the GA belong to the TC.

Draw a Venn diagram to illustrate this, entering the number of people in each region.

3 Functions f, g and h are defined by $f{:}x \to 2x - 5$, $g{:}x \to \frac{1}{2}x$, $h{:}x \to x^2 + 3$ for all real values of x.
(a) If $f = uv$ (where u and v are two simpler functions) identify u and v.
(b) Describe in words the function h.
(c) Draw flow diagrams to illustrate the composite functions fg and gf.
(d) Find the values of $f(4)$, $g(8)$, $h(3)$, $fg(10)$, $fh(5)$, $hg(4)$ and $fgh(1)$.
(e) Write down the inverses of f and g.

4 Write down (in the form $f^{-1}: x \to \ldots$) the inverses of the following functions.

$$p : x \to 7x + 3, \quad q : x \to 4 - 3x, \quad r : x \to \frac{x+3}{4}, \quad s : x \to \frac{5}{1+9x}$$

5 The operation $x * y$ is defined by $x * y = (x-y)^2$ for all non-negative integers x and y.

(a) Find the values of $2 * 5, 5 * 2, 4 * 4, 1 * 8$ and $7 * 0$.

(b) Find the values of $2 * (3 * 6)$ and $(2 * 3) * 6$.

(c) Is the operation $*$ associative, commutative or closed over non-negative integers?

(d) Does this operation have an identity? If so, what is it?

(e) Do any of the non-negative integers have inverses under this operation?

6 The operation $\sim$ is defined on two sets U and V by $U \sim V = (U \cup V)'$.

(a) Draw Venn diagrams to show $U \sim V, V \sim U, U \sim (V \sim W)$ and $(U \sim V) \sim W$.

(b) What can you say about the operation $\sim$?

(c) Simplify $U \sim$ & and $U \sim \varnothing$.

(d) Is there an identity for this operation?

2.4 Equations, orderings, and formulas (Chapters 1 and 2 of *Algebra 2: Equations, Formulas and Graphs*)

Chapter 1

Many simple equations in one unknown may be solved by using a reversed flow diagram containing the inverse operations.

For example; the flow diagram for $3x - 5 = 16$ is

x ⟶ [multiply by 3] ⟶ [subtract 5] ⟶ 16.

The reversed flow diagram gives

16 ⟶ [add 5] ⟶ [divide by 3] ⟶ $x = 7$.

Alternatively, inverse elements may be used. Rewrite the equation above as

$$3x + {}^{-}5 = 16$$

add $^{+}5$ to both sides $3x + {}^{-}5 + {}^{+}5 = 16 + {}^{+}5$

i.e. $3x = 21$

multiply both sides by $\frac{1}{3}$ $\quad \frac{1}{3}(3x) = \frac{1}{3}(21)$

i.e. $x = 7$.

Inequalities may also be solved by using inverse elements, but remember that, if both sides are multiplied by a negative number, the direction of the inequality is changed. For example, if $^{-}3x < 18$

then $^{-}\frac{1}{3}(^{-}3x) > (^{-}\frac{1}{3})(18)$

i.e. $x > {}^{-}6$.

The solution set of simultaneous one-dimensional inequalities is the intersection of the two separate solution sets.

For example, if $2x - 1 < 3x + 5 < 19 - 4x$

then $2x - 1 < 3x + 5$ and $3x + 5 < 19 - 4x$

i.e. $^{-}6 < x$ and $7x < 14$ (or $x < 2$).

The intersection of these separate solutions is $^{-}6 < x < 2$.

(The solution set may be illustrated on a number line.)

An equation in two unknowns is shown graphically by a curved or straight line.

An inequality in two unknowns is a region of the graph paper whose boundary is the line obtained by changing the inequality into an equation.

Simultaneous equations in two unknowns may be solved:

graphically; algebraically; or by the use of matrices.

Algebraic methods involve substitution and/or elimination.

Simultaneous inequalities in two unknowns should be solved graphically.

(It is usually better to shade out the unwanted regions.
The solution set is then the area left unshaded.)

Chapter 2

A formula is a relation connecting two or more variable quantities.

The formula $V = \pi r^2 h$ connects the volume of a cylinder (V) with its radius (r) and its height (h).

Formulas are used to calculate the value of one of the variables when the values of the other variables are known.

To do this it is sometimes easier to 'change the subject' of the formula.

As it stands, the subject of the formula above is V.

To find a value for h the formula may be rearranged as

$$h = \frac{V}{\pi r^2}.$$

The subject of the formula is now h.

Exercise D

1 Write down the equations represented by the flow diagrams shown in Figure 8.

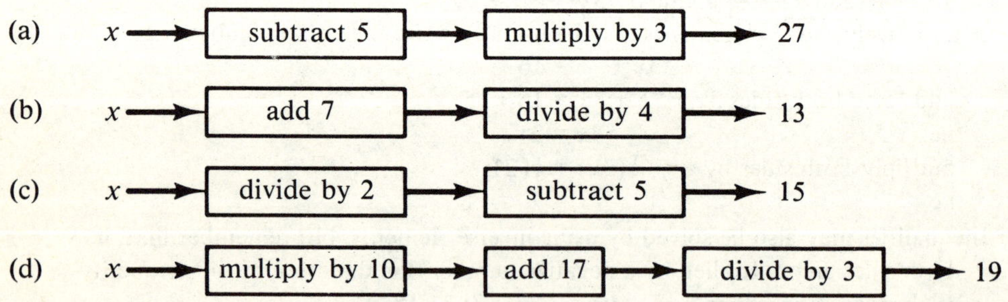

Figure 8

2 Construct flow diagrams corresponding to the following equations.

(a) $5(x - 2) = 35$ (b) $\dfrac{2x + 7}{5} = 12$

(c) $\frac{3}{4}(x - 9) = 15$ (d) $4(3x - 11) = 100$

3 Reverse the flow diagrams in question 1, and hence solve the equations they represent.

4 Use reversed flow diagrams to solve the equations listed in question 2.

5 Use reversed flow diagrams to solve the following equations.

(a) $\dfrac{5}{x+3} = 1$ (b) $3(4-x) = 36$

(c) $26 - 3x = 5$ (d) $\dfrac{24}{5-7x} = 16$

6 Solve the equations in question 2 by using inverse elements.

7 Solve the following inequalities.

(a) $2x - 5 > 7$ (b) $6 + 5x < 41$ (c) $\dfrac{2+3x}{4} \geqslant 14$

(d) $1 - 4x \leqslant 25$ (e) $2 + 3x < 34 - 5x$ (f) $6 - x \geqslant \frac{1}{2}x$

8 Where possible, solve the following, illustrating the solutions on number lines.

(a) $3x - 2 < 10 < x + 9$ (b) $5 + 2x > 13 > 4 - x$

(c) $x + 12 < 0 > 3 - x$ (d) $5 - 2x > {}^{-}11 < 4x - 3$

9 Solve the following pairs of simultaneous equations graphically.

(a) $2x + y = 10$
$3y = x + 9$

(b) $3x - y = 5$
$x + y = 4$

10 Solve the two pairs of simultaneous equations in question 9 by algebraic methods.

11 Write down the pair of simultaneous inequalities for which Figure 9 is the graphical solution.

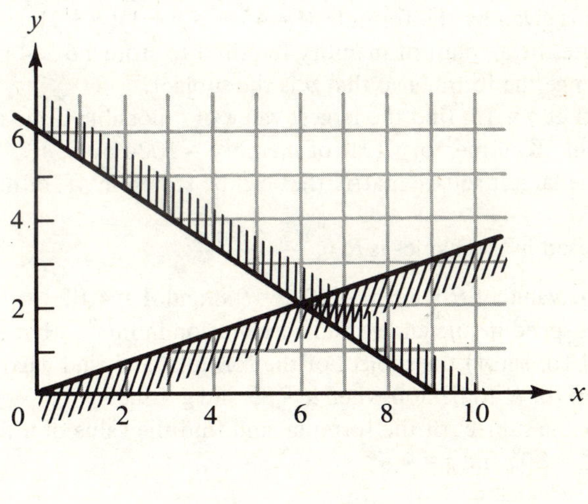

Figure 9

12 The approximate capacity (V ml) of a cylindrical tin, whose diameter and height are measured in centimetres, is found by squaring the diameter and then multiplying by three-quarters of the height.

(a) Write down the formula for the approximate capacity of a tin of height h cm whose base is a circle of diameter d cm.

(b) Calculate the capacity of a tin 14 cm high that has a base of diameter 8 cm.

(c) Re-arrange the formula to make h the subject.

(d) A tin whose base has a diameter of 10 cm is required to have a capacity of 600 ml. How high should the tin be?

13 Write down the five simultaneous inequalities for which Figure 10 is the graphical solution.

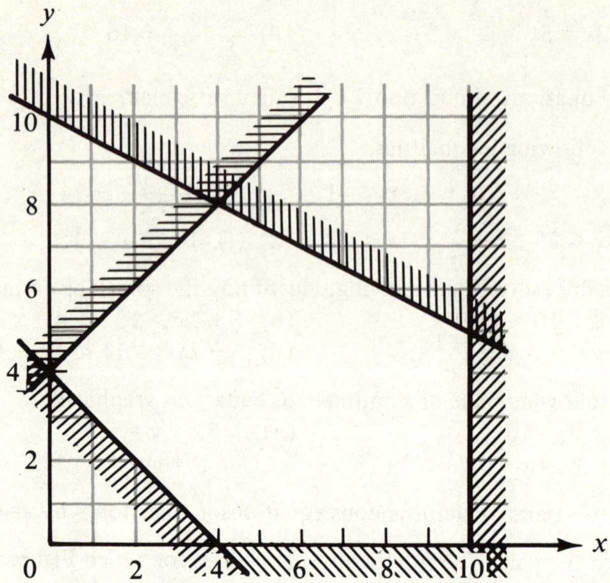

Figure 10

14 The minimum memory (M bytes) required by a computer to store a matrix of order $p \times q$ is given by the formula $M = 45 + 2(p + 1)(q + 1)$.

(a) Calculate the amount of memory required to store a 6×4 matrix.

(b) Re-arrange the formula so that p is the subject.

(c) Given that $q = 12$, find the largest value of p possible if the matrix is to be stored in 2K of memory. (1K of memory = 1024 bytes.)

(d) Find the largest square matrix that can be stored in 4K of memory.

15 A formula used in mechanics is $R = \dfrac{u^2 \times \sin A}{g}$.

(a) Find the value of R when $u = 70, g = 9.8$ and $A = 40°$.
If u is a speed in m/s and g is an acceleration in m/s^2, what are the units of R?

(b) Make A (or $\sin A$) the subject of the formula, and find what value of A is required for R to be 500 when $u = 85$ and $g = 9.8$.

(c) Make u the subject of the formula, and find the value of u for R to be 1200 when $A = 80°$ and $g = 9.8$.

2.5 Transformations (Chapters 3 and 4 of *Matrix Algebra and Isometric Transformations*)

Chapter 3

In transformation geometries, every point of a plane (or of space) is mapped onto another point under the rules defining a particular geometry.

The original point or shape is called the object, and the final (or transformed) position is called the image.

A point (line, etc.) whose position is not changed under a transformation is said to be invariant.

Properties of shapes (for example, area, parallelism) may also be invariant.

Reflection is one type of transformation. To define a reflection we need to know a mirror line (or line of symmetry) m.

The image of a point P is then the reflection of P in m. It is labelled P'.

(i.e. P' is the point such that m is the mediator of PP'.)

In mathematical reflections, all mirrors are two-sided!

A reflection in a mirror line that passes through the origin may be represented by a 2×2 matrix **M**. If a matrix **X** gives the position vectors of the points of an object, then the position vectors of the images of these points is given by the matrix product **MX**.

Some simple reflection matrices are as follows:

mirror	x-axis ($y = 0$)	y-axis ($x = 0$)	$y = x$	$x + y = 0$
image of (x, y)	$(x, {}^-y)$	$({}^-x, y)$	(y, x)	$({}^-y, {}^-x)$
matrix	$\begin{bmatrix} 1 & 0 \\ 0 & {}^-1 \end{bmatrix}$	$\begin{bmatrix} {}^-1 & 0 \\ 0 & 1 \end{bmatrix}$	$\begin{bmatrix} 0 & 1 \\ 1 & 0 \end{bmatrix}$	$\begin{bmatrix} 0 & {}^-1 \\ {}^-1 & 0 \end{bmatrix}$

Under reflection, size and shape (and hence lengths, angles and areas) are invariant.

Sense is reversed (i.e. clockwise to anti-clockwise).

All points on the mirror line are invariant.

All lines at right-angles to the mirror line are invariant (although individual points on these lines are not invariant).

Reflection is a self-inverse operation/transformation.

Chapter 4

Rotation is a transformation under which a shape (or object) is rotated about a point (or axis) through an angle θ (usually measured anti-clockwise).

For a rotation in the plane (i.e. in two dimensions) the point is called the centre of rotation.

A rotation is defined by its centre, and the angle of rotation.

Every line in an object is rotated through the same angle under a rotation.

Shape, size and sense are invariant under rotation.

The centre of rotation is equidistant from any point and its image.

Hence all the mediators of the lines joining points to their respective images are concurrent at (i.e. go through) the centre of rotation.

The inverse of a rotation of θ about a centre C is another rotation, a rotation of ${}^-\theta$ about the same centre C.

A rotation whose centre is at the origin may be represented by a 2×2 matrix.

Some simple rotation matrices are as follows:

angle of rotation	$90°$	$180°$	$270°$
image of (x, y)	$({}^-y, x)$	$({}^-x, {}^-y)$	$(y, {}^-x)$
matrix	$\begin{bmatrix} 0 & {}^-1 \\ 1 & 0 \end{bmatrix}$	$\begin{bmatrix} {}^-1 & 0 \\ 0 & {}^-1 \end{bmatrix}$	$\begin{bmatrix} 0 & 1 \\ {}^-1 & 0 \end{bmatrix}$

A rotation of $0°$, $360°$, $720°$, etc., is an identity (rotation) with matrix $\begin{bmatrix} 1 & 0 \\ 0 & 1 \end{bmatrix}$.

Exercise E

1 Copy Figure 11, and draw in the mirror lines (lines of symmetry).

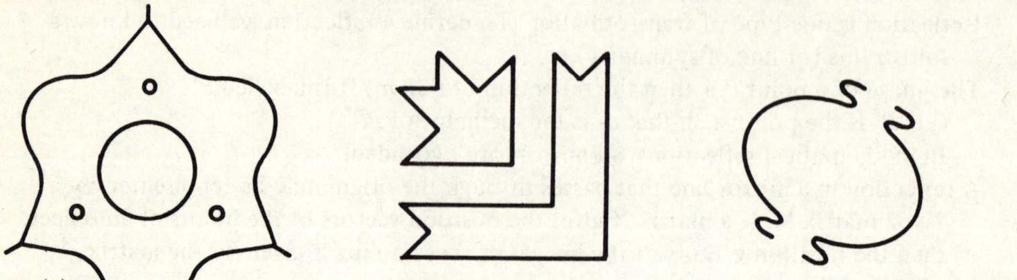

(a) (b) (c) Figure 11

2 Copy Figure 12, and draw in the image of the flag in each of the mirror lines.

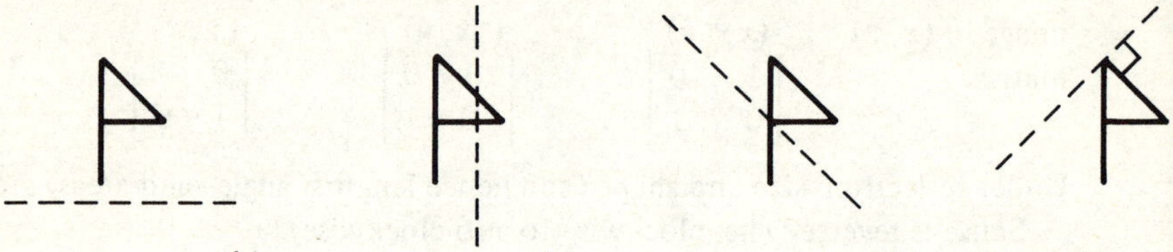

(a) (b) (c) (d) Figure 12

3 Each part of Figure 13 shows an object and its image under a reflection.
Copy Figure 13, and construct accurately the mirror line for each reflection.

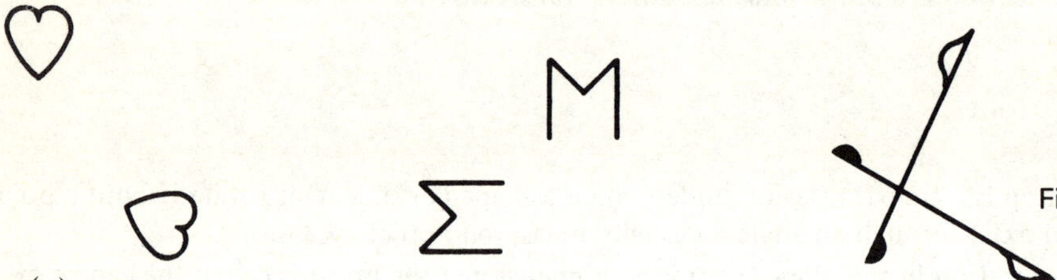

Figure 13

(a) (b) (c)

4 Write down the coordinates of the images of P, Q and R (see Figure 14) when reflected in each of the following mirror lines.

(a) $y = 0$ (the x-axis) (b) $x + y = 0$ (c) $x = 2$

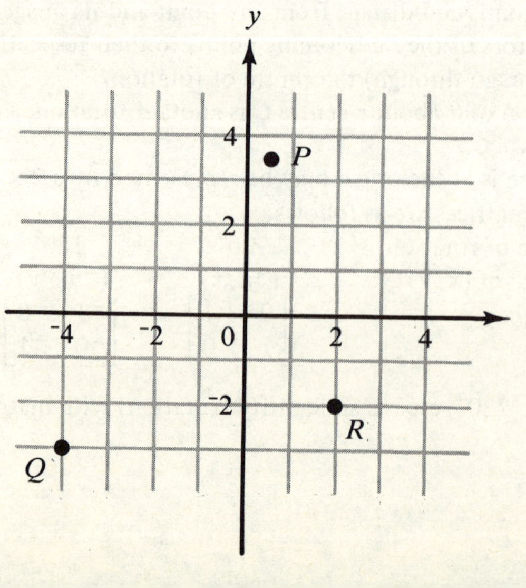

Figure 14

5 Check your answers to parts (a) and (b) of question 4 by pre-multiplying the position vectors of P, Q and R by the following matrices.

(a) $\begin{bmatrix} 1 & 0 \\ 0 & ^-1 \end{bmatrix}$ (b) $\begin{bmatrix} 0 & ^-1 \\ ^-1 & 0 \end{bmatrix}$

Why is it not possible to check part (c) of question 4 by this method?

6 Figure 15 shows an object F and its images L, M and N under three reflections. Write down the equations of the mirror lines for these reflections.

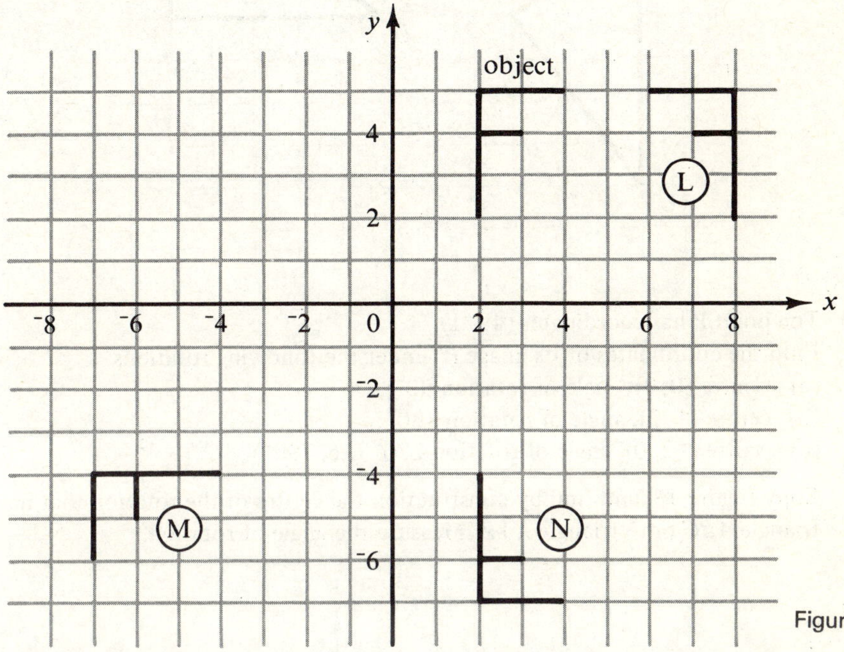

Figure 15

7 (a) Pre-multiply the position vectors of P, Q and R (see question 4) by the matrix $\begin{bmatrix} 0.28 & 0.96 \\ 0.96 & ^-0.28 \end{bmatrix}$ to give the position vectors of points P', Q' and R'.

(b) Draw a diagram to show triangles PQR and $P'Q'R'$.

(c) Describe the transformation that maps triangle PQR onto triangle $P'Q'R'$.

8 Copy Figure 16, and for each part construct the image of triangle FGH when rotated through an angle of 90° about the point C.
(Note that this is a positive, i.e. anti-clockwise, rotation.)

Figure 16

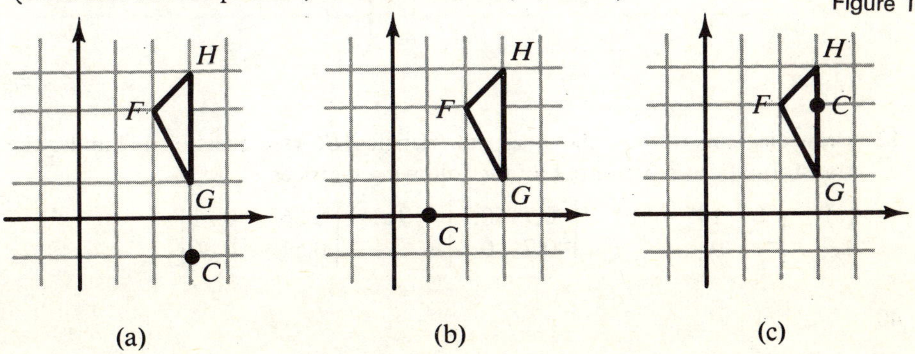

(a) (b) (c)

9 From Figure 17 find, by measuring a suitable angle, the amount (angle) of the rotation that maps triangle UVW onto triangle $U'V'W'$.

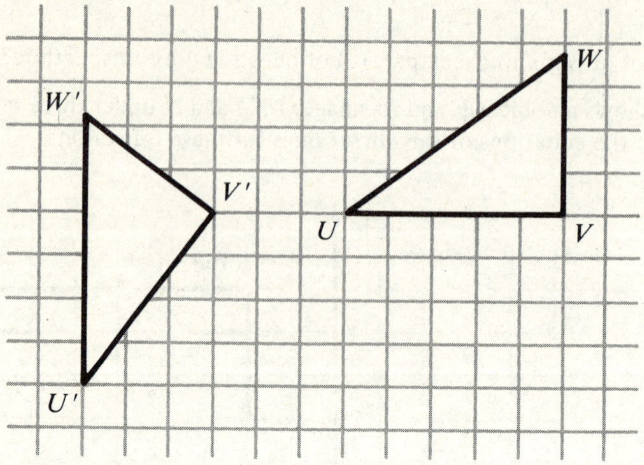

Figure 17

10 The point P has coordinates $(4, ^-1)$.
Find the coordinates of its image P' under the following rotations.
(a) Centre (0, 0), angle of rotation 90°;
(b) centre (1, 2), angle of rotation 180°;
(c) centre $(^-2, 0)$, angle of rotation 270° (i.e. $^-90°$).

11 Copy Figure 18, and find by construction the centre of the rotation that maps triangle ABC onto triangle XYZ. Measure the angle of rotation.

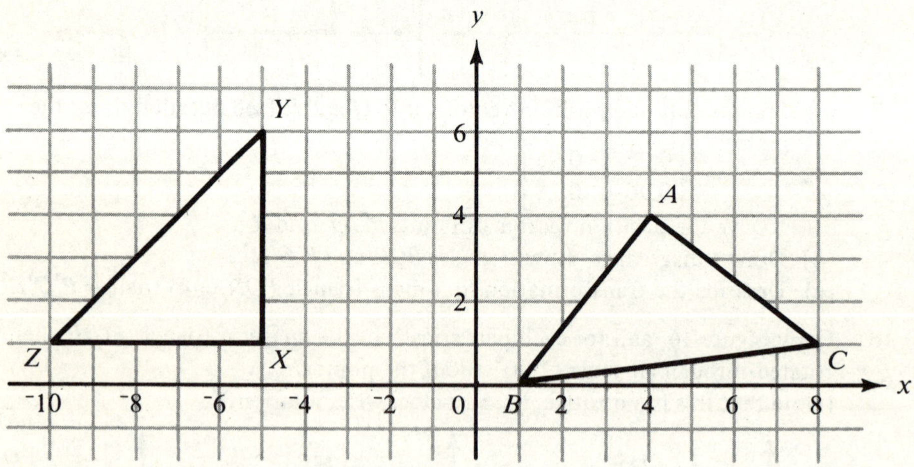

Figure 18

12 Draw diagrams to show the images of triangle ABC (see question 11) under the transformations represented by the following matrices.

(a) $\begin{bmatrix} 0 & 1 \\ ^-1 & 0 \end{bmatrix}$ (b) $\begin{bmatrix} 0.7 & 0.7 \\ ^-0.7 & 0.7 \end{bmatrix}$ (c) $\begin{bmatrix} 0.86 & ^-0.51 \\ 0.51 & 0.86 \end{bmatrix}$

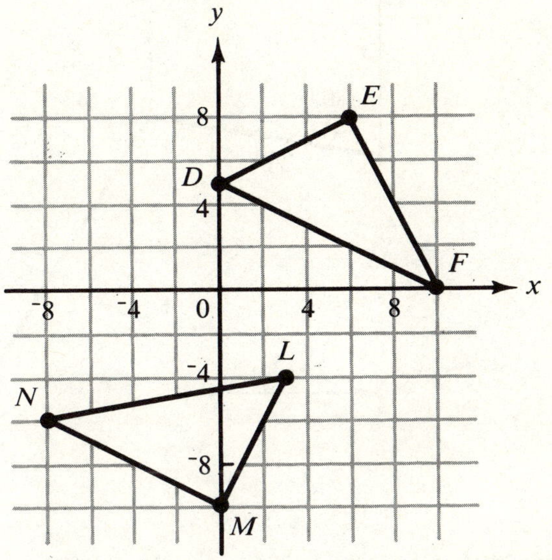

Figure 19

13 Triangle *LMN* is the image of triangle *DEF* under a certain rotation about the origin. (See Figure 19.)
Determine the image of the unit square under this rotation, and hence write down the matrix for the transformation.

Answers

Exercise A

(In the trigonometrical part of this exercise most answers are given correct to 3 s.f.)

1 (a) 13, 23, 63, 64, 83 (b) 57, 79, 197, 255, 256

2 (a) 11, 17, 40, 77, 144 (in base eight) (b) 9, F, 20, 3F, 64 (in base sixteen)

3 16, 25, 36, 49, 64, 81, 100
Yes; since $121_n = 1 \times n^2 + 2n + 1$, which is $(n + 1)^2$.

4 (a) 1203 (b) 73 (c) 322 (d) 14402 (e) 615

5 (a) 8*e*8 (b) 533 (c) 11 (d) 2562 (e) 30*e*9

6 $PR = 12 \text{ cm} \times \cos 36°$ (or $\sin 54°$) $= 12 \times 0.809\ldots \text{ cm} = 9.71 \text{ cm}$
$QR = 12 \text{ cm} \times \sin 36°$ (or $\cos 54°$) $= 12 \times 0.588\ldots \text{ cm} = 7.05 \text{ cm}$ or 7.06 cm

7 See Figure A.
The calculated distances, correct to the nearest kilometre, are shown in the answer to question 8. Answers from a scale drawing should be correct to the nearest 10 km.

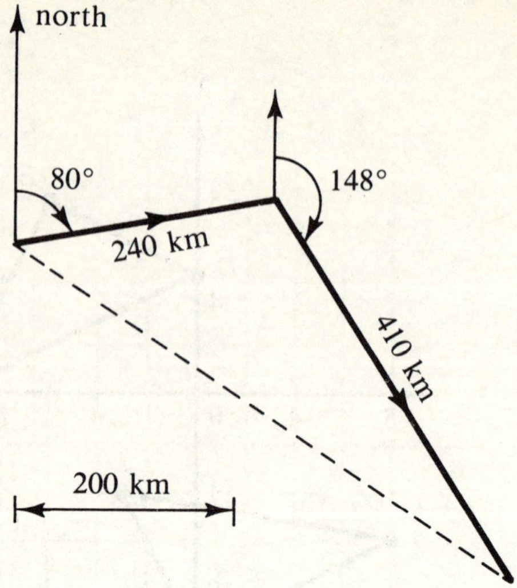

Figure A

8 (a) 1st stage: 240 km × sin 80° = 236 km east, and 240 km × cos 80° = 42 km north
2nd stage: 410 km × sin 148° = 217 km east, and 410 × cos 148° = ⁻348 km north (or 348 km south)
(b) Combined: (236 + 217) km east = 453 km east;
and (42 − 348) km north = ⁻306 km north, i.e. 306 km south
(c) Total distance = $\sqrt{(453^2 + 306^2)}$ km = $\sqrt{299\,000}$ km = 547 km.

9 (a) $x = 13 \times \sin 27° = 5.90$ (b) $x = 14 \times \sin 77° = 13.6$
(c) $x = 15 \times \cos 33° = 12.6$ (d) $x = 16 \times \cos 81° = 2.50$
(e) $x = \dfrac{17}{\cos 40°} = 22.2$ (f) $x = \dfrac{18}{\sin 51°} = 23.2$

10 (a) $\sin y° = \frac{5}{7} = 0.714$; $y = 45.6$
(b) $\cos y° = \frac{5}{8} = 0.625$; $y = 51.3$
(c) 26.4 (d) 55.1 (e) 24.6 (f) 65.4

11 (a) sin 220° = ⁻sin (220 − 180)° = ⁻sin 40° = ⁻0.643;
sin 330° = ⁻sin 30° = ⁻0.500; sin 440° = sin 80° = 0.985
(b) cos 220° = ⁻cos (220 − 180)° = ⁻cos 40° = ⁻0.766;
cos 330° = cos 30° = 0.866; cos 440° = cos 80° = 0.174

12 (a) If sin θ = 0.250, then θ = 14° or (180 − 14)° or (360 + 14)°, etc. $x = 374$
(b) If sin θ = ⁻0.250, then θ = ⁻14° or (180 + 14)° or (360 − 14)°, etc. $x = 346$
(c) If cos θ = 0.600, then θ = 53° or (360 − 53)° or (360 + 53)°, etc. $x = 307$
(d) If cos θ = ⁻0.600, then θ = (180 − 53)° or (180 + 53)° or (540 − 53)°, etc. $x = 233$

Exercise B

1 (a) 4 (b) 6 (c) 25 (d) 61 or more (e) 1
(f) 2 (the '13th child' has 2 pets) (g) 61/25 = 2.4 (1 d.p.)

2 See Figure B.

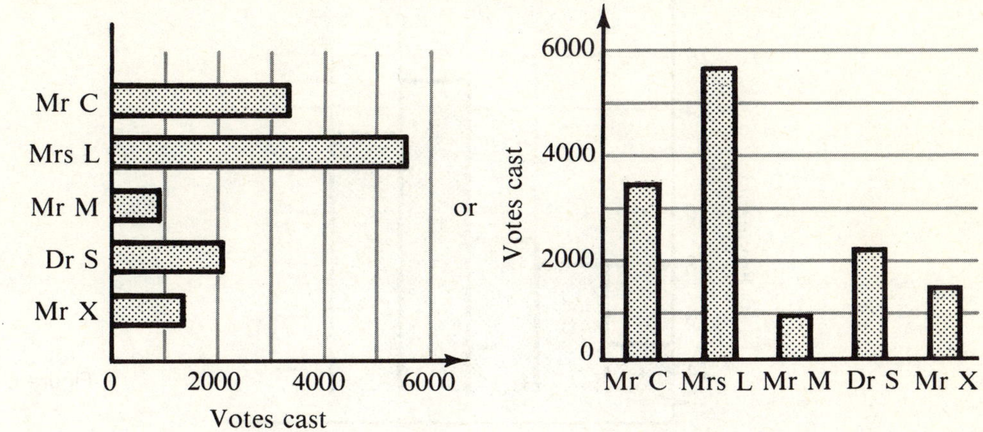

(a)

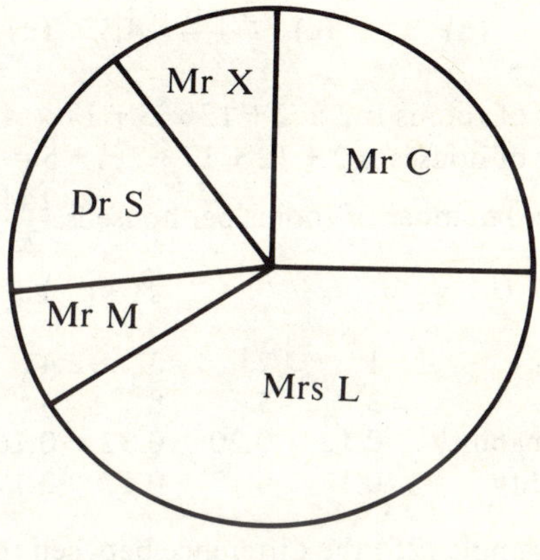

Figure B

(b)

The order of the candidates does not matter. In Figure B they are listed alphabetically.

For (b) the angle for each candidate = $\dfrac{\text{number of votes}}{13673} \times 360°$.

This gives angles of 90 (or 91)°, 148°, 26°, 58°, and 38° respectively.

3 (a) $\frac{99}{360} \times 100\% = 27.5\%$ (b) $\frac{124}{360} \times 34\,650$ tonnes = 11 950 tonnes (approximately)

4 (a)

Registration	T	V	W	X	Y
Frequency	15	18	19	25	23

(b) See Figure C.

(c) The modal (commonest) registration was X.

5 The numbers arranged in order of size are 4 5 8 8 8 8 9 9 12 13 13 15 18.

(a) $\dfrac{4+18}{2} = 11$ (b) 8 (c) 9 (d) $\dfrac{130}{13} = 10$

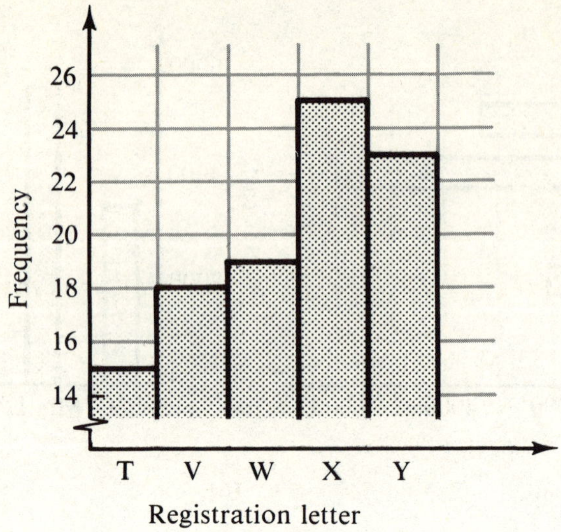

Figure C

6 (a) $\frac{3+3}{2} = 3$ (b) 3 (c) $\frac{3+6}{2} = 4.5$ (d) 6

7 The total number of rooms is $2 \times 2 + 12 \times 3 + 17 \times 4 + \ldots + 5 \times 10 = 1444$.
The total number of houses is $2 + 12 + 17 + \ldots + 5 = 232$.
The mean (average) number of rooms per house is $\frac{1444}{232} = 6.2$ (correct to 1 d.p.).

8 (a) $\frac{10}{52}$ or $\frac{5}{26}$ (b) $\frac{6}{52}$ or $\frac{3}{26}$ (c) $\frac{2}{52}$ or $\frac{1}{26}$

9

Score	1	2	3	4	5	6
Frequency	3	5	8	4	3	2
Experimental probability	0.12	0.20	0.32	0.16	0.12	0.08
Expected probability	0.17	0.17	0.17	0.17	0.17	0.17

For such a small sample (25) the difference between the experimental result and the expected result is probably not significant.

10 (a)

Second spinner					
5	6	7	8	9	10
4	5	6	7	8	9
3	4	5	6	7	8
2	3	4	5	6	7
1	2	3	4	5	6
	1	2	3	4	5

First spinner

prob(total score of 6) = $\frac{5}{25} = \frac{1}{5}$ (0.20)

prob(total score > 6) = $\frac{10}{25} = \frac{2}{5}$ (0.40)

(b)

Second spinner					
5	6	7	7	8	10
3	4	5	5	6	8
3	4	5	5	6	8
2	3	4	4	5	7
1	2	3	3	4	6
	1	2	2	3	5

First spinner

prob(total score of 6) = $\frac{4}{25}$ (0.16)

prob(total score > 6) = $\frac{7}{25}$ (0.28)

Exercise C

1 (a) $P = \{11, 13, 17, 19, 23\}$
$Q = \{12, 15, 18, 21, 24\}$
$R = \{11, 13, 15, 17, 19, 21, 23, 25\}$
$S = \{10, 12, 14, 16, 18, 20, 22, 24\}$

See Figure D(a).

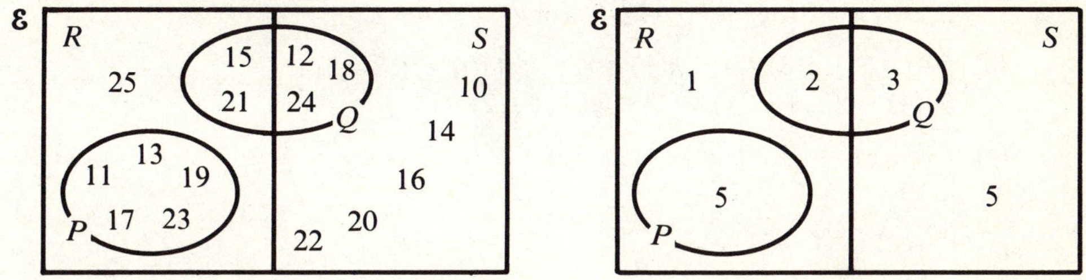

(a) (b) Figure D

(b) No element (member) belongs to both P and Q (i.e. P and Q are disjoint); $P \cap Q = \varnothing$
(c) All elements of P are also members of R (i.e. P is a subset of R); $P \subset R$ (or $R \supset P$)
(d) $Q \cup R = \{11, 12, 13, 15, 17, 18, 19, 21, 23, 24, 25\}$
(e) $Q \cap S = \{12, 18, 24\}$
(f) Together, R and S contain all the elements of ℰ; but R and S are disjoint. Hence R and S are complementary (to each other). $R = S'$ and $S = R'$.
(g) 25 is the only element of R that does not belong to either P or Q. Hence $\{25\} = R \cap P' \cap Q'$ or $\{25\} = R \cap (P \cup Q)'$.
(h) $n(P) = 5$ $n(Q \cup R) = 11$ $n(R \cap S) = 0$ $n(S \cap Q) = 3$
(i) See Figure D(b).

2 See Figure E.
Figure E(a) shows the intermediate stage, when most of the information given in fractional form has been entered. Figure E(b) is the final form.

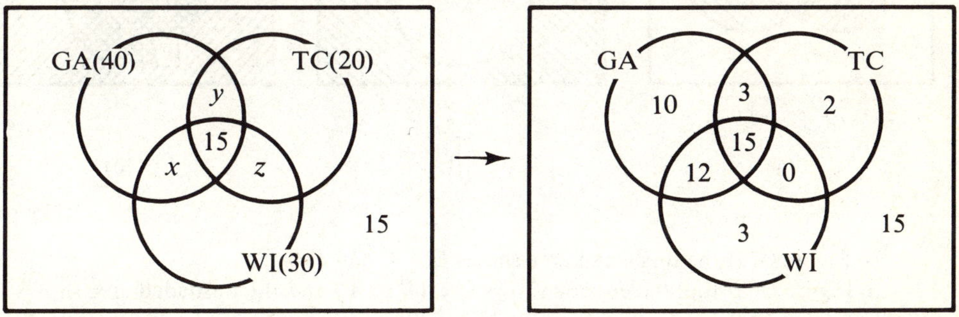

(a) (b) Figure E

3 (a) $u:x \to x - 5$, $v:x \to 2x$ (Remember that uv means 'v first, u second'.)
(b) 'Square, and then add three'
(c) See Figure F.

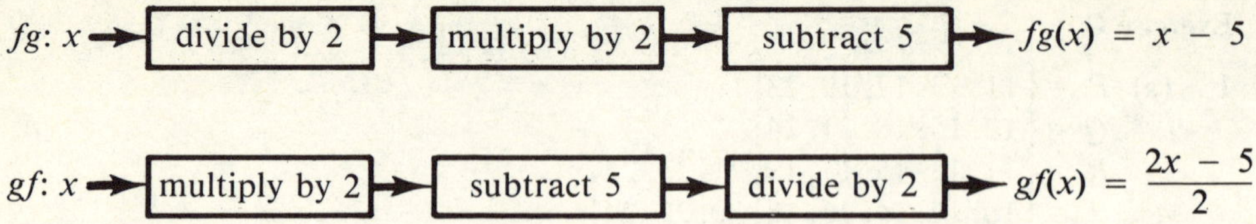

Figure F

$$fg: x \to x - 5 \quad gf: x \to \frac{2x-5}{2} \quad (\text{or } gf: x \to x - 2.5)$$

(d) $f(4) = 3$; $g(8) = 4$; $h(3) = 12$; $fg(10) = f(5) = 5$;
$hg(4) = h(2) = 7$; $fgh(1) = fg(4) = f(2) = {}^{-}1$

(e) $f^{-1}: x \to \dfrac{x+5}{2}$ $\quad g^{-1}: x \to 2x$

4 $p^{-1}: x \to \dfrac{x-3}{7}$ $\quad q^{-1}: x \to \dfrac{4-x}{3}$

$r^{-1}: x \to 4x - 3$ $\quad s^{-1}: x \to \dfrac{\frac{5}{x} - 1}{9}$ $\quad \left(\text{or } \dfrac{5-x}{9x}\right)$

5 (a) 9, 9, 0, 49, 49

(b) $2 * (3 * 6) = 2 * 9 = 49$, $(2 * 3) * 6 = 1 * 6 = 25$

(c) It is not associative (see part (b)), it is commutative (e.g. $2 * 5 = 5 * 2$), and it is closed (the result is always a non-negative integer).

(d) No. (Note that, unless $x = 1$, $x * 0$ is not equal to x.)

(e) As there is no identity, inverses cannot exist.

6 (a) See Figure G.

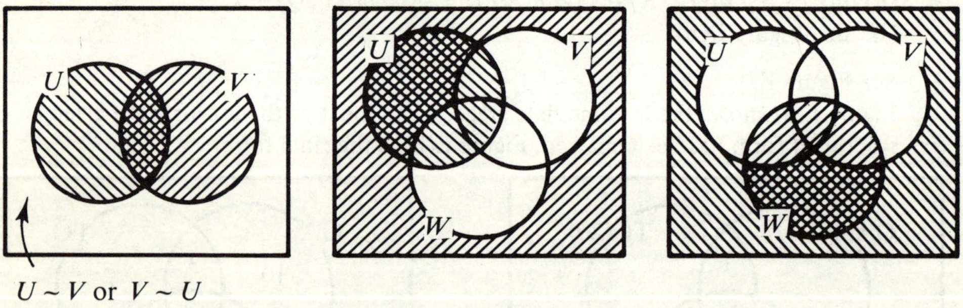

(a) (b) (c)

Figure G

In Figure G(a) the unshaded area shows $U \sim V$ and $V \sim U$.
In Figure G(b) the shaded area shows $U \cup (V \sim W)$ and the unshaded area shows $U \sim (V \sim W)$.
Similarly, in Figure G(c) $(U \sim V) \sim W$ is shown by the unshaded area.

(b) The operation is commutative, but not associative.

(c) $U \sim \mathcal{E} = (U \cup \mathcal{E})' = \varnothing$; $U \sim \varnothing = (U \cup \varnothing)' = U'$

(d) No. The only possible elements that could be the identity are $\varnothing$ and $\mathcal{E}$.
Part (c) shows that neither of these is the identity.

Exercise D

1 (a) $3(x - 5) = 27$ (b) $\frac{x + 7}{4} = 13$

(c) $\frac{x}{2} - 5 = 15$ (d) $\frac{10x + 17}{3} = 19$

2 See Figure H.

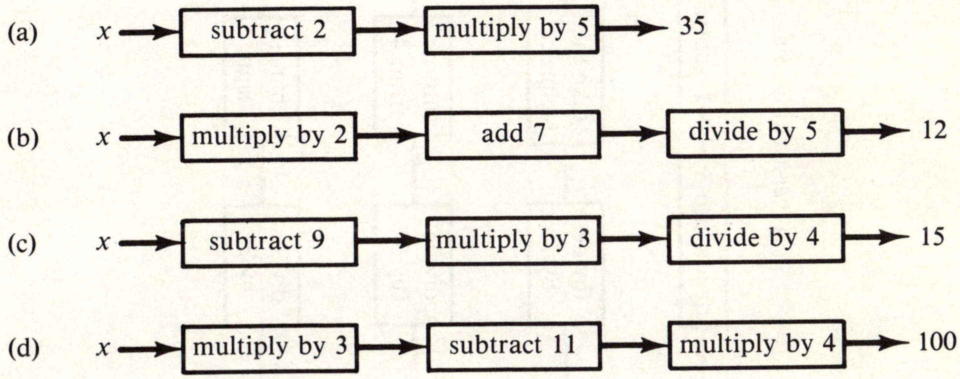

Figure H

3 See Figure I.

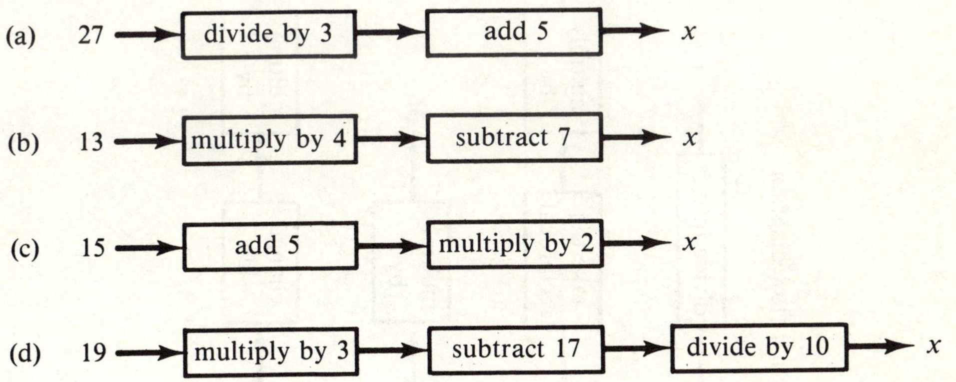

Figure I

(a) $x = 14$ (b) $x = 45$ (c) $x = 40$ (d) $x = 4$

4 (a) $x = 9$ (b) $x = 26.5$ (c) $x = 29$ (d) $x = 12$

5 (a) $x = 2$ (b) $x = {}^{-}8$ (c) $x = 7$ (d) $x = 0.5$

Figure J shows the original and reversed flow diagrams for parts (a) and (b).

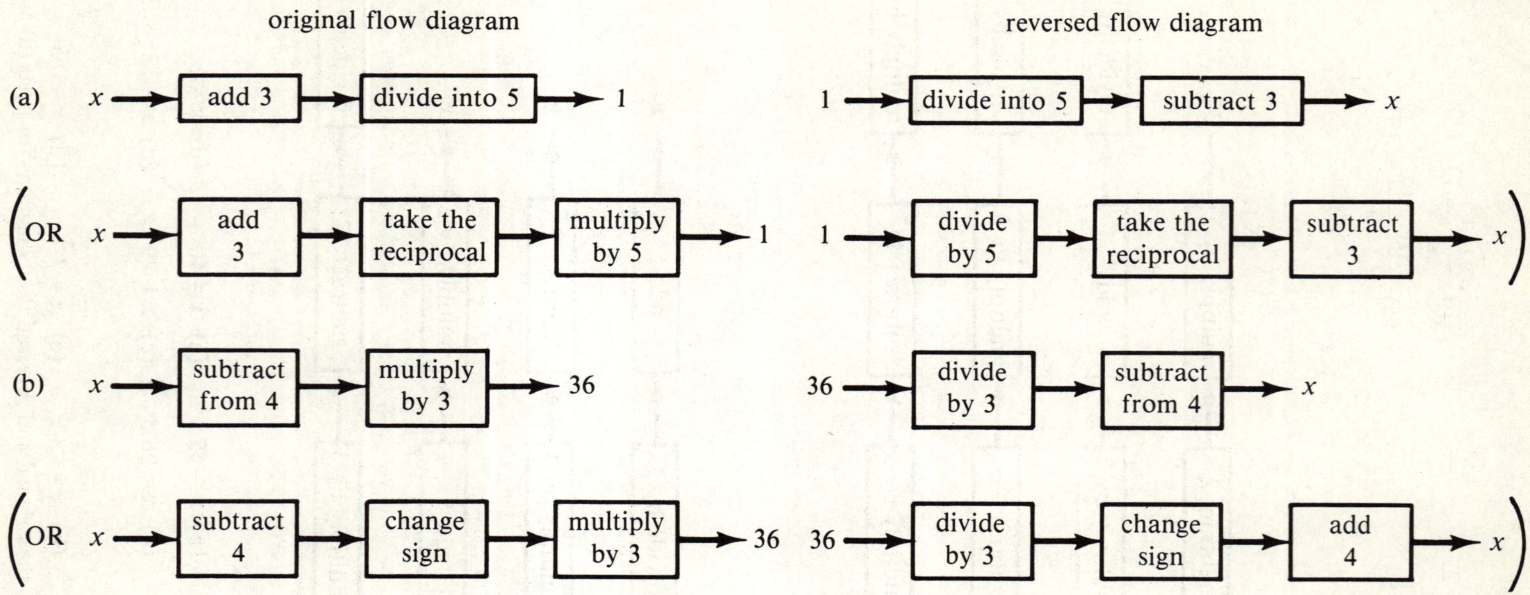
original flow diagram
reversed flow diagram
(a)
x
add 3
divide into 5
1
1
divide into 5
subtract 3
x
OR
x
add
3
take the
reciprocal
multiply
by 5
1
1
divide
by 5
take the
reciprocal
subtract
3
x
(b)
x
subtract
from 4
multiply
by 3
36
36
divide
by 3
subtract
from 4
x
OR
x
subtract
4
change
sign
multiply
by 3
36
36
divide
by 3
change
sign
add
4
x

Figure J

6 (a)

$$5(x-2) = 35$$
$[\times \frac{1}{5}]$ $x - 2 = 7$
$[+2]$ $x = 9$

(b)

$$\frac{2x+7}{5} = 12$$
$[\times 5]$ $2x + 7 = 60$
$[+^{-}7]$ $2x = 53$
$[\times \frac{1}{2}]$ $x = 26.5$

(c)

$$\frac{3(x-9)}{4} = 15$$
$[\times 4]$ $3(x-9) = 60$
$[\times \frac{1}{3}]$ $x - 9 = 20$
$[+9]$ $x = 29$

(d)

$$4(3x - 11) = 100$$
$[\times \frac{1}{4}]$ $3x - 11 = 25$
$[+11]$ $3x = 36$
$[\times \frac{1}{3}]$ $x = 12$

7 (a) $x > 6$ (b) $x < 7$ (c) $x \geqslant 18$ (d) $^{-}x \leqslant 6$; i.e. $x \geqslant {}^{-}6$
(e) $x < 4$ (f) $12 - 2x \geqslant x$; $^{-}3x \geqslant {}^{-}12$; i.e. $x \leqslant 4$

8 (a) $3x - 2 < 10$ gives $x < 4$; $10 < x + 9$ gives $x > 1$. Combined: $1 < x < 4$.
(b) $x > 4$ and $x > {}^{-}9$ give a combined result of $x > 4$.
(c) $x < {}^{-}12$ and $x > 3$ cannot be satisfied simultaneously. No solution.
(d) $x < 8$ and $x > {}^{-}2$ give a combined result of $^{-}2 < x < 8$.
See Figure K.

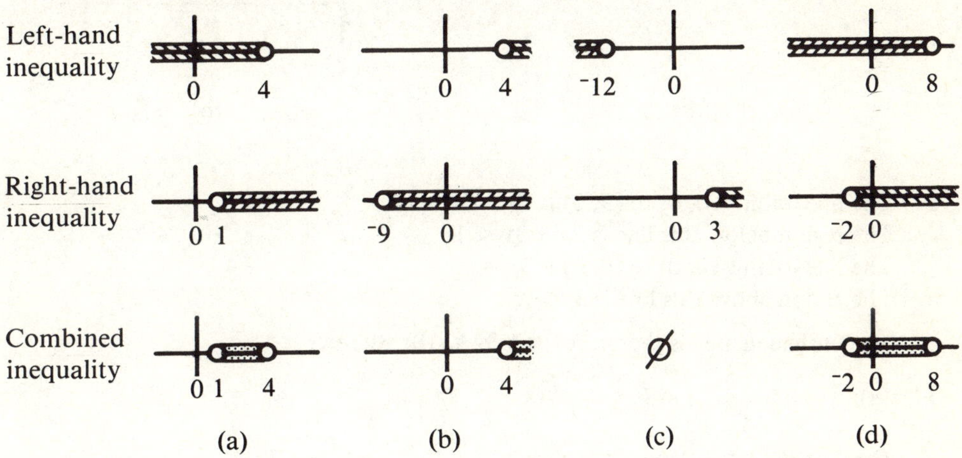

Figure K

9 See Figure L.
(a) $x = 3$, $y = 4$ (b) $x = 2.25$, $y = 1.75$

10 (a) Multiply the first by 3, and then substitute $x + 9$ for $3y$.
$6x + 3y = 30$; $6x + (x + 9) = 30$; $7x = 21$; $x = 3$.
Substituting 3 for x in the second equation gives $3y = 12$; i.e. $y = 4$.
Check in the first equation. When $x = 3$ and $y = 4$, LHS $= 2 \times 3 + 4 = 10 =$ RHS.
(An alternative start is to substitute $(3y - 9)$ for x in the first equation.)
(b) Add the equations together. $4x + 0y = 9$; $x = \frac{9}{4} = 2.25$
Substituting 2.25 for x in the second equation gives $2.25 + y = 4$;
i.e. $y = 1.75$. Check in the first equation. LHS $= 3 \times 2.25 - 1.75 =$ RHS.

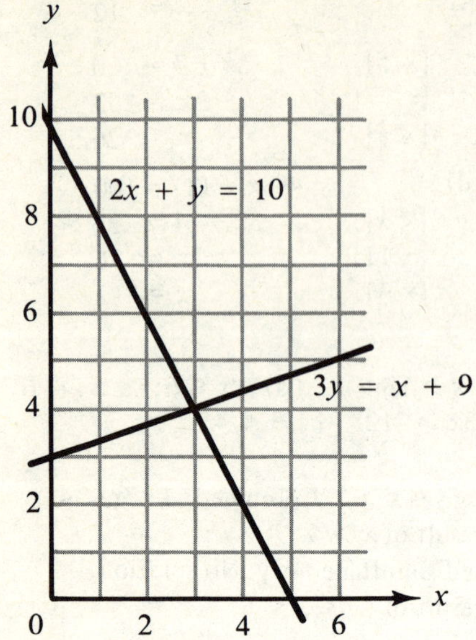

(a)

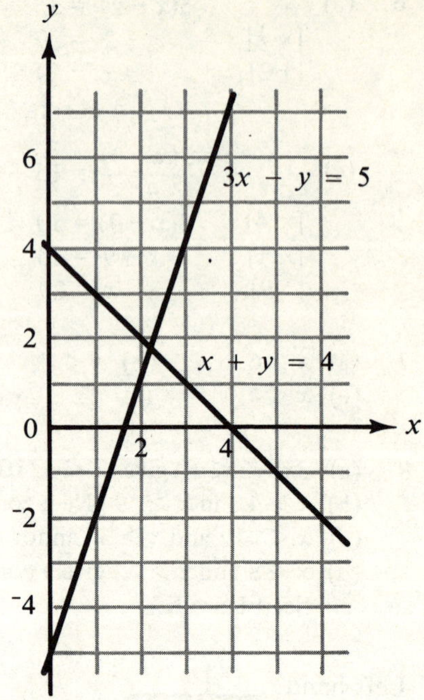

(b)

11 The line joining (0, 6) to (9, 0) is $2x + 3y = 18$.
The region below this line is $2x + 3y < 18$.
The line joining (0, 0) to (9, 3) is $3y = x$.
The region above this line is $3y > x$.

The unshaded area is therefore $2x + 3y < 18$; $3y > x$.

12 (a) $V = d^2 \times \frac{3}{4}h$, i.e. $V = \dfrac{3d^2h}{4}$

(b) Putting $h = 14$ and $d = 8$ gives $V = \dfrac{3 \times 8^2 \times 14}{4} = 672$.

The capacity is approximately 670 ml.

(c) $h = \dfrac{4V}{3d^2}$

(d) Putting $d = 10$ and $V = 600$ gives $h = \dfrac{4 \times 600}{3 \times 100} = 8$.

The tin should be 8 cm high.

13 The boundary lines (working anti-clockwise from the x-axis) are:
$y = 0$; $x = 10$; $x + 2y = 20$; $y = x + 4$; and $x + y = 4$.
The region is therefore described by:
$y > 0$; $x < 10$; $x + 2y < 20$; $y < x + 4$; $x + y > 4$.

14 (a) $M = 45 + 2 \times 7 \times 5 = 115$
115 bytes of memory are required.

(b) $p + 1 = \dfrac{M - 45}{2(q+1)}$, or $p = \dfrac{M - 45}{2(q+1)} - 1$

(c) Putting $q = 12$ and $M = 2048$ gives $p = \dfrac{2003}{26} - 1 = 76.04$.

The largest possible integral value of p is 76.

(d) If $p = q$ then $2(p + 1)^2 + 45 = 4096$

$$(p + 1)^2 = \frac{4051}{2} = 2025.5$$

$$p + 1 = 45, \text{ giving } p = 44.$$

The largest square matrix that can be stored is 44×44.

15 (a) $R = \dfrac{70^2 \times \sin 40^\circ}{9.8} = 321.4 = 320$ (correct to 2 s.f.)

The units of R are metres.

(b) $\sin A = \dfrac{gR}{u^2}$ or $A = \arcsin\left(\dfrac{gR}{u^2}\right)$ $\left(A = \sin^{-1}\left(\dfrac{gR}{u^2}\right)\right)$

$\sin A = \dfrac{9.8 \times 500}{85 \times 85} = 0.6782 \quad A = 42.7^\circ$

(c) $u = \pm\sqrt{\left(\dfrac{gR}{\sin A}\right)}$

Assuming u to be positive, $u = \sqrt{\left(\dfrac{9.8 \times 1200}{\sin 80^\circ}\right)} = 109.3$

The value of u is approximately 110 (2 s.f.).

Exercise E

1 See Figure M.

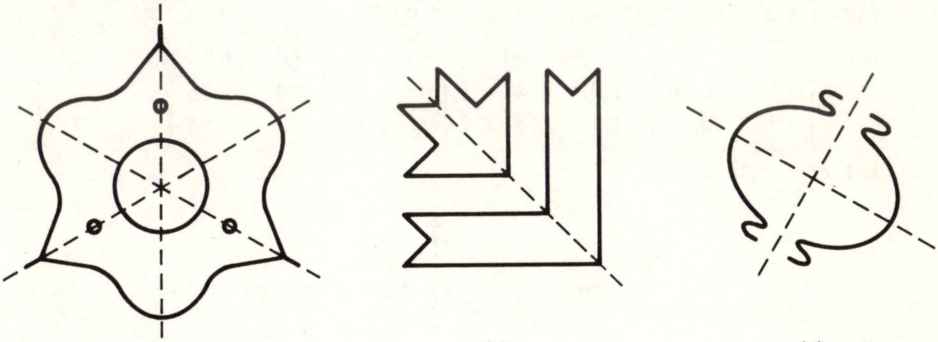

(a) (b) (c) Figure M

2 See Figure N.

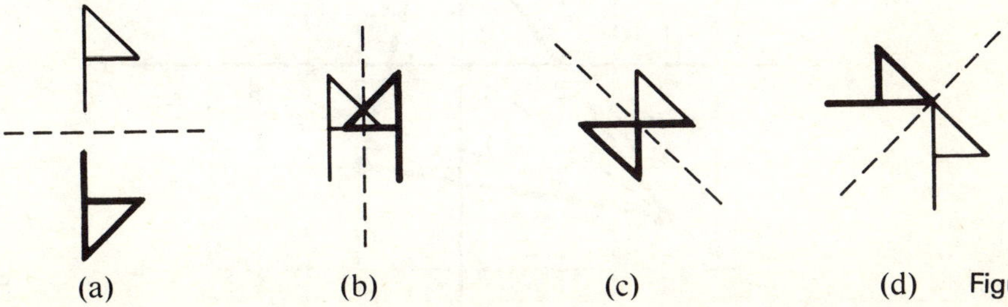

(a) (b) (c) (d) Figure N

3 See Figure O.

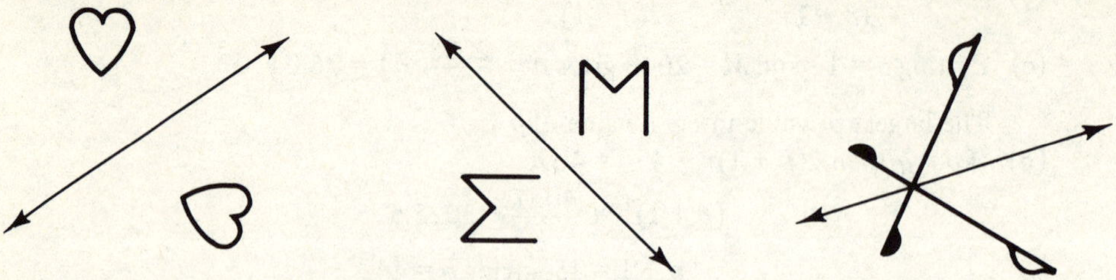

Figure O

4

Point	Image (a)	Image (b)	Image (c)
$P(0.5, 3.5)$	$(0.5, {}^-3.5)$	$({}^-3.5, {}^-0.5)$	$(3.5, 3.5)$
$Q({}^-4, {}^-3)$	$({}^-4, 3)$	$(3, 4)$	$(8, {}^-3)$
$R(2, {}^-2)$	$(2, 2)$	$(2, {}^-2)$	$(2, {}^-2)$

5 (a)

$$\begin{bmatrix} 1 & 0 \\ 0 & {}^-1 \end{bmatrix} \overset{\quad P \quad Q \quad R}{\begin{bmatrix} 0.5 & {}^-4 & 2 \\ 3.5 & {}^-3 & {}^-2 \end{bmatrix}} = \overset{\quad P' \quad Q' \quad R'}{\begin{bmatrix} 0.5 & {}^-4 & 2 \\ {}^-3.5 & 3 & 2 \end{bmatrix}}$$

(b)

$$\begin{bmatrix} 0 & {}^-1 \\ {}^-1 & 0 \end{bmatrix} \overset{\quad P \quad Q \quad R}{\begin{bmatrix} 0.5 & {}^-4 & 2 \\ 3.5 & {}^-3 & {}^-2 \end{bmatrix}} = \overset{\quad P' \quad Q' \quad R'}{\begin{bmatrix} {}^-3.5 & 3 & 2 \\ {}^-0.5 & 4 & {}^-2 \end{bmatrix}}$$

(c) As the origin is not invariant under reflection in the line $x = 2$, it is not possible to represent 'reflection in $x = 2$' by a 2×2 matrix.

6

Reflection	L	M	N
Mirror line	$x = 5$	$x + y = {}^-2$	$y = {}^-1$

7 (a)

$$\begin{bmatrix} 0.28 & 0.96 \\ 0.96 & {}^-0.28 \end{bmatrix} \overset{\quad P \quad Q \quad R}{\begin{bmatrix} 0.5 & {}^-4 & 2 \\ 3.5 & {}^-3 & {}^-2 \end{bmatrix}} = \overset{\quad P' \quad Q' \quad R'}{\begin{bmatrix} 3.5 & {}^-4 & {}^-1.36 \\ {}^-0.5 & {}^-3 & 2.48 \end{bmatrix}}$$

(b) See Figure P.

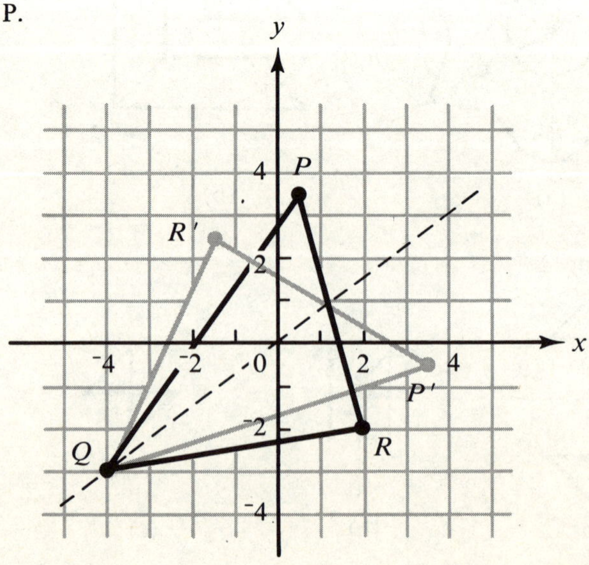

Figure P

(c) The transformation is a reflection.
The origin O is invariant, as the transformation is represented by a 2×2 matrix; the point Q is also invariant. Hence the mirror line is OQ, or $4y = 3x$.

8 See Figure Q.

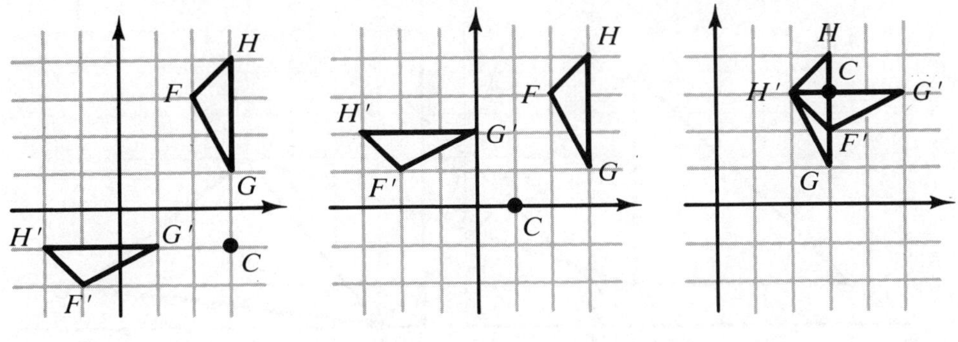

(a) (b) (c) Figure Q

9 Produce WV and $W'V'$ (or UV and $U'V'$, or UW and $U'W'$) to meet at the point X. Angle WXW' will then measure the **amount** of turn. (Note that X is **not** the centre of rotation.)

In this question the angle of rotation is approximately 53°.

10 See Figure R.

(a) (1, 4)
(b) ($^-2$, 5)
(c) ($^-3$, $^-6$)

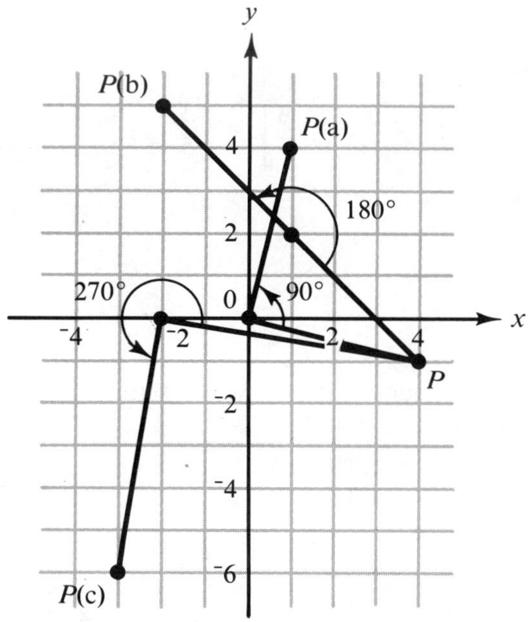

Figure R

11 See Figure S.

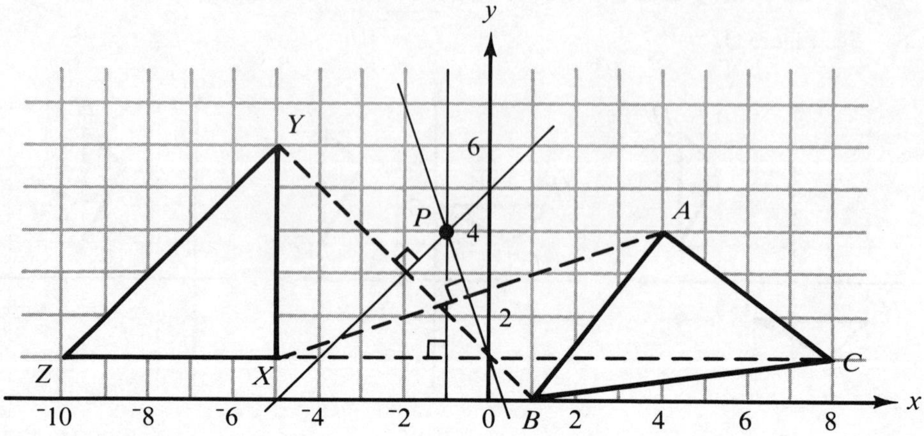

Figure S

The centre of rotation is $P(^-1, 4)$.
The angle of rotation is approximately 217°.

12 (a) $\begin{bmatrix} 0 & 1 \\ ^-1 & 0 \end{bmatrix} \begin{bmatrix} 4 & 1 & 8 \\ 4 & 0 & 1 \end{bmatrix} = \begin{bmatrix} 4 & 0 & 1 \\ ^-4 & ^-1 & ^-8 \end{bmatrix}$

A rotation of 270°.

(b) $\begin{bmatrix} 0.7 & 0.7 \\ ^-0.7 & 0.7 \end{bmatrix} \begin{bmatrix} 4 & 1 & 8 \\ 4 & 0 & 1 \end{bmatrix} = \begin{bmatrix} 5.6 & 0.7 & 6.3 \\ 0 & ^-0.7 & ^-4.9 \end{bmatrix}$

A rotation of 315°.

(c) $\begin{bmatrix} 0.86 & ^-0.51 \\ 0.51 & 0.86 \end{bmatrix} \begin{bmatrix} 4 & 1 & 8 \\ 4 & 0 & 1 \end{bmatrix} = \begin{bmatrix} 1.4 & 0.86 & 6.37 \\ 5.48 & 0.51 & 4.94 \end{bmatrix}$

A rotation of 30°.

See Figure T.

13 As O is the centre of rotation, the image of $I(1, 0)$ is $(^-0.8, ^-0.6)$ and the image of $J(0, 1)$ is $(0.6, ^-0.8)$.

The matrix is $\begin{bmatrix} ^-0.8 & 0.6 \\ ^-0.6 & ^-0.8 \end{bmatrix}$

Check:

$$\begin{bmatrix} ^-0.8 & 0.6 \\ ^-0.6 & ^-0.8 \end{bmatrix} \overset{\begin{matrix} D & E & F \end{matrix}}{\begin{bmatrix} 0 & 6 & 10 \\ 5 & 8 & 0 \end{bmatrix}} = \overset{\begin{matrix} L & M & N \end{matrix}}{\begin{bmatrix} 3 & 0 & ^-8 \\ ^-4 & ^-10 & ^-6 \end{bmatrix}}$$

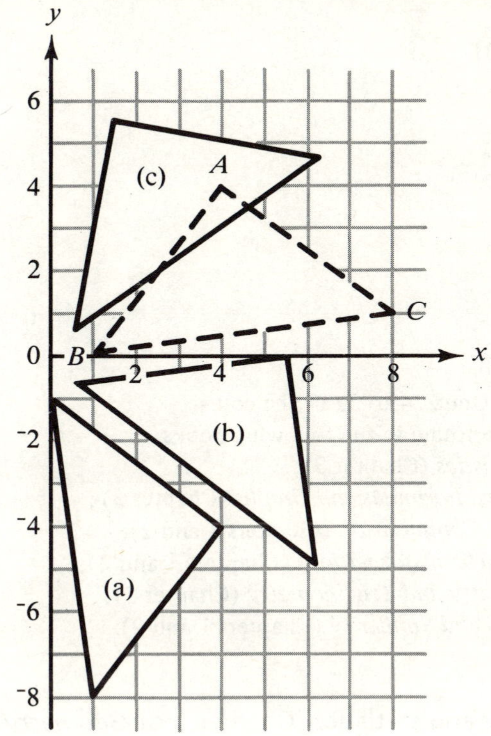

Figure T

Consolidation 3

This chapter covers Units 24 to 32 of the course.
These units are to be found in the following books:
Probability and Statistics (Chapter 3);
Algebra 2: Equations, Formulas and Graphs (Chapter 3);
Further Algebra and Computation (Chapters 1 and 2);
Further Matrices and Transformations (Chapters 1 and 2);
Geometry 1: Symmetry and Trigonometry (Chapter 5);
Geometry 2: Shapes and Similarity (Chapters 1 and 2).

3.1 Trigonometry and statistics (Chapter 5 of *Geometry 1: Symmetry and Trigonometry* and Chapter 3 of *Probability and Statistics*)

Trigonometry

In a right-angled triangle the tangent relation connects the two sides containing the right-angle and one of the angles.
The 'tangent picture' is shown in Figure 1.

Figure 1

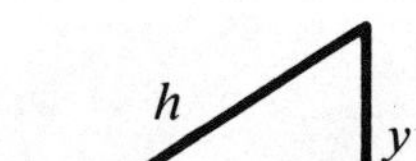

Figure 2

$y = x \tan\theta \qquad \tan\theta = \dfrac{y}{x}$

Pythagoras' theorem states that in a right-angled triangle $x^2 + y^2 = h^2$. (See Figure 2.)
If the cartesian coordinates of a point are (x, y) and the polar coordinates are (r, θ),

then $x = r\cos\theta, \quad y = r\sin\theta, \quad r^2 = x^2 + y^2, \quad \tan\theta = \dfrac{y}{x}$. (See Figure 3.)

These relations define the sine and cosine functions.
The tangent function is defined by the relation $\tan\theta = \dfrac{\sin\theta}{\cos\theta}$.

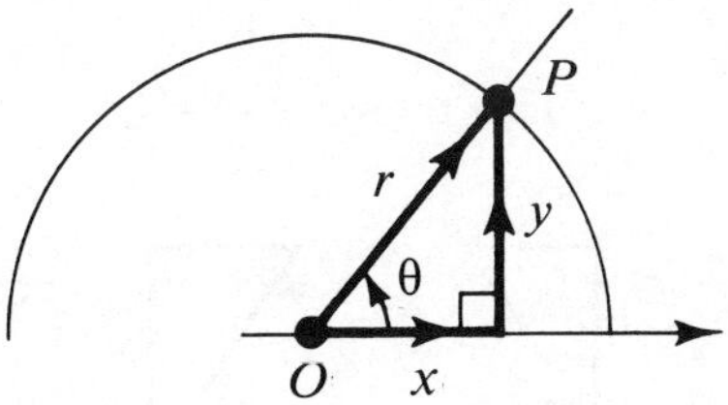

Figure 3

The formulas that you should know for right-angled triangles are as follows.

$x = r\cos\theta$, $y = r\sin\theta$, $y = x\tan\theta$, $x^2 + y^2 = r^2$,

$\cos\theta = \dfrac{x}{r}$ $\sin\theta = \dfrac{y}{r}$ $\tan\theta = \dfrac{y}{x}$ (See Figure 3.)

In 'solving' right-angled triangles, two measurements (other than the right-angle) are required.
If no other angles are given or required, use Pythagoras' theorem;
if the hypotenuse is not given or required, use a tangent relation;
otherwise use sine or cosine relations (the choice is yours).

The line of symmetry of an isosceles triangle divides the triangle into two identical right-angled triangles.
Some 'exact' values that are worth remembering are as follows.

$\cos 45° = \sin 45° = \dfrac{1}{\sqrt{2}}$ $\tan 45° = 1$

$\cos 30° = \sin 60° = \dfrac{\sqrt{3}}{2}$ $\sin 30° = \cos 60° = \frac{1}{2}$

$\tan 30° = \dfrac{1}{\sqrt{3}}$ $\tan 60° = \sqrt{3}$

Statistics

Information is usually displayed in frequency diagrams or bar charts.
If the number of columns (bars) would be more than ten, the data should be grouped into classes so that there are between five and ten classes (columns).
The mean (average) of data presented in grouped frequencies is estimated by assuming that the average of the data in any one group is the middle of that group.
The cumulative frequency curve is the graph of the total frequency of the measurements (equal or) less than x. Medians and quartiles are easily read from such a graph.
The quartiles divide the data (after they have been arranged in order of size) into four equal parts (as far as possible).

For a population of 25 measurements (arranged in order of size),
the median is the 13th measurement;
the lower quartile is between the 6th and 7th measurements;
the upper quartile is between the 19th and 20th measurements.
The inter-quartile range is the difference between the values of the upper and lower quartiles. It is a measure of the spread of the data.
The modal class is the class with the largest frequency.

Exercise A

1 For each part of Figure 4 calculate the value of x.

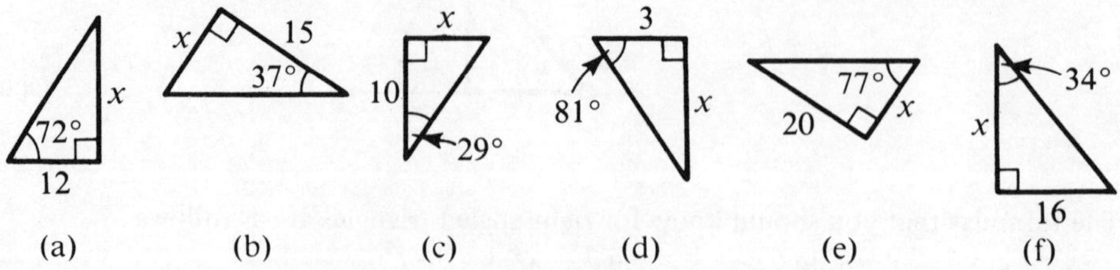

Figure 4

2 For each part of Figure 5 calculate the value of θ.

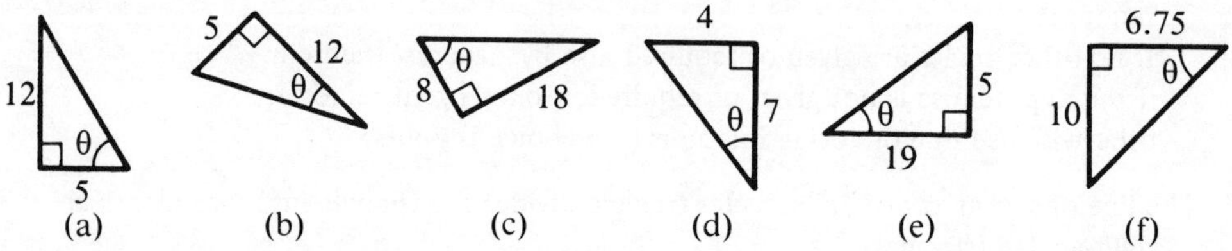

Figure 5

3 XY is a vertical television mast standing on level ground. From a point P, 1300 metres from X (the foot of the mast), the angle of elevation of Y is 23°. From a point S directly between P and X the angle of elevation of Y is 46°. Calculate the height of the mast XY, and the distance between P and S.

4 A ship sails 24 km on a bearing of 085°, and then 16 km on a bearing of 156°. Calculate the distance and bearing of its final position from its starting point.

5 (a) Write down the values of the following, correct to three significant figures: tan 111°, tan 234°, tan 335°, tan 500°.

(b) Solve the following equations.

$\tan x^\circ = 2.4 \quad (200 < x < 300)$

$\tan x^\circ = {}^{-}0.65 \quad (300 < x < 400)$

$\tan x^\circ = 2.0 \quad ({}^{-}300 < x < {}^{-}200)$

$\tan x^\circ = {}^{-}1 \quad ({}^{-}100 < x < 100)$

6 (a) Write down some possible values for x given that $\sin x^\circ = \frac{8}{17}$ and $\cos x^\circ = \frac{{}^{-}15}{17}$.

(b) Write down, as a fraction, the value of $\tan y^\circ$ given that $\sin y^\circ = \frac{11}{61}$ and $90 < y < 180$.

7 For each part of Figure 6 calculate the value of x.

Figure 6

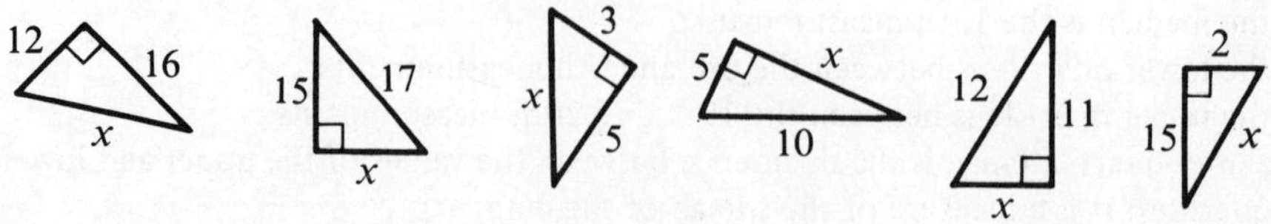

8 (a) Find the polar coordinates of the points whose cartesian coordinates are as follows.

$(4, 7)$, $(3, {}^{-}5)$, $({}^{-}1, 6)$, $({}^{-}3, {}^{-}3)$

(b) Find the cartesian coordinates of the points whose polar coordinates are as follows.

$(5, 66°)$, $(6, 125°)$, $(10, 222°)$, $(4, 305°)$

9 Draw frequency diagrams to illustrate the following information.

(a)

Age (years)	1–5	6–10	11–15	16–20	21–25	26–30	31–35
Number of people	38	45	120	132	158	104	95

(b)

Height (cm)	0–20	20–40	40–60	60–80	80–100	100–120
Number of plants	13	23	56	12	5	3

(c)

Number of people on a ferry	0–3	4–7	8–11	12–15	16–19	20–23
Number of times in one week	7	6	15	12	10	4

10 Figure 7 shows the numbers of different types of commemorative stamps issued by Great Britain for five-year periods from 1950 to 1984.

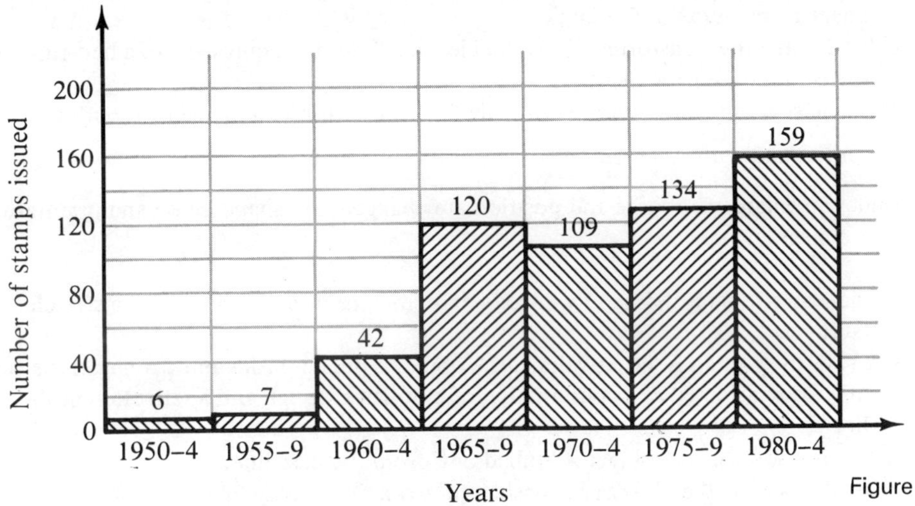

Figure 7

(a) In which period was the number of different stamps the greatest? What was the average **annual** number during this period?

(b) Calculate the mean average annual number of different types of stamps issued between 1950 and 1984.

11 For each part of question 9 calculate the mean, and show this value on your diagram.

12 For each part of question 9 state the modal class.

13 For each part of question 9:

construct the cumulative frequency table;
draw the cumulative frequency curve;
estimate the median.

3.2 More transformations (Chapters 1 and 2 of *Further Matrices and Transformations*)

Chapter 1

An enlargement is defined by a centre (C) and a scale factor (k).
The image of the point P is the point P′ such that $\mathbf{CP}' = k\,\mathbf{CP}$.

For any point P of the object, the line joining P to its image P' passes through the centre of enlargement C. $\dfrac{CP'}{CP} = k$.

If $k < 0$ then the enlargement is negative. The centre C lies between P and P'. (i.e. the image is on the opposite side of the centre of enlargement to the object). A negative enlargement may be considered as a combination of a positive enlargement and a half-turn about C.

If the centre of enlargement is the origin, the matrix $\begin{bmatrix} k & 0 \\ 0 & k \end{bmatrix}$ represents an enlargement of scale factor k.

If $k > 1$, or $k < {}^-1$, then the image is larger than the object; but if ${}^-1 < k < 1$, then the image is smaller than the object.

If $k = 1$, then the transformation is the identity; $k = {}^-1$ is equivalent to a half-turn about the centre of 'enlargement'.

The inverse of an enlargement with scale factor k is another enlargement with the same centre, and with scale factor $\dfrac{1}{k}$.

Under an enlargement, size and position are changed; but shape, sense and orientation are invariant.

A one-way stretch is defined by an axis (base line, or invariant line), and a stretch factor k.

If $k < 0$, the stretch is 'negative'; i.e. the object is pulled 'inside-out'. A negative stretch may be considered as a combination of a positive stretch and a reflection in the base line.

If $k > 1$ or $k < {}^-1$, the object is 'pulled out' from the base line; if ${}^-1 < k < 1$, the object is 'squashed in' towards the base line.

If $k = 1$, the transformation is the identity;
$k = {}^-1$ is equivalent to a reflection in the base line.

If M is the point on the base line such that MP is at right-angles to the base line, then the image of P is the point P' such that $MP' = k \times MP$.

If the base line is the y-axis ($x = 0$), the matrix for the stretch is $\begin{bmatrix} k & 0 \\ 0 & 1 \end{bmatrix}$;

if the base line is the x-axis ($y = 0$), the matrix is $\begin{bmatrix} 1 & 0 \\ 0 & k \end{bmatrix}$.

The inverse of a one-way stretch is another one-way stretch from the same base line, but with stretch factor $\dfrac{1}{k}$.

A two-way stretch is a combination of two one-way stretches. (We consider only those cases in which the base lines of the one-way stretches are perpendicular.) The centre is the intersection of these base lines.

If the base lines are the x- and y-axes, the matrix for the stretch is $\begin{bmatrix} k & 0 \\ 0 & m \end{bmatrix}$;

where k is the stretch factor from the y-axis,
and m is the stretch factor from the x-axis.

The inverse of a two-way stretch is another two-way stretch from the same base lines, but with stretch factors $\frac{1}{k}$ and $\frac{1}{m}$.

Enlargements ($k = m$) and one-way stretches (either $k = 1$ or $m = 1$) may be considered as special cases of two-way stretches.

The area factor for a transformation is given by the ratio $\frac{\text{area of image}}{\text{area of object}}$.

For a two-way stretch, the area factor is km. For an enlargement it is k^2.

The area factor for any transformation is given by the determinant of the matrix for that transformation. If the area factor is negative, the sense of the image is opposite to that of the object (i.e. at some stage the object has been 'turned over').

Chapter 2

A shear is defined by an axis (invariant line or base line), and a shear factor (or power) k.

Under a shear all points move parallel to the base line; the distance moved being proportional to the perpendicular distance from the base line. If the distance of P from the base line is d, the distance that P moves is kd.

Under a shear:

straight lines map onto straight lines;
line segments that were originally parallel to the base line remain parallel to the base line, and are unaltered in length;
area is unaltered, giving rise to the following formulas

area of a parallelogram = base × perpendicular height;
area of a triangle = $\frac{1}{2}$ base × perpendicular height.

The matrix for a shear with base line $y = 0$ and shear factor s is $\begin{bmatrix} 1 & s \\ 0 & 1 \end{bmatrix}$;

if the base line is $x = 0$ the matrix is $\begin{bmatrix} 1 & 0 \\ s & 1 \end{bmatrix}$.

In three dimensions, a shear has an invariant plane.
Under such a shear all other points move parallel to that plane.
In three dimensions volume is invariant under a shear.

Exercise B

1 Make one copy of Figure 8, and on it construct the following enlargements of the flag:

(a) centre (2, 6), scale factor 2;
(b) centre (10, 8), scale factor $1\frac{1}{2}$;
(c) centre (8, 0), scale factor $\frac{1}{2}$;
(d) centre (5, 5), scale factor $^-3$.

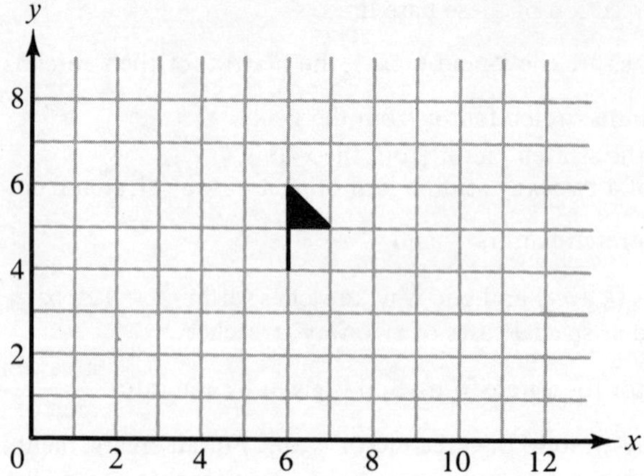

Figure 8

2 For each image in Figure 9, find the centre and the scale factor of the enlargement.

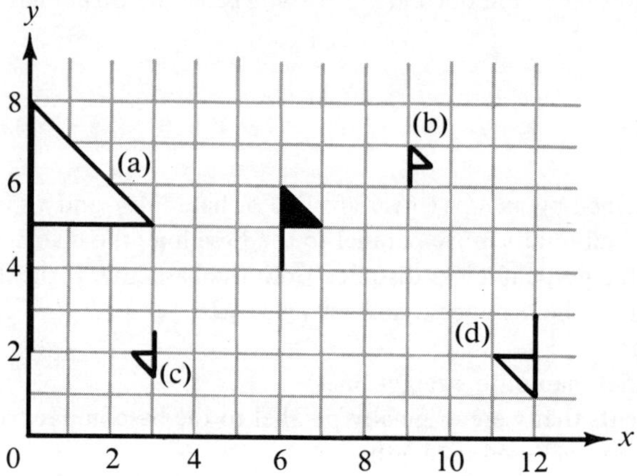

Figure 9

3 Copy the table below, and complete it by filling in the coordinates of the images of A, B and C under the given enlargements.

Centre	Scale factor	$A(4, 0)$	$B(3, {}^{-}4)$	$C(0, {}^{-}5)$
(0, 0)	4			
(2, 2)	$^{-}1$			
(5, $^{-}$1)	2.5			
(0, 3)	$^{-}0.2$			

4 (a) Draw x-axis for values from $^{-}12$ to 10 and y-axis for values from $^{-}10$ to 10. Draw the squares $A(2, 0)$, $B(10, 0)$, $C(10, 8)$, $D(2, 8)$ and $P(^{-}1, 0)$, $Q(^{-}1, ^{-}4)$, $R(^{-}5, ^{-}4)$, $S(^{-}5, 0)$.

(b) Describe two enlargements that map the smaller square onto the larger square.

5 (a) Copy Figure 10 and draw the enlargement of T from the centre $(8, 0)$ with scale factor 2. Label this image T'.

(b) Now draw T'', the enlargement of T' from the centre $(0, 8)$ with scale factor $^{-}1.5$.

(c) Describe the transformation that maps T'' onto T.

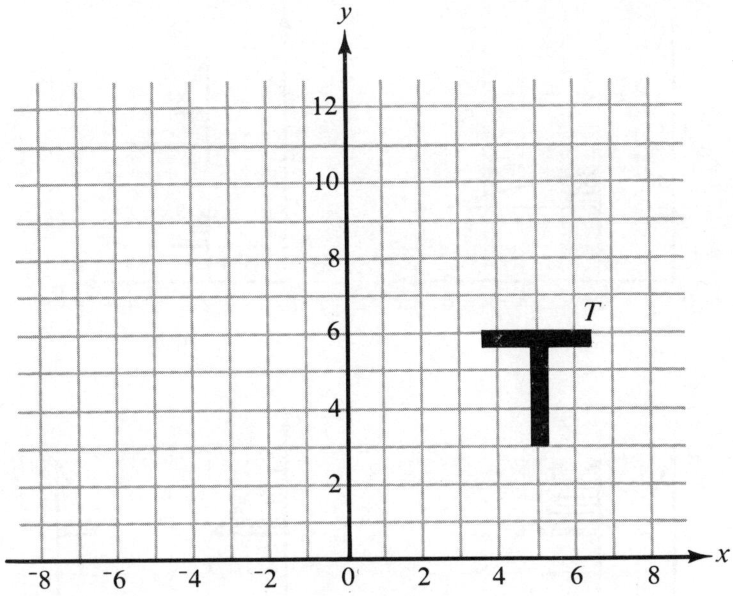

Figure 10

6 The vertices of a triangle are $F(2, 4)$, $G(2, 8)$, and $H(6, 2)$.

(a) Find the image of triangle FGH under the transformation whose matrix is $\begin{bmatrix} 0.25 & 0 \\ 0 & 0.25 \end{bmatrix}$.

(b) Describe this transformation.

7 Repeat question 6 for the transformations with the following matrices. (You may find a diagram helpful in describing the transformations.)

(a) $\begin{bmatrix} 2 & 0 \\ 0 & 1 \end{bmatrix}$ (b) $\begin{bmatrix} 0.25 & 0 \\ 0 & 1 \end{bmatrix}$ (c) $\begin{bmatrix} 1 & 0 \\ 0 & 1.5 \end{bmatrix}$ (d) $\begin{bmatrix} 1 & 0 \\ 0 & ^-0.5 \end{bmatrix}$

8 Draw the triangle $T(2, 0)$, $U(4, 0)$, $V(1, 6)$ and construct its images under the following stretches.

(a) One-way stretch from the line $y = 2$, with scale factor $\frac{1}{2}$.

(b) One-way stretch from the line $x = 0$, with scale factor $^-2$.

(c) Two-way stretch from the lines $x = {}^-1$ (scale factor 2) and $y = 0$ (scale factor $^-1$).

9 For each part of question 8 calculate or measure the ratio $\dfrac{\text{area of image}}{\text{area of object}}$.

10 Draw the triangle TUV (described in question 8) and its images under the transformations whose matrices are as follows. Describe each transformation as fully as possible.

(a) $\begin{bmatrix} 1 & 0 \\ 0.5 & 1 \end{bmatrix}$ (b) $\begin{bmatrix} 1 & ^-2 \\ 0 & 1 \end{bmatrix}$ (c) $\begin{bmatrix} 1 & 0 \\ ^-1.5 & 1 \end{bmatrix}$

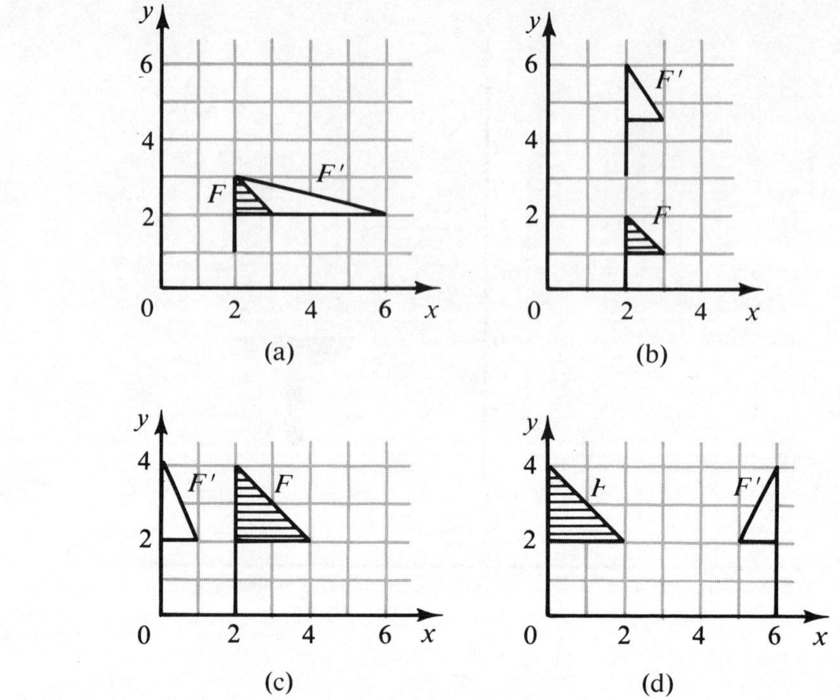

Figure 11

11 Each part of Figure 11 shows an object F and its image F' under a one-way stretch. For each part, write down the scale factor, and the equation of the base line (invariant line), of the stretch.

12 Each part of Figure 12 shows an object F and its image F' under a shear. For each part, name or describe the base line of the shear, and state the image of the point (2, 2).

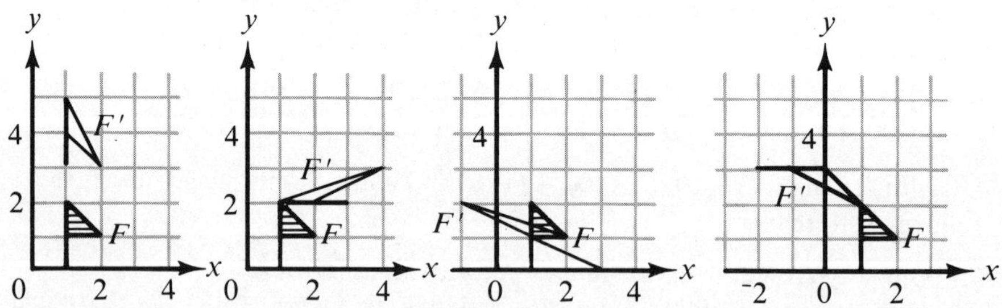

Figure 12

3.3 Geometry (Chapters 1 and 2 of *Geometry 2: Shapes and Similarity*)

Chapter 1

Geometrical figures or objects are similar if they have the same shape.
If two figures are similar, then corresponding lengths are in proportion (and the ratio

of any two corresponding lengths gives the scale factor) and corresponding angles are equal in size.

Two triangles are similar if:

three pairs of sides are in proportion;

or the triangles are equiangular;

or two pairs of sides are in proportion, and the angles between them are equal in size.

An enlargement is a special case of similarity in which no rotation is involved.

In a similarity (including an enlargement):

the area factor is the square of the scale factor;

the volume factor is the cube of the scale factor.

Chapter 2

The mid-point theorem for triangles states that

'the line joining the mid-points of two sides of a triangle is parallel to the third side and half the length of that side'.

The converse result is also true.

A median of a triangle joins a vertex to the mid-point of the opposite side.

The three medians of a triangle are concurrent (all pass through one point).

This point G is called the centroid (centre of gravity) of the triangle, and it divides each median in the ratio 2:1.

The mediator (perpendicular bisector) of a side of a triangle is the line through the mid-point of the side, at right-angles to that side.

The three mediators of a triangle are concurrent.

The point O where they meet is called the circumcentre of the triangle.

It is the centre of a circle (the circumscribed circle) that can be drawn to pass through all three vertices of the triangle.

The bisectors of the three angles of a triangle are concurrent.

The point I where they meet is called the incentre of the triangle.

With I as centre, a circle (the inscribed circle) can be drawn inside the triangle to touch all three sides of the triangle.

Some special types of quadrilaterals (shapes with four sides) are as follows:

A trapezium has one pair of (opposite) sides parallel. If the non-parallel sides are equal in length the trapezium is isosceles. Isosceles trapeziums have one line of symmetry (joining the mid-points of the parallel sides); other trapeziums have no symmetry.

A parallelogram has both pairs of opposite sides parallel. The opposite sides are equal in length, and the opposite angles are equal in size. The diagonals bisect each other, and each bisects the area. There is point symmetry about the intersection of the diagonals. An 'ordinary' parallelogram has no lines of symmetry.

A kite is a quadrilateral in which one of the diagonals is a line of symmetry. This diagonal is the mediator of the other diagonal. Adjacent sides that meet at an end of this diagonal are equal in length. The line of symmetry bisects the angles at its ends. The other two angles are equal to each other in size.

If one of the interior angles at the end of the line of symmetry of a kite is reflex (i.e. the quadrilateral has a re-entrant angle), then the quadrilateral is usually called an *arrowhead*.

A rhombus is a quadrilateral in which both diagonals are lines of symmetry. It may be regarded as a special case of a parallelogram or a kite in which all the sides have the same length. The diagonals are perpendicular to each other; and each bisects the angles of the rhombus.

A rectangle is a parallelogram with one (and hence all) angles right-angles. The diagonals are equal in length (but they do not bisect the angles). A rectangle has two lines of symmetry, each joining the mid-points of a pair of opposite sides.

A square is a parallelogram with all of its sides equal in length, and all of its angles equal in size (and therefore right-angles). It is also a special case of a kite, a rhombus or a rectangle. It has four lines of symmetry and rotational symmetry of order four.

Exercise C

1 For each part of Figure 13 state whether the two triangles are similar or not. For those that are similar, state the image of triangle *FGH* (taking care to write down the vertices of the image in the corresponding order) and the scale factor of the mapping.

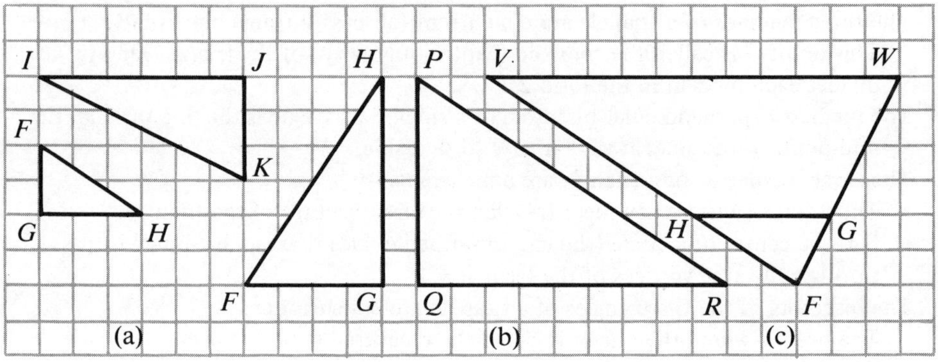

Figure 13

2 Each part of Figure 14 shows a pair of similar triangles *FGH* and *PQR*. For each part calculate the values of x and y, and the scale factor of the mapping $FGH \to PQR$.

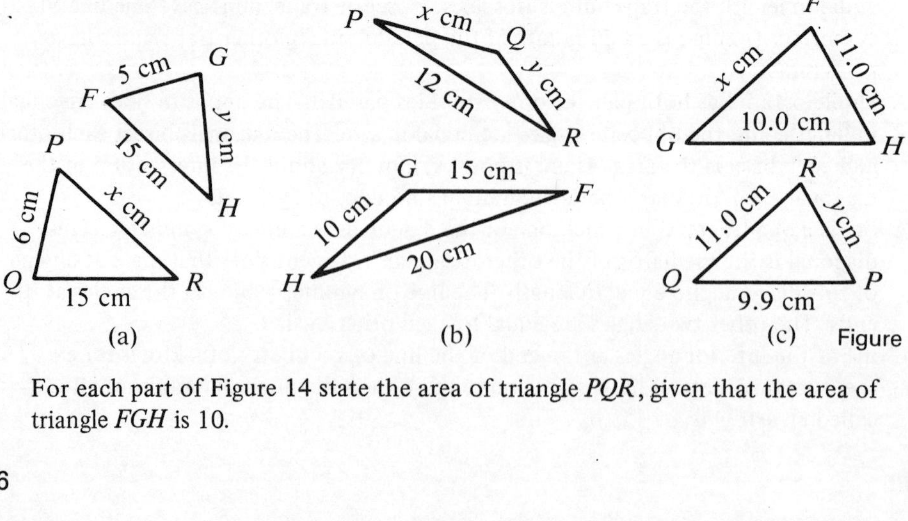

(a) (b) (c) Figure 14

3 For each part of Figure 14 state the area of triangle *PQR*, given that the area of triangle *FGH* is 10.

4 A pyramid, with a square base of side 10 cm and a height of 15 cm, is divided into two parts by a plane cut that is parallel to the base, and 3 cm from the base.

(a) Describe the shape produced by the cut.
(b) Calculate the volume of the original pyramid, and of the two parts into which it is divided.
(c) Use a calculator to find (by trial and error, or otherwise) how far from the base (correct to two significant figures) the cut should be for the two parts to have the same volume.

5 In Figure 15 the line PQ is parallel to BC.
$AB = 12$ cm, $AC = 15$ cm, and $BC = 20$ cm.
(a) If $PQ = 16$ cm, calculate the lengths of AP and QC.
(b) If $PB = 3$ cm, calculate the lengths of AQ and PQ.

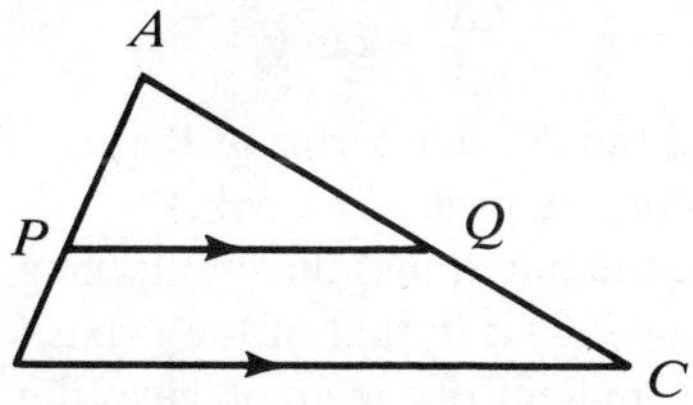

Figure 15

6 Triangle RST is right-angled at S, and angles R and T are both 45°.
Draw an accurate diagram to show the positions of the circumcentre O, the incentre I, and the centroid (centre of gravity) G.

7 From Figure 16(a) name a non-isosceles trapezium, an isosceles trapezium, a kite, an arrowhead, a rhombus, and a rectangle.

8 From Figure 16(b) state what special type of quadrilateral each of the following is.
ABCD, *ABPS*, *ABQS*, *BCRQ*, *QRDS*, and *BPSQ*

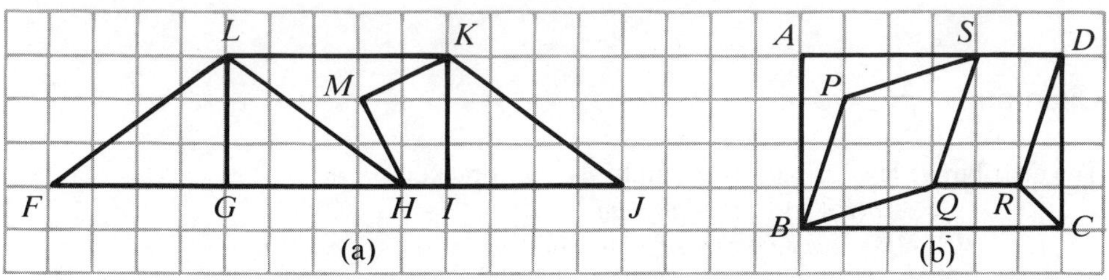

Figure 16

9 For each part of Figure 17 state the sizes of the angles marked x, y and z.

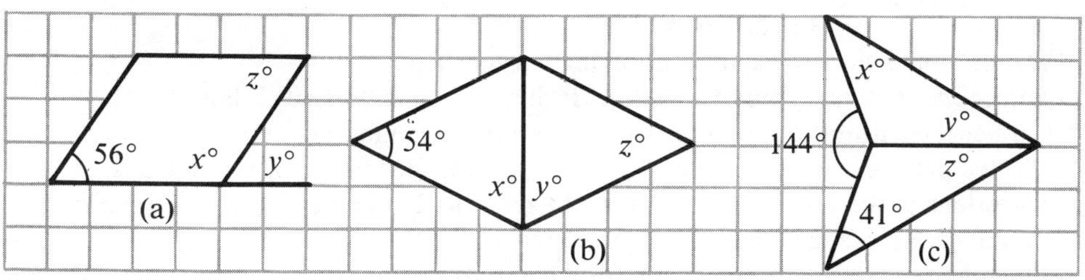

Figure 17

3.4 **Algebra** (Chapter 3 of *Algebra 2: Equations, Formulas and Graphs* and Chapter 1 of *Further Algebra and Computation*)

Gradients

The gradient of a straight line is the ratio $\frac{LN}{MN}$ (see Figure 18).

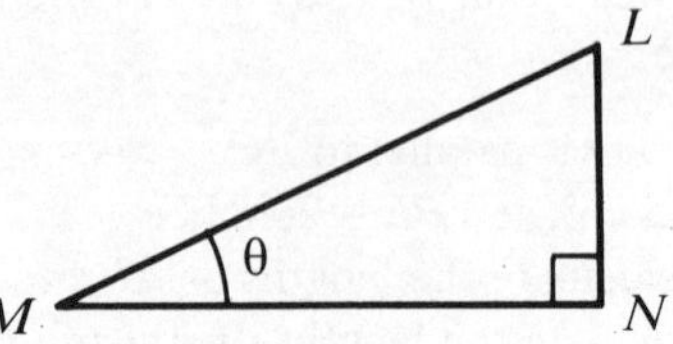

Figure 18

$$\text{gradient} = m = \frac{LN}{MN} = \tan\theta$$

(The values of LN, MN and $\tan\theta$ are in terms of the coordinates of L, M and N; **not** the actual lengths or angles on the page of a book.)

If, going from left to right, the line slopes downhill, the gradient is negative.

The gradient of the x-axis ($y = 0$) is 0; that of the y-axis ($x = 0$) is infinite.

For any relation $x \to y$ the gradient of the graph gives the rate of change of y with respect to x (measured in the units of the graph).

For a linear function $f{:}x \to mx + c$ (or an equation $y = mx + c$) the gradient is given by the value of m, the coefficient of x.

For a non-linear function (i.e. one whose graph is a curve) the gradient is not constant. In such cases we can give either the average gradient over an interval of x; or an estimate of the gradient at a point.
(The latter may be found by drawing a tangent to the curve at the point.)

The gradient at a point on a distance-time graph gives the speed at that instant; the gradient of a speed-time graph gives the acceleration.

Quadratic expressions

The distributive law enables us to 'multiply out' brackets:

$$a(b + c) = ab + ac$$
$$(p + q)(r + s) = pr + ps + qr + qs.$$

Some special examples worth remembering are

$$(a + b)^2 = a^2 + 2ab + b^2$$
$$(a - b)^2 = a^2 - 2ab + b^2$$
$$(a + b)(a - b) = a^2 - b^2.$$

Factorisation is the reverse of multiplying out brackets.

Expressions containing only two terms (if they can be factorised) follow:
either the pattern $ab + ac = a(b + c)$ (a is the 'common factor');
or the pattern $x^2 - y^2 = (x + y)(x - y)$ (the 'difference of two squares').

Expressions of the form $x^2 + px + q$ can be factorised as $(x + s)(x + t)$ if we can find numbers s and t such that $s + t = p$ and $st = q$.

A quadratic expression is one of the form $ax^2 + bx + c$.

A quadratic function is of the form $f\!:x \rightarrow ax^2 + bx + c$ or $y = ax^2 + bx + c$.
(The graph of a quadratic function is a parabola.)

A quadratic equation is an equation of the form $ax^2 + bx + c = 0$.
A quadratic equation may have two, one, or no solutions (roots, answers).

Quadratic equations may be solved graphically, or by factorisation.
(There are other methods, including 'using the formula'.)

The factorisation method uses the result that if the product of two numbers is zero, then one (or both) of those numbers is zero.

Exercise D

1 For each part of Figure 19 find the rate of change of the variable shown, stating the units in which the change is measured.

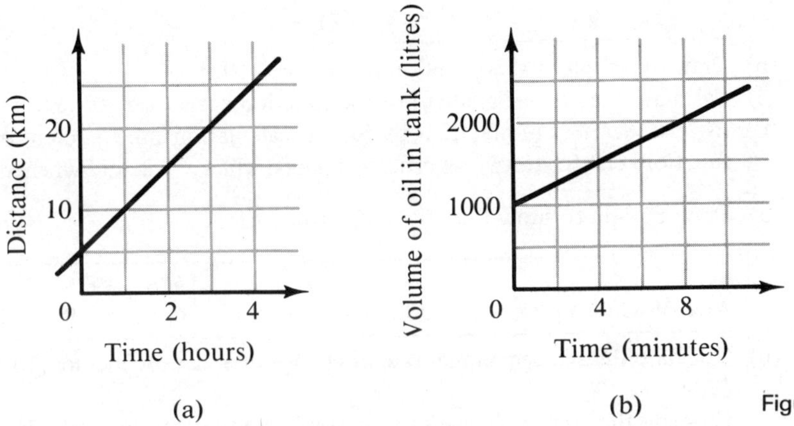

Figure 19

2 Show the following information graphically, and read from your graph the rate of change of growth with respect to height above sea level.

Height above sea level (metres)	200	300	500	750	1000
Annual growth (cm)	48	44	37	28	19

3 (a) The upper part of Perran Hill is 200 metres long; and the sign at the top states that it has a gradient of 12.5%.
Express this as a gradient in the form *1 in n* (where n is an integer), and calculate the change in height above sea level when driving down this section.

(b) The lower part of the hill has a gradient of 1 in 6; and the change in vertical height is the same as the top part.
Express the gradient of the lower part as a percentage (correct to one decimal place); and calculate the length of the lower part of the hill.

4 Write down the gradients of the following lines.

(a) $y = 2x - 7$ (b) $y = 3 + 4x$ (c) $x = 2y$ (d) $3x + y = 9$
(e) $y = 5 - 6x$ (f) $2y - 3x = 10$ (g) $y = 8$ (h) $7x + 11 = 0$

5 For each part of Figure 20 write down the gradient of the line shown.

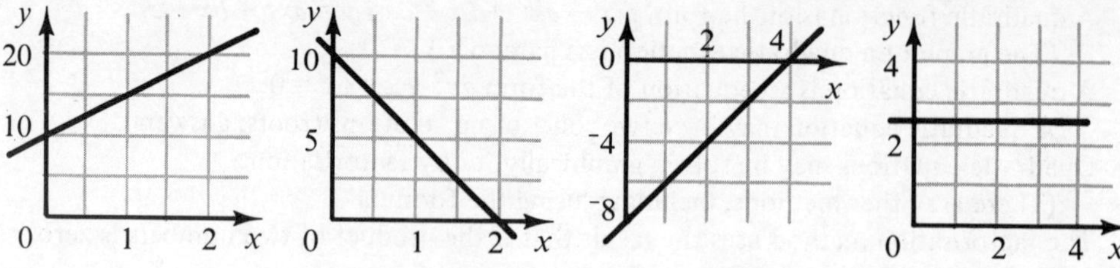

(a) (b) (c) (d)

Figure 20

6 (a) Copy and complete the table below for the function $y = 0.5x^2 + 3x + 1$.

x	0	2	4	6	8	10
y	1	9				81

(b) Draw the graph of this function for $0 \leqslant x \leqslant 10$.
(c) Calculate the average gradient of the function between $x = 2$ and $x = 8$.
(d) Estimate from your graph, or by further calculations, the gradient of the function, correct to two significant figures, when $x = 2$, and when $x = 8$.

7 (a) Draw a graph to show the following information.

Year	1976	1978	1980	1982	1984
Area of wildlands ($km^2 \times 1000$) at end of year	628	553	504	465	442

(b) Calculate the average annual rate of change of area of wildlands from 1976 to 1984.
(c) Estimate the rate of change of area of wildlands at the end of 1976, and at the end of 1984.

8 For the following journey draw (a) the speed–time graph; (b) the distance–time graph.
Starting from rest a constant acceleration of 2 m/s^2 for 9 seconds;
a steady (constant) speed for 90 metres;
a constant deceleration so that it takes 3 seconds to come to rest.

9 Work out the following.
(a) $(x + 6)(x - 4)$ (b) $(x - 3)(2x + 7)$ (c) $(t + 5)(8 - 3t)$
(d) $(2w + 5)(3w + 7)$ (e) $(3 + 2s)(8s + 1)$ (f) $(4 - 3y)(5 - 2y)$
(g) $(3 - 2q)(5q + 1)$ (h) $(x + 5y)(2x - y)$ (i) $(3s - 2t)(5t + s)$

10 Write down the expansions of the following.
(a) $(x - 4)^2$ (b) $(w + 2v)^2$ (c) $(2q + 5s)^2$ (d) $(a + 3b)(3b - a)$

11 Factorise the following.
(a) $5p + 40$ (b) $36 - 9q$ (c) $24s^2 + 16st$ (d) $3xyz + 12xz$
(e) $11 + 11w$ (f) $13t - qt$ (g) $18gh + 24fh$ (h) $20 - 10xyz$

12 Factorise the following.
(a) $x^2 + 7x + 10$ (b) $y^2 - 11y + 24$ (c) $z^2 + 5z - 24$ (d) $t^2 - 6t - 16$
(e) $s^2 + 2s - 24$ (f) $w^2 - 11w + 30$ (g) $d^2 - 9d - 10$ (h) $x^2 + 17x + 72$

13 (a) Complete the following table, and then draw the graph of $y = x^2 - 6x + 5$ for values of x between $^-1$ and 7.

x	$^-1$	0	1	2	3	4	5	6	7
y		5	0						12

(b) Write down the equation of the line of symmetry of this graph. What is the minimum value of the function $f: x \rightarrow x^2 - 6x + 5$?

14 Use the graph you have drawn for question 13 to solve the following equations.
(a) $x^2 - 6x + 5 = 0$ (b) $x^2 - 6x + 8 = 0$ (c) $x^2 - 6x = 1$

15 (a) On the same axes draw the graphs of $y = x^2$ and $y = 6x + 1$, for values of x between $^-1$ and 7.
(b) Write down the x-coordinates of the points where the two graphs cross. Write down a quadratic equation that has these values of x as its solutions.

16 Solve the following equations by factorisation.
(a) $s^2 - 2s - 15 = 0$ (b) $t^2 + 10t + 21 = 0$ (c) $16 - 8w + w^2 = 0$

3.5 Using a calculator (Chapter 2 of *Further Algebra and Computation*)

When using a calculator:
(a) write down the question/sum on paper;
(b) consider the most effective order of carrying out the stages;
(c) work to the full capacity of the machine;
(d) check your work by doing the calculation in another order;
(e) give the answer to a suitable degree of accuracy.

Calculators may usefully be used in numerical problems involving matrices;
compiling tables for points to be plotted on a graph;
determining accuracy of results, and limits of accuracy; etc.

In complex calculations or problems a flow diagram can be helpful.
A flow diagram shows the stages to be worked through, but it does not always list every key-stroke required to evaluate that stage.

A loop in a flow diagram indicates that a sequence of operations has to be performed several times. The number obtained at the end of each operation of the loop should be recorded (written down) each time.

The end of a loop is usually a decision box, the answer to which determines whether the loop should be followed again, or not.

A calculator may be used to solve some equations by iterative methods.
The equation is first re-written in the form $x = F(x)$.
Then, using the 'iteration' (relation) $x_{n+1} = F(x_n)$, successive approximations to a solution are found from an initial value x_0.

Exercise E

1 Use a calculator to evaluate the following, correct to four significant figures.
(a) $(23.45)^2 + (18.03)^2 - 2 \times 23.45 \times 18.03 \times \cos 56°$

(b) The square root of $\frac{4 \times 3.1416^2 \times 101.4}{9.81}$

(c) $\frac{(82.3)^2 - (50.5)^2 + (16.7)^2}{(345.6 + 199.5)(12.52 - 9.89)}$

2 A pyramid has a square base of side 10 cm, and a height of 8.4 cm, all measurements being correct to two significant figures.

(a) Calculate, correct to five significant figures, the maximum and minimum possible volumes.

(b) Let V be the volume obtained by treating the above measurements as exact. Calculate the difference between the maximum possible volume and the value of V as a percentage of V (correct to three significant figures).

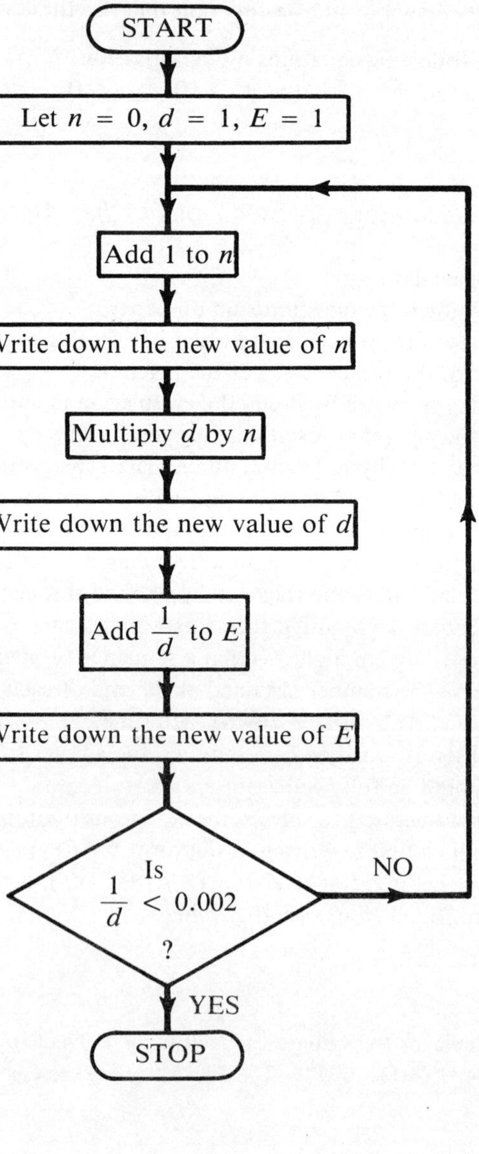

Figure 21

3 Evaluate $\begin{bmatrix} 1.2 & 3.7 & ^-2.5 \\ 0.8 & ^-6.2 & 4.5 \end{bmatrix} \begin{bmatrix} 4.5 & ^-1.15 & 2.5 \\ 0 & 7.4 & 0 \\ ^-0.8 & 10.4 & 1.2 \end{bmatrix}$

4 (a) Copy and complete the table below for the function $f: x \rightarrow x^3 - 15.2x + 7.8$.

x	3.5	3.55	3.6	3.65	3.7	3.75	3.8
y	$^-2.525$						4.912

(b) By further calculation, or by drawing a graph, solve the equation $f(x) = 0$, for $3.5 \leqslant x \leqslant 3.8$, correct to three significant figures.

5 Copy the table below, and use the flow diagram shown in Figure 21 to complete it.

n	d	$\frac{1}{d}$	E
0	1	1	1
...			
...			

6 Starting with $x_0 = 3.6$, use the iteration $x_{n+1} = \dfrac{15.2x_n - 7.8}{x_n^2}$ to solve the equation in question 4(b) correct to two decimal places.

7 (a) Write down the iteration represented by Figure 22.
(b) Starting with $x = 1$, use the flow diagram in Figure 22 to find one solution, correct to four significant figures, of the equation $x^3 + 5x^2 - 10 = 0$.

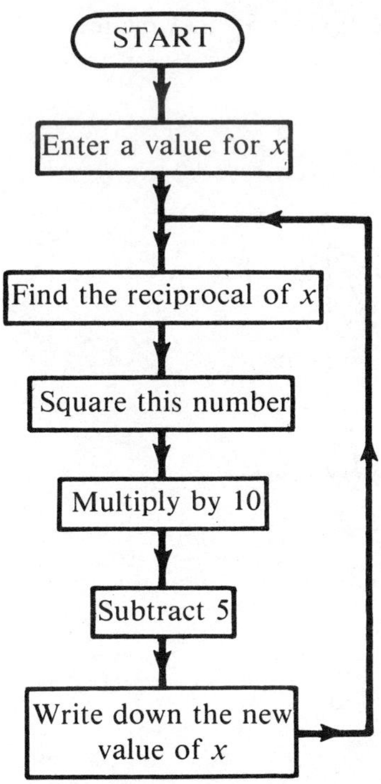

Figure 22

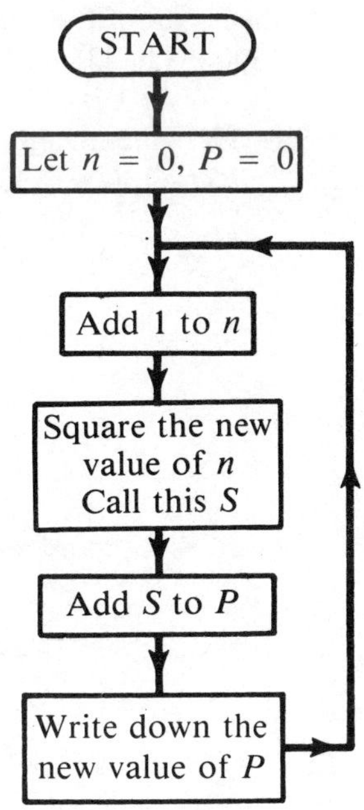

Figure 23

8 (a) Find the first eleven numbers produced by the flow diagram shown in Figure 23.
(b) Can you identify this sequence of numbers?

Answers

Exercise A

(All answers are given correct to three significant figures unless otherwise stated.)

1 (a) $x = 12 \tan 72° = 36.9$ (b) $x = 15 \tan 37° = 11.3$
(c) $x = 10 \tan 29° = 5.54$ (d) $x = 3 \tan 81° = 18.9$

(e) $\frac{20}{x} = \tan 77°$; i.e. $x = \frac{20}{\tan 77°} = 4.62$

(f) $\frac{16}{x} = \tan 34°$; i.e. $x = \frac{16}{\tan 34°} = 23.7$

An alternative method for (e) and (f), particularly if a calculator is not available, is to use the complementary angle. This gives $x = 20 \times \tan 13°$ in (e), and $x = 16 \times \tan 56°$ in (f).

2 (a) 67.4° (b) 22.6° (c) 66.0° (d) 29.7° (e) 14.7° (f) 56.0°
(If a calculator is not available, parts (e) and (f) are solved more easily by finding the complementary angles first. In (e), for example, $\tan c° = \frac{19}{5} = 3.80$; which gives $c = 75.3$, and hence $x = 14.7$)

3 See Figure A.
Let the height of the mast be h metres, and the distance SX be x metres.
$h = 1300 \times \tan 23° = 552$
$x = h \times \tan SYX = 552 \times \tan 44° = 533$
Hence $SX = 533$ m, and
$PS = (1300 - 533)$ m $= 767$ m.

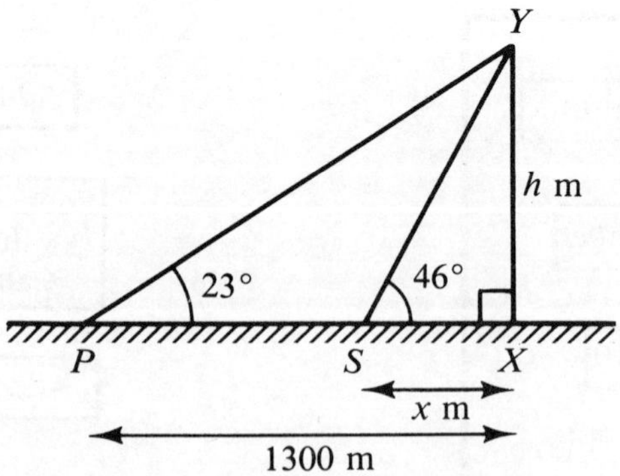

Figure A

4 See Figure B.
$PT = (24 \times \cos 5° + 16 \times \cos 66°)$ km $= 30.4$ km
$RT = (16 \times \sin 66° - 24 \times \sin 5°)$ km $= 12.5$ km
$PR^2 = PT^2 + RT^2 = 1080$ km^2
$PR = \sqrt{(1080)}$ km $= 32.9$ km

$\tan TPR = \dfrac{12.5}{30.4} = 0.411$; angle $TPR = 22.4°$
The bearing of R from P is $(90 + 22.4)° = 112°$.

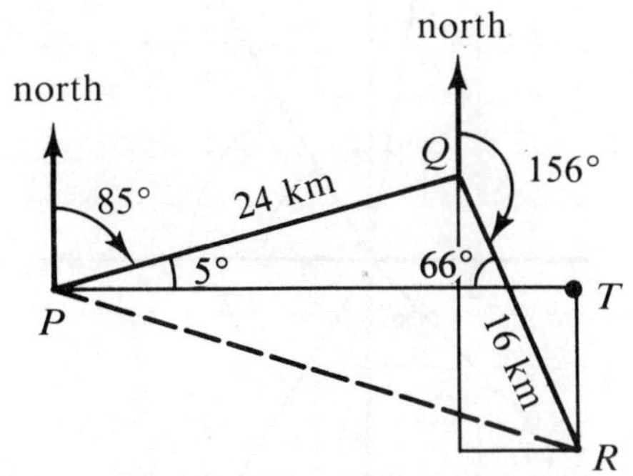

Figure B

5 Find the difference between the given angle and the nearest multiple of 180°, and then use the graph of the tangent function to decide the sign (+ or −).
(a) $^{-}\tan 69° = {}^{-}2.61$; $\tan 54°$ or 1.38; $^{-}0.466$; $^{-}0.839$
(b) If $\tan x° = 2.4$, then $x = 67.4 + 180n$, where n is an integer. Hence if $200 < x < 300$, the required answer is 247°.
The other answers are 327°, $^{-}297°$, and $^{-}45°$.

6 (a) Since $\tan x = \dfrac{\sin x}{\cos x}$, $\tan x = {}^{-}\frac{8}{15}$; $x = ({}^{-}28 + 180n)°$. As $\sin x > 0$, and $\cos x < 0$, x must be in the second quadrant. Hence possible values are 152°, 512°, . . . ; i.e. $(152 + 360n)°$. See Figure C(a).
(b) See Figure C(b).
Pythagoras' theorem gives $d = 60$. Hence $\tan y = {}^{-}\frac{11}{60}$.

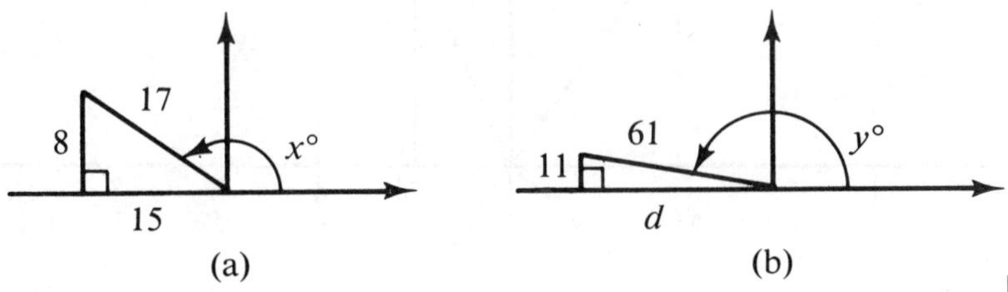

Figure C

7 (a) $x^2 = 12^2 + 16^2 = 400$; $x = 20$
(b) $x^2 = 17^2 - 15^2 = 64$; $x = 8$
(c) $x = \sqrt{34} = 5.83$ (d) $x = \sqrt{75} = 8.66$ (e) $x = 4.80$ (f) $x = 15.1$
Parts (a) and (b) are 'exact' answers, as 12, 16, 20 and 8, 15, 17 are Pythagorean triples. Part (d) is a 30°, 60°, 90° triangle; hence $x = 5\sqrt{3}$.

8 (a) (8.06, 60.3°); (5.83, $^{-}59°$); (6.08, 99.5°); (4.24, 225°) (or (4.24, $^{-}135°$))
(b) (2.03, 4.57); ($^{-}3.44$, 4.91); ($^{-}7.43$, $^{-}6.69$); (2.29, $^{-}3.28$)
See Figure D.

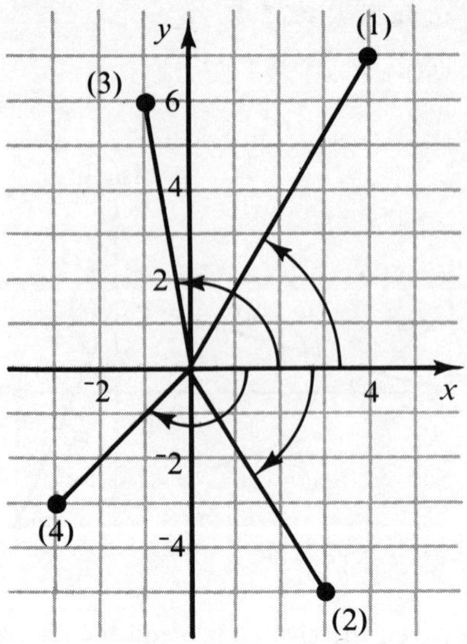

(a)

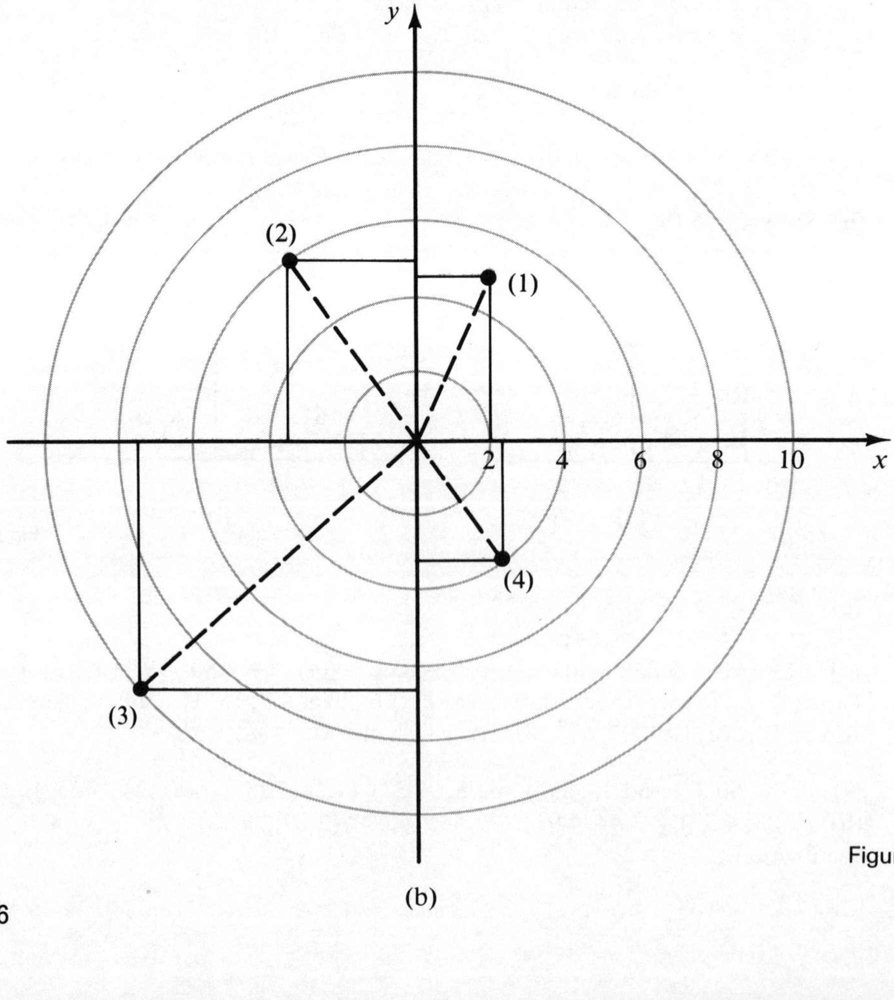

(b)

Figure D

9 See Figure E.

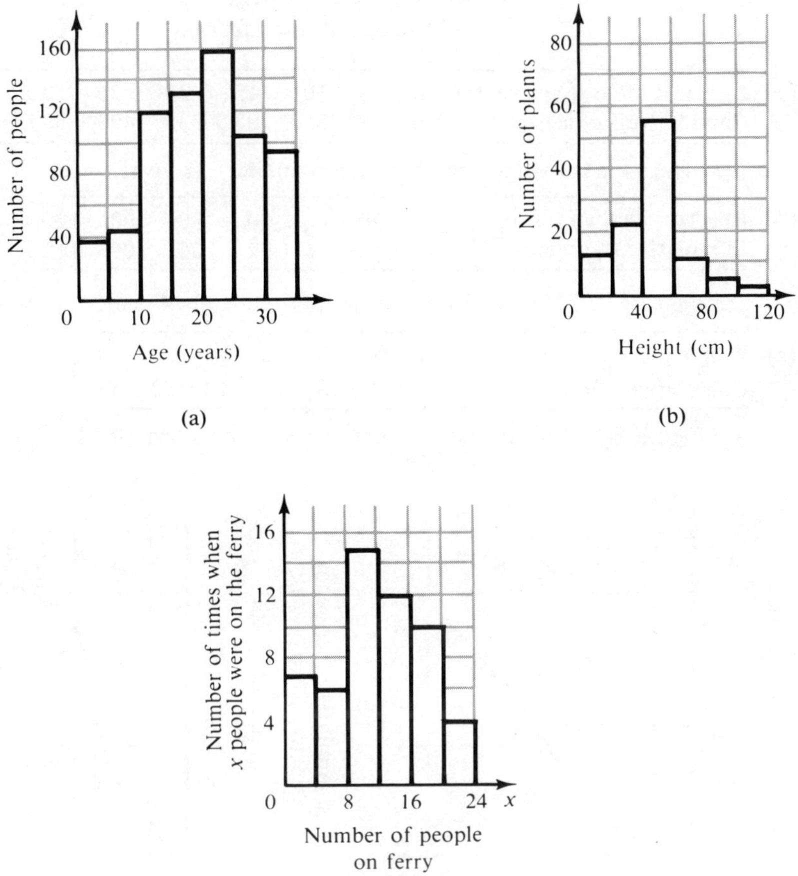

(a) (b) (c)

Figure E

10 (a) The number of different types of stamps was greatest in the 1980–4 period.

The average annual number in this period was $\frac{159}{5} = 32$ (to the nearest integer).

(b) $\frac{6 + 7 + 42 + 120 + 109 + 134 + 159}{35} = \frac{577}{35} = 16.5$ (to 3 s.f.)

11 (a) The total number of people was $(38 + 45 + \ldots + 95) = 692$;
the sum of all the ages was $(38 \times 3 + 45 \times 8 + \ldots + 95 \times 33)$ years
$= 14\,091$ years;

the mean age was $\frac{14\,091}{692} = 20.4$ years.

(b) Total number of plants = 112; sum of all the heights = 5240 cm;

the mean height = $\frac{5240 \text{ cm}}{112} = 46.8$ cm.

(c) Total number of ferry sailings = 54; total number of passengers = 609;

the mean number of passengers per crossing = $\frac{609}{54} = 11.3$.

12 The modal classes are (a) 21–25 year-olds;
(b) 40-60 cm high plants;
(c) 8–11 people (on the ferry).

13 (a)

Age: not older than (years)	0	5	10	15	20	25	30	35
Cumulative frequency	0	38	83	203	335	493	597	692

See Figure F(a). The median age is approximately 21 years.

(b)

Height: less than (cm)	0	20	40	60	80	100	120
Cumulative frequency	0	13	36	92	104	109	112

See Figure F(b). The median height is approximately 48 cm.

(c)

People per ferry: less than	0	4	8	12	16	20	24
Cumulative frequency	0	7	13	28	40	50	54

See Figure F(c). The median number of people on a ferry is 11.

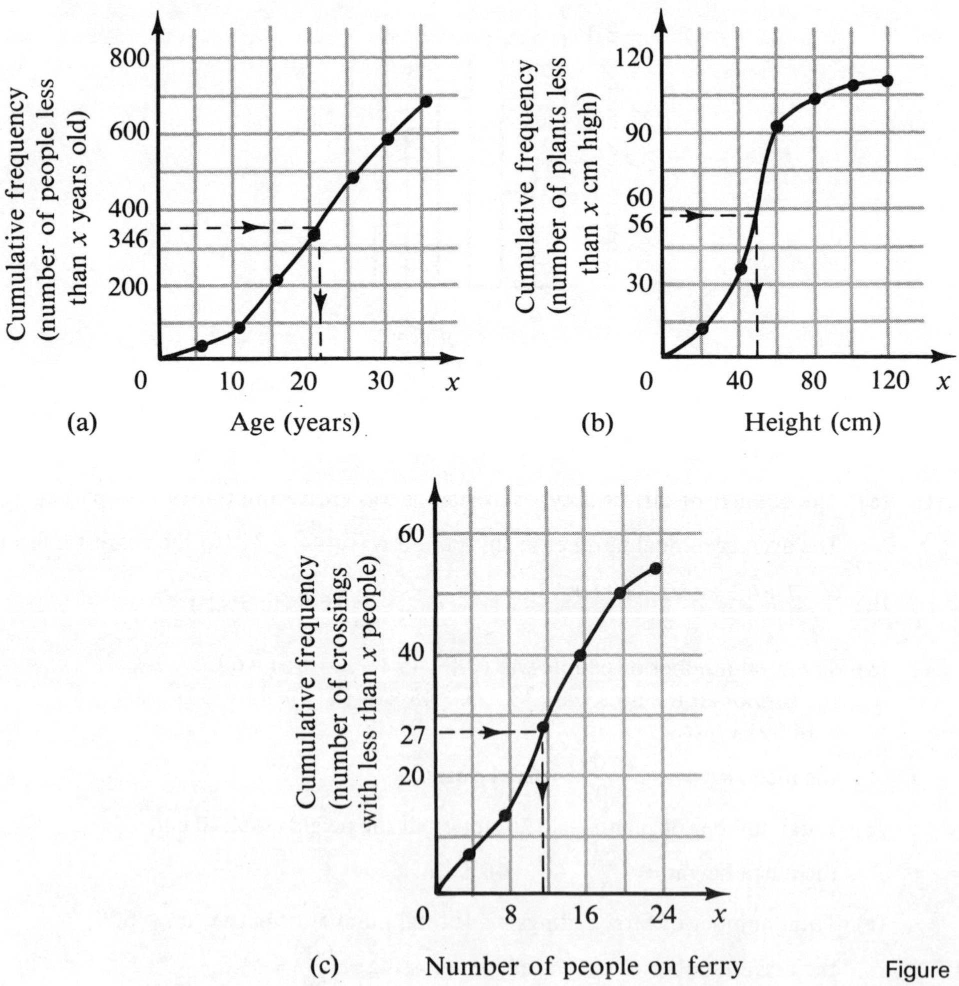

Figure F

Exercise B

1 See Figure G.

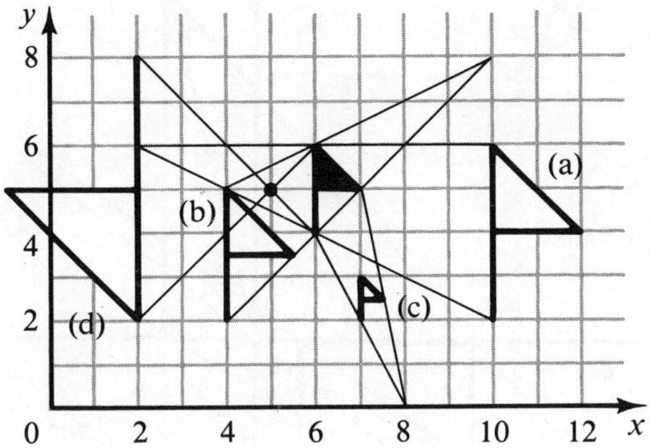

Figure G

2 See Figure H.

(a) centre (9, 5), scale factor 3

(b) centre (12, 8), scale factor $\frac{1}{2}$

(c) centre (4, 3), scale factor $^{-}\frac{1}{2}$

(d) centre $(9, 3\frac{1}{2})$, scale factor $^{-}1$

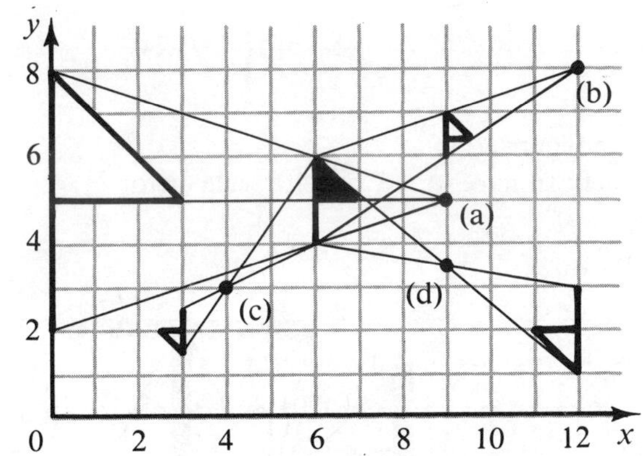

Figure H

3

Centre	Scale factor	$A(4, 0)$	$B(3, ^{-}4)$	$C(0, ^{-}5)$
(0, 0)	4	(16, 0)	(12, $^{-}$16)	(0, $^{-}$20)
(2, 2)	$^{-}$1	(0, 4)	(1, 8)	(4, 9)
(5, $^{-}$1)	2.5	(2.5, 1.5)	(0, $^{-}$8.5)	($^{-}$7.5, $^{-}$11)
(0, 3)	$^{-}$0.2	($^{-}$0.8, 3.6)	($^{-}$0.6, 4.4)	(0, 4.6)

4 (a) See Figure I.

(b) Enlargement from centre ($^{-}$12, $^{-}$8) with scale factor 2; and enlargement from centre (0, 0) with scale factor $^{-}$2.

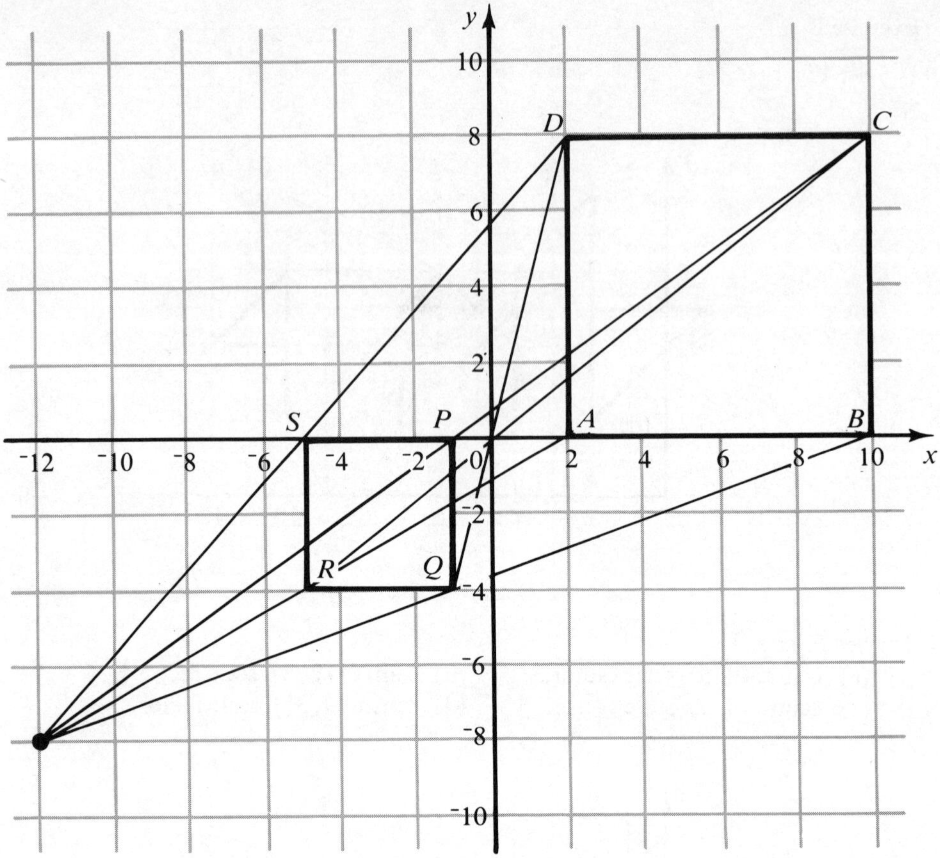

Figure I

5 (a) and (b) See Figure J.

(c) Enlargement from centre (3, 5) with scale factor $^{-}\frac{1}{3}$.

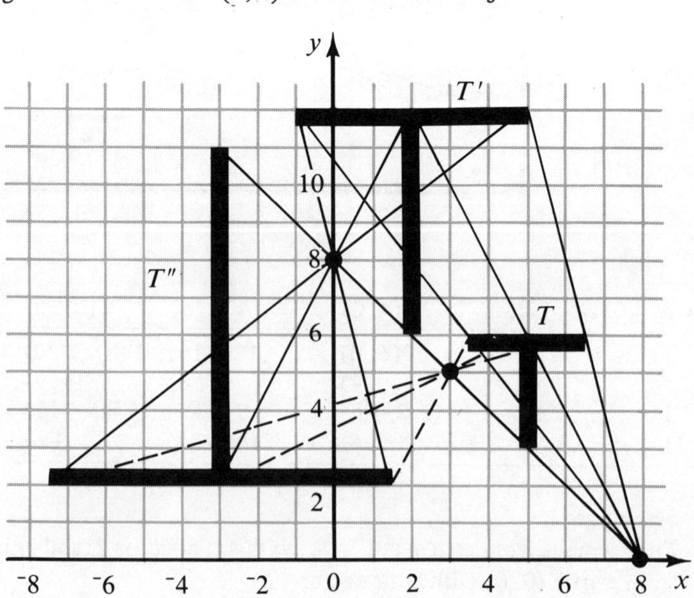

Figure J

6 (a)

$$\begin{bmatrix} 0.25 & 0 \\ 0 & 0.25 \end{bmatrix} \begin{bmatrix} \overset{F}{2} & \overset{G}{2} & \overset{H}{6} \\ 4 & 8 & 2 \end{bmatrix} = \begin{bmatrix} \overset{F'}{0.5} & \overset{G'}{0.5} & \overset{H'}{1.5} \\ 1 & 2 & 0.5 \end{bmatrix}$$

(b) Enlargement from the origin with scale factor 0.25

7

	(a)	(b)	(c)	(d)
F'	(4, 4)	(0.5, 4)	(2, 6)	(2, ⁻2)
G'	(4, 8)	(0.5, 8)	(2, 12)	(2, ⁻4)
H'	(12, 2)	(1.5, 2)	(6, 3)	(6, ⁻1)

All these transformations are one-way stretches. See Figure K.

	(a)	(b)	(c)	(d)
Base line	$x = 0$	$x = 0$	$y = 0$	$y = 0$
Scale factor	2	0.25	1.5	⁻0.5

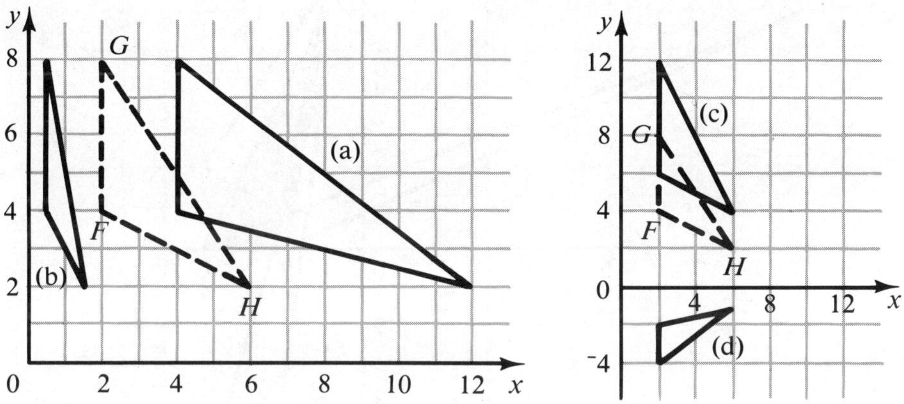

Figure K

8 See Figure L.

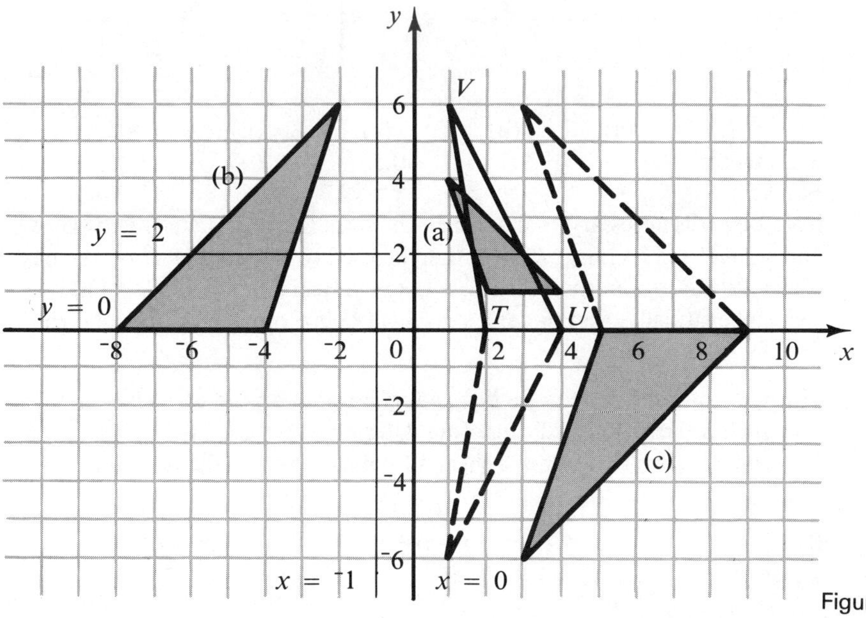

Figure L

In (c) the two stretches may be performed in either order. The broken outlines show the two possible intermediate positions.

9 (a) 1:2 (or $\frac{1}{2}$) (b) and (c) 2:1 (strictly, $^-2$:1)

10 See Figure M. All the transformations are shears.

	T'	U'	V'	Base line	Shear factor
(a)	(2, 1)	(4, 2)	$(1, 6\frac{1}{2})$	$x = 0$	$\frac{1}{2}$
(b)	(2, 0)	(4, 0)	$(^-11, 6)$	$y = 0$	$^-2$
(c)	$(2, ^-3)$	$(4, ^-6)$	$(1, 4\frac{1}{2})$	$x = 0$	$^-1\frac{1}{2}$

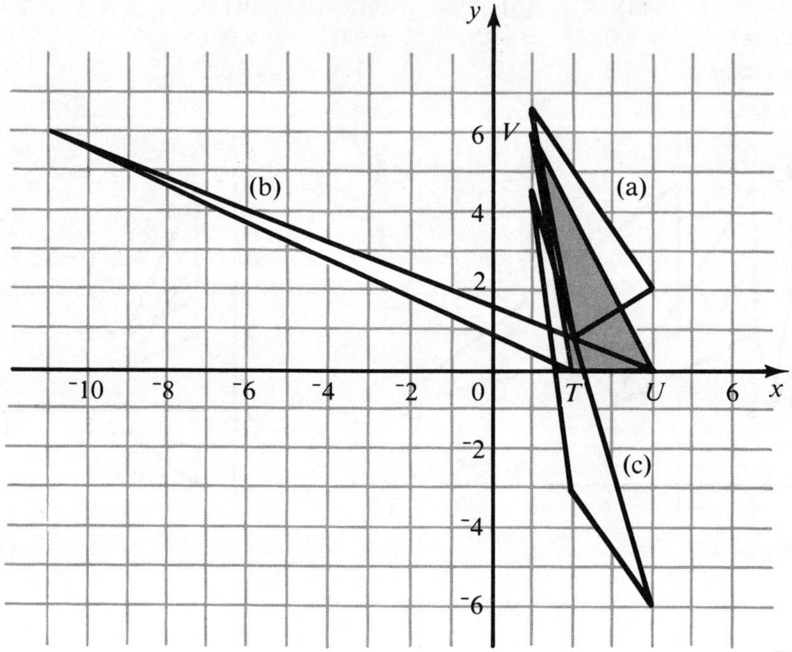

Figure M

		(a)	(b)	(c)	(d)
11	Scale factor	4	1.5	0.5	$^-0.5$
	Base line	$x = 2$	$y = ^-6$	$x = ^-2$	$x = 4$

Note that it is necessary to determine the scale factor k first. The distance between one point P and its image P' may then be used to find a point B on the base line. (Since $BP{:}BP' = 1{:}k$, then $BP{:}PP' = 1{:}k - 1$. Hence $BP = PP'/(k - 1)$.)
Remember, finally, that under a stretch all points move perpendicular to the base line.

12 The point of intersection of a **line** and its image is on the base line.
Two such intersections will therefore determine the base line.
(Remember, also, that under a shear all points move parallel to the base line.)

	(a)	(b)	(c)	(d)
Base line	$x = 4$	$y = x + 1$	$y = 1$	$x + y = 4$
Image of (2, 2)	(2, 4)	(3, 3)	(0, 2)	(2, 2)

Exercise C

1 (a) Triangle FGH is not similar to triangle KJI.
($FG:GH = 2:3$, but $KJ:JI = 3:6$ or $1.5:3$.)
(b) Triangle FGH is similar to triangle PQR with a scale factor of 1.5.
($FG:GH = 4:6 = 2:3$; $PQ:QR = 6:9 = 2:3$; and angles G and Q are right-angles.)
(c) Triangle FGH is similar to triangle FWV with a scale factor of 3.
(As GH is parallel to WV, the triangles are equiangular and therefore similar.)

2 If triangle FGH is similar to triangle PQR,
then $PQ:FG = PR:FH = QR:GH =$ scale factor. This gives
(a) $6:5 = x:15 = 15:y$
$x = 15 \times \frac{6}{5} = 18$; $y = 15 \times \frac{5}{6} = 12.5$; scale factor $= \frac{6}{5} = 1.2$
(b) $x:15 = 12:20 = y:10$
$x = 9$; $y = 6$, scale factor $= 0.6$
(c) $9.9:x = y:11.0 = 11.0:10.0$
$x = 9.0$; $y = 12.1$; scale factor $= 1.1$

3 The ratio of the areas of similar triangles is the square of the scale factor.
Hence the area of triangle $PQR = k^2 \times$ area of triangle $FGH = 10k^2$.
(a) Area of triangle $PQR = 10 \times (1.2)^2 = 14.4$
(b) 3.6 (c) 12.1

4 (a) A square of side 8 cm (the square $WXYZ$ in Figure N). If this square has a side of x cm then $x:10 = 12:15$.
(b) Volume of original pyramid ($VABCD$) $= \frac{1}{3} \times 10^2 \times 15\ \text{cm}^3 = 500\ \text{cm}^3$.
The two pyramids ($VABCD$ and $VWXYZ$) are similar, with a scale factor of $12:15 = 0.8$; hence the volume of the smaller pyramid is $(0.8)^3 \times 500\ \text{cm}^3 = 256\ \text{cm}^3$; and the volume of the truncuated pyramid ($WXYZABCD$) is $(500 - 256)\ \text{cm}^3 = 244\ \text{cm}^3$.

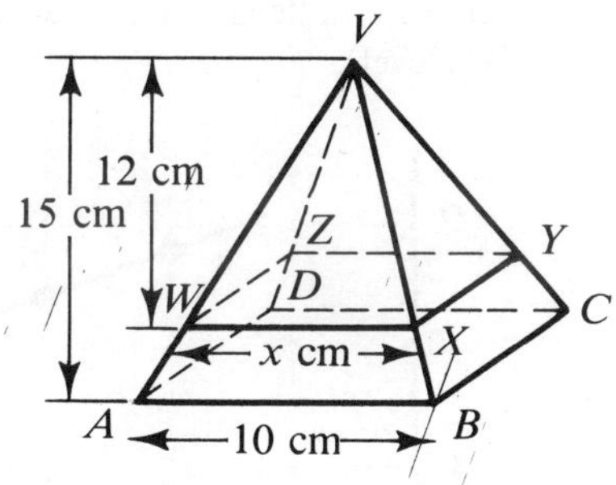

Figure N

(c) At present, the cut is not quite high enough. For equal volumes the volume factor will be 0.5, and the scale factor will be the cube root of $0.5 = 0.7937\ldots$
Hence the height of $VWXYZ$ will be approximately $0.7937 \times 15\ \text{cm} = 11.9\ \text{cm}$ (to three significant figures). The cut should be approximately 3.1 cm above the base.

5 As PQ is parallel to BC, triangles APQ and ABC are similar, and so $AP:AB = AQ:AC = PQ:BC$.
(a) $AP:12\ \text{cm} = AQ:15\ \text{cm} = 16\ \text{cm}:20\ \text{cm}$. $AP = 9.6$ cm and $AQ = 12.0$ cm
Hence $QC = (15.0 - 12.0)\ \text{cm} = 3.0$ cm.
(b) If $PB = 3$ cm, then $AP = 9$ cm.
$9\ \text{cm}:12\ \text{cm} = AQ:15\ \text{cm} = PQ:20\ \text{cm}$. $AQ = 11.25$ cm and $PQ = 15.0$ cm

6 See Figure O.
(O, M and N are the mid-points of the sides of the triangle RST.
RY and TX are the bisectors of angles R and T.)

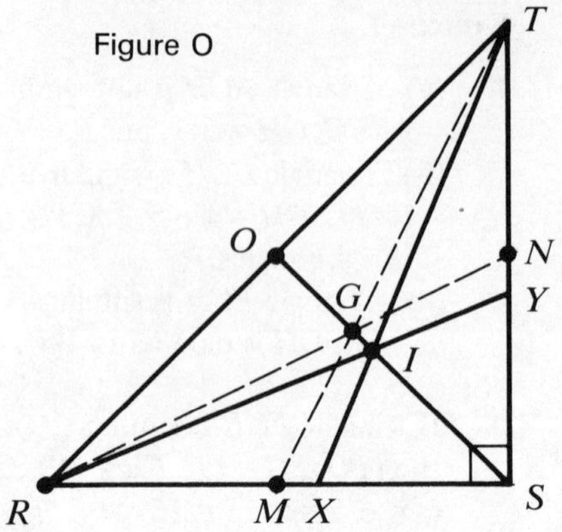

Figure O

7 Non-isosceles trapeziums: *FIKL* or *GJKL*
Kite: *HJKM* Arrowhead: *HMKL*

Isosceles trapezium: *FJKL*
Rhombus: *HJKL* Rectangle: *GIKL*

8 Rectangle, arrowhead, kite, (non-isosceles) trapezium, parallelogram, rhombus

9 (a) $x = 124; y = z = 56$ (b) $x = y = 63; z = 54$ (c) $x = 41; y = z = 72 - 41 = 31$

Exercise D

1 (a) The change is 20 km in 4 hours, giving a *rate of change* of 5 km per hour (5 km/h).
(b) The change is 1000 litres in 8 minutes, i.e. 125 litres per minute.

2 See Figure P.
The decrease in growth from (for example) 500 m above sea level to 1000 m above sea level is 18 cm/year, i.e. a rate of decrease of annual growth of 3.6 cm per 100 m increase in height above sea level (or 0.036 cm per metre increase in height above sea level).

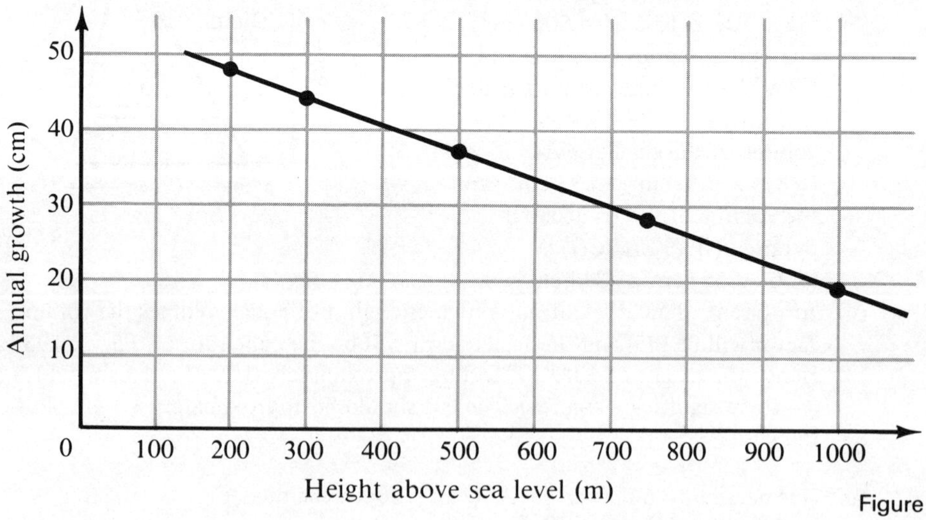

Figure P

3 (a) 12.5% = 12.5 in 100, i.e. 1 in 8.
At this degree of accuracy this may be regarded as 1 vertically for every 8 along the road. Hence a stretch of 200 m of road drops $\frac{200}{8}$ m = 25 m vertically.

(b) 1 in 6 = $\frac{1}{6} \times 100$ in 100, or approximately 16.7 in 100; i.e. 16.7%.
The vertical drop in height is 25 m (from part (a)), hence the actual length of the road will be 6×25 m = 150 m. (See Figure Q.)

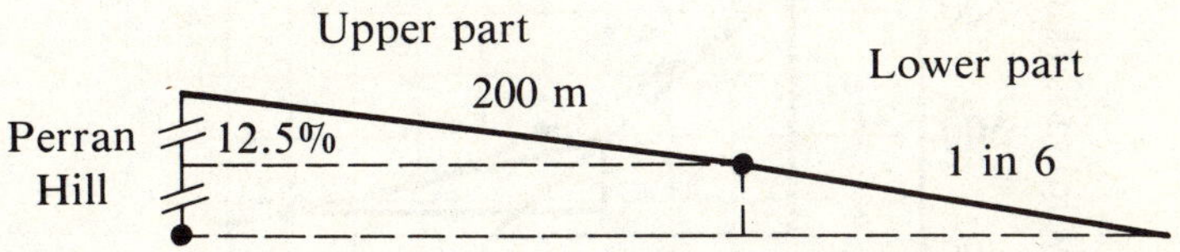

Figure Q

4 When the equation of a straight line is written in the form $y = mx + c$, the gradient of the line is given by the value of m.
(a) 2 (b) 4 (c) $\frac{1}{2} = 0.5$ (d) $^-3$ (e) $^-6$ (f) $\frac{3}{2} = 1.5$
(g) 0 (h) infinite

5 (a) 10 in 2; i.e. a gradient of 5 (b) $^-10$ in 2; i.e. a gradient of $^-5$
(c) 8 in 4; i.e. a gradient of 2 (d) 0

6 (a)

x	0	2	4	6	8	10
y	1	9	21	37	57	81

(b) See Figure R.
(c) The change in y is $57 - 9 = 48$. The change in x is $8 - 2 = 6$.
The average gradient is $\frac{48}{6} = 8$.
(d) See Figure R. The line PQ is the tangent to the curve at the point (8, 57).

The gradient of this tangent is
$$\frac{QR}{PR} = \frac{77 - 22}{10 - 5} = \frac{55}{5} = 11.$$
(Alternatively, using a calculator, $y = 58.105$ when $x = 8.1$;
$y = 55.905$ when $x = 7.9$.
Hence the gradient at T is approximately $(58.105 - 55.905)/(8.1 - 7.9) = 11$.)
The gradient at the point (2, 9) is approximately 5.

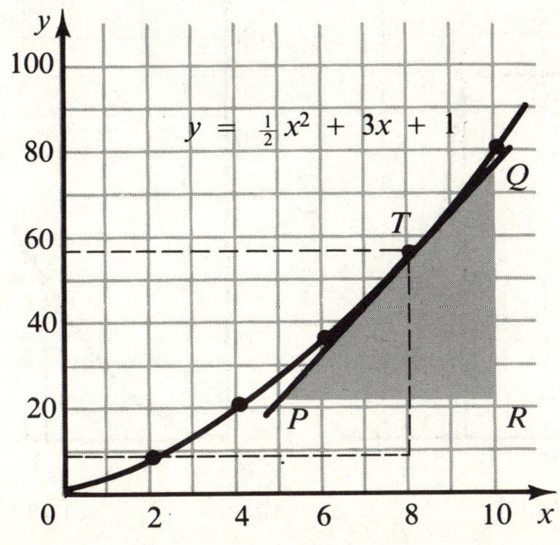

Figure R

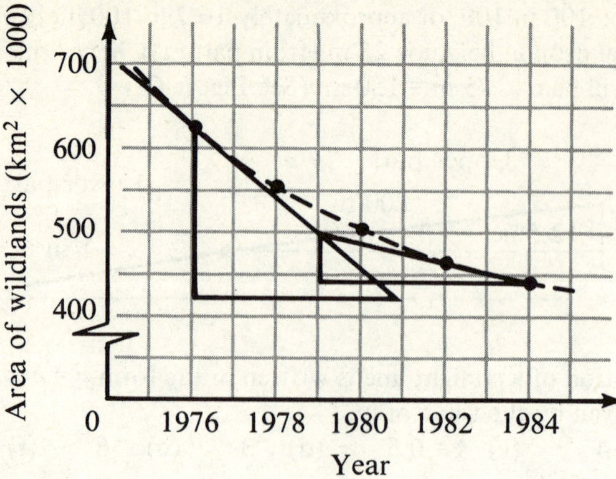

Figure S

7 (a) See Figure S.

(b) A decrease of $(628 - 442) \times 1000\ \text{km}^2$ in 8 years gives an average annual decrease of $\dfrac{186\,000}{8}\ \text{km}^2 = 23\,250\ \text{km}^2$ ($23\,000\ \text{km}^2$, correct to two significant figures).

(c) Figure S shows tangents drawn at the points corresponding to 1976 and 1984. The first has a gradient of approximately 40 000 (km^2 per year); the second a gradient of approximately 12 000 (km^2 per year).

8 See Figure T.

(a) After 9 seconds the speed is 18 m/s; and so it takes 5 seconds to cover the 90 m at constant speed.

(b) The distance travelled is given by the area under the speed–time graph, Figure T(a). Some possible measurements from Figure T(a) are

Time (seconds)	0	3	6	9	10	12	14	15	16	17
Area (i.e. distance in metres)	0	9	36	81	99	135	171	186	195	198

These are used to draw Figure T(b).

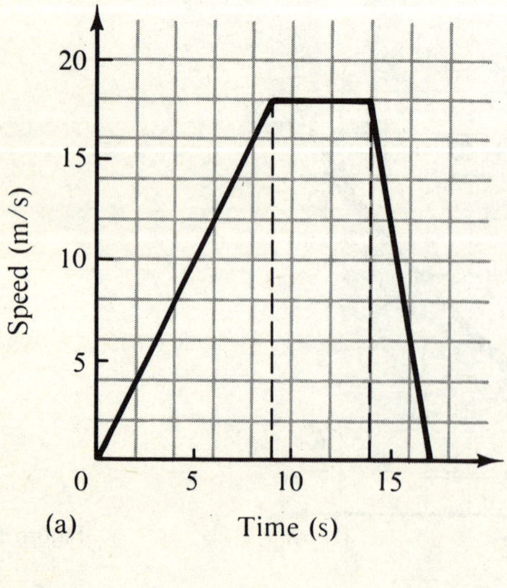

(a)

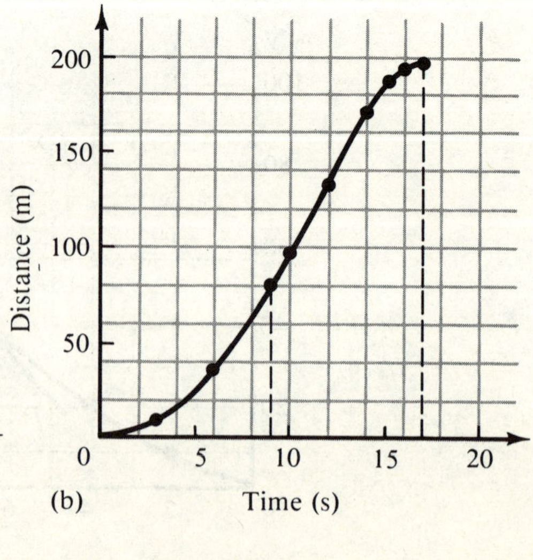

(b)

9 (a) $x^2 + 2x - 24$ (b) $2x^2 + x - 21$ (c) $40 - 7t - 3t^2$
(d) $6w^2 + 29w + 35$ (e) $16s^2 + 26s + 3$ (f) $20 - 23y + 6y^2$
(g) $3 + 13q - 10q^2$ (h) $2x^2 + 9xy - 5y^2$ (i) $3s^2 + 13st - 10t^2$

10 (a) $x^2 - 8x + 16$ (b) $w^2 + 4wv + 4v^2$
(c) $4q^2 + 20qs + 25s^2$ (d) $^{-}a^2 + 9b^2$

11 (a) $5(p+8)$ (b) $9(4-q)$ (c) $8s(3s+2t)$ (d) $3xz(y+4)$
(e) $11(1+w)$ (f) $t(13-q)$ (g) $6h(3g+4f)$ (h) $10(2-xyz)$

12 (a) $(x+2)(x+5)$ (b) $(y-3)(y-8)$ (c) $(z-3)(z+8)$
(d) $(t+2)(t-8)$ (e) $(s-4)(s+6)$ (f) $(w-5)(w-6)$
(g) $(d+1)(d-10)$ (h) $(x+8)(x+9)$

13 (a)

x	$^{-}1$	0	1	2	3	4	5	6	7
y	12	5	0	$^{-}3$	$^{-}4$	$^{-}3$	0	5	12

See Figure U.

(b) The line of symmetry is $x = 3$. The minimum value of $f(x)$ is $^{-}4$.

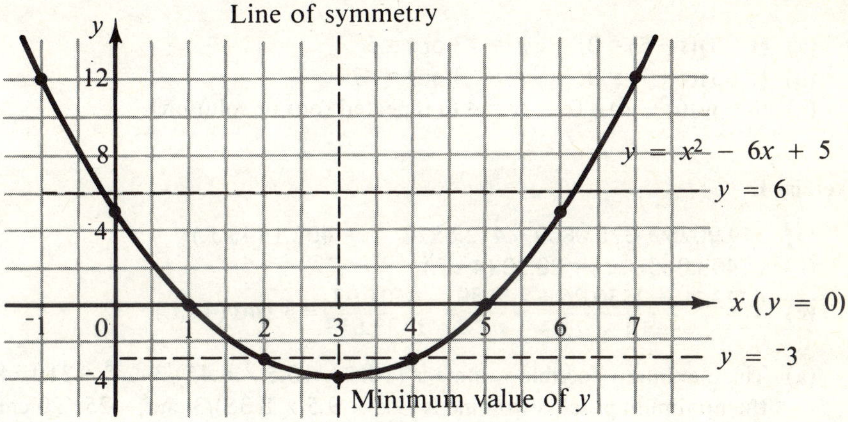

Figure U

14 (a) If $x^2 - 6x + 5 = 0$, then $y = 0$. This occurs when $x = 1$ and when $x = 5$.
(b) $x^2 - 6x + 5 = {}^{-}3$, i.e. $y = {}^{-}3$. The solutions are $x = 2$ and $x = 4$.
(c) $x^2 - 6x + 5 = 6$; i.e. $y = 6$. The solutions are approximately $^{-}0.2$ and 6.2.

15 (a) See Figure V.

x	$^{-}1$	0	1	2	3	4	5	6	7
x^2	1	0	1	4	9	16	25	36	49
$6x + 1$	$^{-}5$	1	7	13	19	25	31	37	43

(b) The x-coordinate of P is approximately $^{-}0.2$, and that of Q is approximately 6.2. At the points of intersection, $y = x^2$ and $y = 6x + 1$; i.e. $x^2 = 6x + 1$ or $x^2 - 6x - 1 = 0$. Note that this is the same equation as in question 14(c).

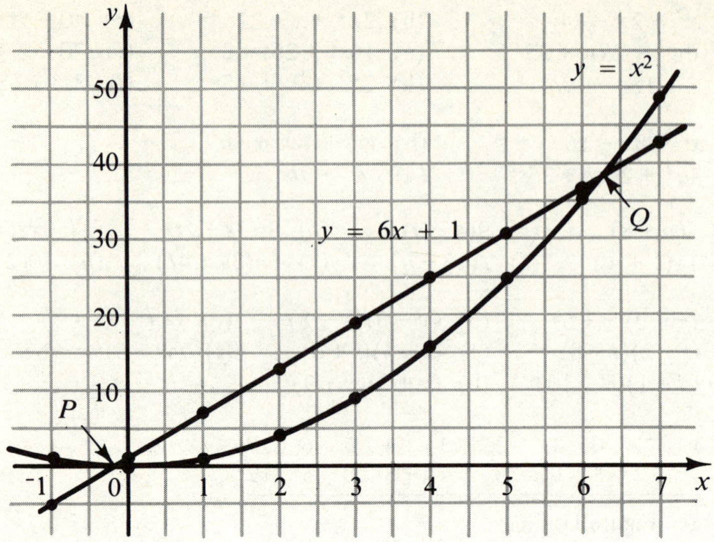

Figure V

16 (a) $(s+3)(s-5)=0$; $s = {}^-3$ or $s = 5$
(b) $(t+3)(t+7)=0$; $t = {}^-3$ or $t = {}^-7$
(c) $(4-w)(4-w)=0$; $w = 4$ (a repeated root or solution)

Exercise E

1 (a) $549.9025 + 325.0809 - 472.8574\ldots = 402.1$ (4 s.f.)
(b) $\sqrt{(408.066\ldots)} = 20.20$ (4 s.f.)
(c) $\dfrac{6773.29 - 2550.25 + 278.89}{545.1 \times 2.63} = \dfrac{4501.93}{1433.613} = 3.140$ (4 s.f.)

2 (a) The maximum possible volume is $(10.5 \times 10.5 \times 8.45)/3\ \text{cm}^3 = 310.54\ \text{cm}^3$, the minimum possible volume is $(9.5 \times 9.5 \times 8.35)/3\ \text{cm}^3 = 251.20\ \text{cm}^3$.
(b) $V = \dfrac{10 \times 10 \times 8.4}{3}\ \text{cm}^3 = 280\ \text{cm}^3$.

The percentage difference is $\dfrac{310.54 - 280}{280} \times 100\% = 10.9\%$.

3 $\begin{bmatrix} 7.4 & 0 & 0 \\ 0 & 0 & 7.4 \end{bmatrix}$

4 (a)

x	3.5	3.55	3.6	3.65	3.7	3.75	3.8
y	⁻2.525	⁻1.421	⁻0.264	0.947	2.213	3.534	4.912

(b) If $f(x) = 0$ then $3.6 < x < 3.65$; and by inspection x is approximately one-fifth of the way between 3.60 and 3.65.
$f(3.61) = {}^-0.026$ $f(3.62) = 0.214$
$f(3.611) = {}^-0.002$ $f(3.612) = 0.022$
The solution is $x = 3.61$, correct to three significant figures.

5

n	d	$\frac{1}{d}$	E
0	1	1	1
1	1	1	2
2	2	0.5	2.5
3	6	1.667	2.666
4	24	0.042	2.708
5	120	0.008	2.716
6	720	0.001	2.718

This flow diagram is evaluating the series

$$1 + \frac{1}{1} + \frac{1}{1 \times 2} + \frac{1}{1 \times 2 \times 3} + \frac{1}{1 \times 2 \times 3 \times 4} + \dots$$

It can be seen that the series 'converges' to a finite number 2.718 . . .

6

n	0	1	2	3	4	5	6	7
x_n	3.6	3.620	3.603	3.617	3.605	3.615	3.607	3.614

Correct to two decimal places, $x = 3.61$

7 (a) $x \to \frac{1}{x} \to \left(\frac{1}{x}\right)^2 \to 10\left(\frac{1}{x}\right)^2 \to 10\left(\frac{1}{x}\right)^2 - 5$

Hence the iteration is $x_{n+1} = 10\left(\frac{1}{x_n}\right)^2 - 5$

(b) If $x^3 + 5x^2 - 10 = 0$, then (dividing by x^2)

$x + 5 - \frac{10}{x^2} = 0$, or $x = \frac{10}{x^2} - 5$

which is the iteration derived in part (a).

The successive values of x are: $1, 5, ^-4.6, ^-4.527, ^-4.512, ^-4.508, ^-4.5079$.

Correct to four significant figures, one solution is $x = {}^-4.508$.

8 (a) The values of P are 1, 5, 14, 30, 55, 91, 140, 204, 285, 385, 506.

(b) The numbers being generated are

$$1^2 + 2^2 + 3^2 + 4^2 + \dots + n^2,$$

i.e. the sequence of (square-based) pyramid numbers.

Consolidation 4

This chapter covers Units 34 to 41 of the course.
These units are to be found in the following books:
Probability and Statistics (Chapter 4);
Further Algebra and Computation (Chapter 3);
Further Matrices and Transformations (Chapter 3);
Geometry 2: Shape and Similarity (Chapters 3 and 4);
Geometry 3: Three Dimensions (Chapters 1, 2 and 3).

4.1 Plane geometry (Chapters 3 and 4 of *Geometry 2: Shapes and Similarity*)

Chapter 3

The area of an irregular shape may be found by superimposing a grid (usually of small squares) and counting the number of squares enclosed by the outline. Squares that are 'more in than out' should be counted, but not those that are 'more out than in'.

The formulas for the areas (A) of some shapes are:

rectangle $A = bh$
triangle $A = \frac{1}{2} bh$
trapezium $A = \frac{1}{2}(a + b)h$
parallelogram $A = bh$,
where h is the perpendicular height (i.e. the height at right-angles to the base b).

The area of a polygon may be calculated by a 'subtraction' method: draw a rectangle round the polygon; and from the area of the rectangle subtract the areas of the triangles and rectangles between the polygon and the outside rectangle.

The 'area under a graph' can sometimes be interpreted in terms of the quantities shown on the axes. For example, the area under a speed–time graph represents distance (speed × time).

The 'trapezium method' is often used to estimate the area under a curved graph. Using this method, the area under a curve is approximated to the areas of a number of adjacent trapeziums.

The following terms associated with a circle should be known:

radius	diameter	circumference	chord	arc
sector	segment	tangent	semi-circle.	

The formulas connecting the radius (r), diameter (d), circumference (C) and area (A) are

$$d = 2r, \quad C = \pi d, \quad C = 2\pi r, \quad d = \frac{C}{\pi}, \quad r = \frac{C}{2\pi}, \quad A = \pi r^2, \quad r = \sqrt{\frac{A}{\pi}}$$

In a given circle, the lengths of the arcs, and the areas of the sectors, are proportional to the angles at the centre of the circle.

The area of a segment is found by a subtraction method (sector − triangle).

The tangent at the end of a radius is perpendicular to that radius.

Two tangents from a point outside a circle are equal in length; and they are equally inclined to the line joining the point to the centre.

Pythagoras' theorem is used in calculations involving lengths of chords and tangents, and the distances of chords from the centre of the circle.

The angle subtended by an arc at the centre of a circle is known as 'the angle at the centre'.

The angle subtended by an arc at a point on the circumference is known as 'the angle in a segment'.

If it is possible to draw one circle through all the four corners (vertices) of a quadrilateral then the vertices are said to be (con)cyclic, and the quadrilateral is said to be cyclic.

The principal theorems for angles in circles are as follows:

- I The angle at the centre is twice the angle at the circumference.
- II Angles in the same segment are equal.
- III The angle in a semi-circle is a right-angle.
- IV Opposite angles of a cyclic quadrilateral are supplementary (i.e. their sum is 180°).
- V The exterior angle of a cyclic quadrilateral is equal to the interior opposite angle.

Exercise A

1 Estimate the areas (in number of squares) of the shapes shown in Figure 1.

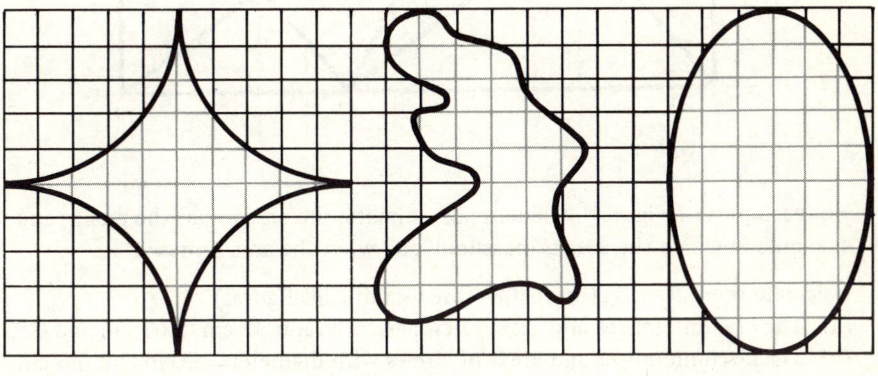

(a) (b) (c) Figure 1

2 Calculate the areas of the shaded shapes shown in Figure 2.

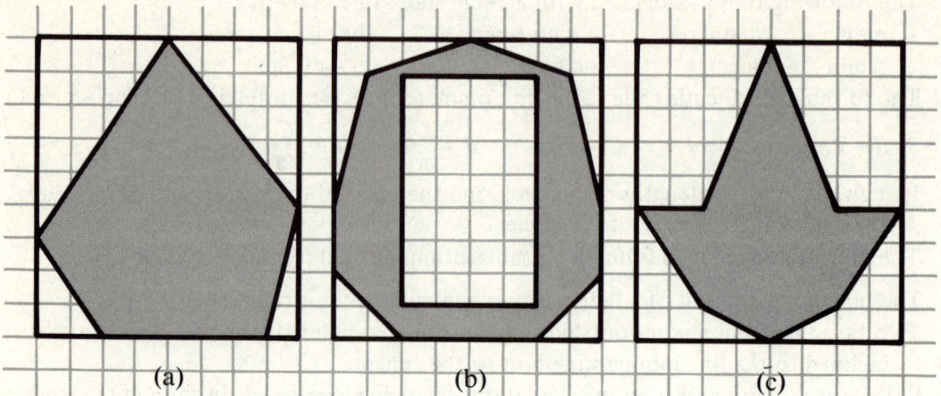

Figure 2

3 (a) Calculate the area of a square whose **diagonals** are each 8 cm long. How long are the sides of this square?
(b) Calculate the area of a rhombus whose **diagonals** are of lengths 10 cm and 24 cm. Calculate the length of one side of this rhombus.

4 From Figure 3 calculate the areas of the following shapes.
(a) triangle *ABC* (b) triangle *ACD* (c) triangle *CDE*
(d) parallelogram *ABCE* (e) trapezium *ABDE* (f) parallelogram *ADCF*

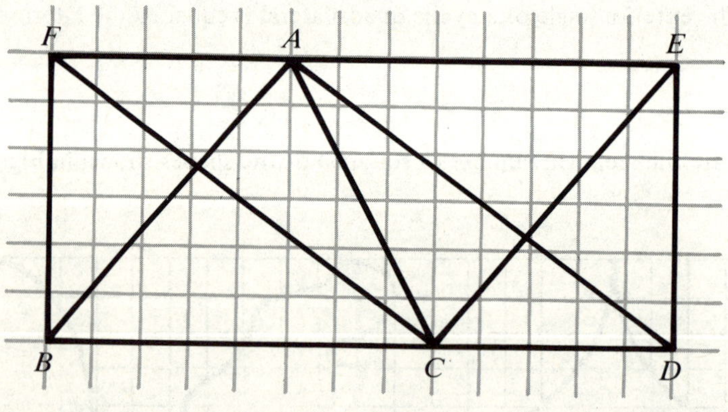

Figure 3

5 For each part of Figure 4 calculate, or estimate, the area under the graph; and state the units in which the area is measured, and what the area represents.

6 Calculate the following (correct to three significant figures)
(a) The circumferences and areas of circles with radii 32 cm, 5.67 cm and 0.92 cm.
(b) The circumferences and areas of circles with diameters 200 m and 0.6 cm.
(c) The radii of circles with circumferences of 56 cm and 0.88 m.
(d) The diameters of circles with areas of 300 cm^2 and 0.05 m^2.

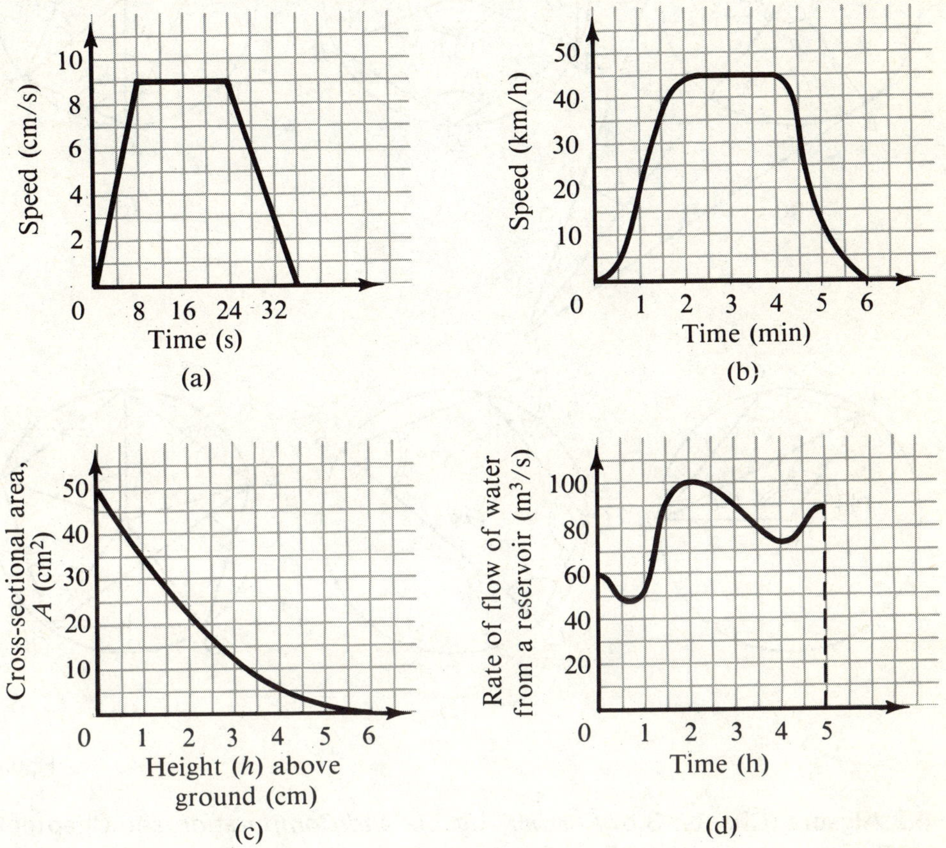

Figure 4

7 *OP* and *OQ* are radii of a circle of diameter 12 cm such that angle *POQ* is 124°. Calculate the following (correct to three significant figures)

(a) The length of the minor arc *PQ*.
(b) The length of the chord *PQ*.
(c) The area of the minor sector *POQ*.
(d) The area of triangle *OPQ*.
(e) The area of the minor segment bounded by the chord *PQ* and the minor arc *PQ*.

8 For each part of Figure 5 calculate the sizes of the lettered angles. (In each diagram *O* is the centre of the circle.)

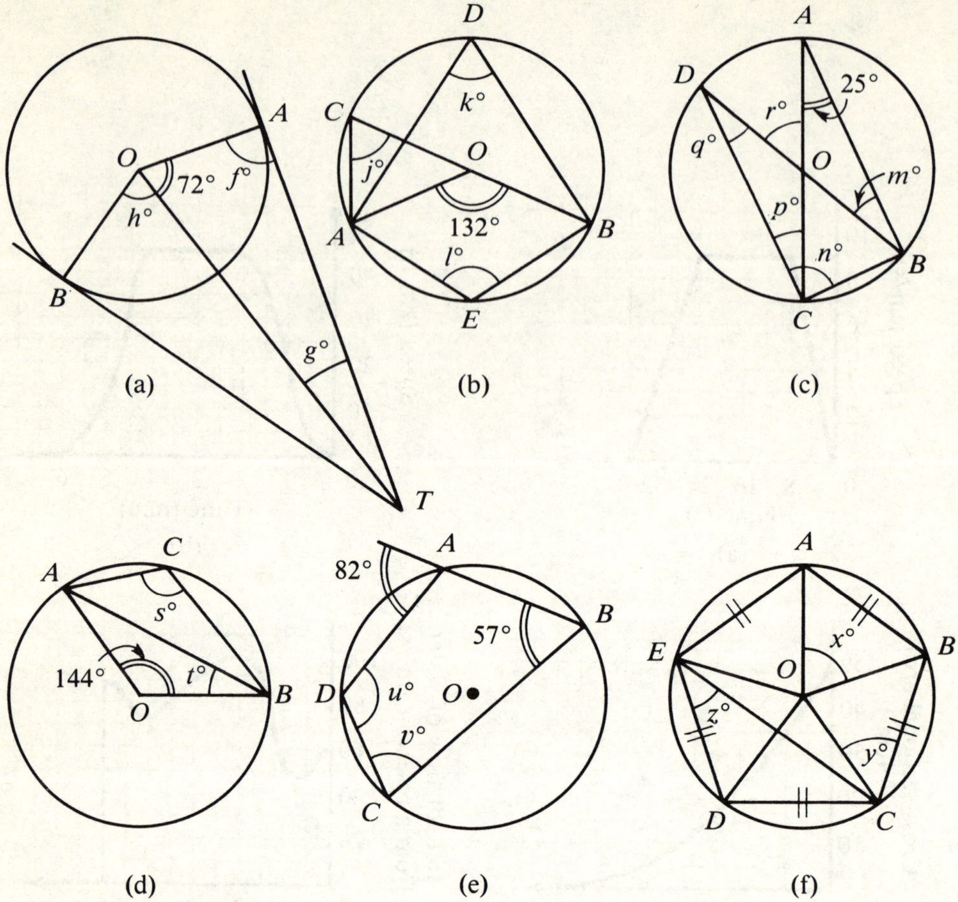

Figure 5

4.2 Algebra (Chapter 3 of *Further Algebra and Computation* and Chapter 3 of *Further Matrices and Transformations*)

Proportion

Two ordered sets $\{x\}$ and $\{y\}$ are directly proportional if corresponding pairs (x, y) are such that $y = kx$, where k is a constant.

In such a case the graph of y against x is a straight line through the origin, with gradient k.

If $\{x\}$ and $\{y\}$ are proportional sets, then
y is proportional to x (written as $y \propto x$), and
x is proportional to y (written as $x \propto y$).

If (x_1, y_1), (x_2, y_2), ... are corresponding pairs from proportional sets, then

$\frac{y_1}{x_1} = \frac{y_2}{x_2} = \ldots = k$; and

$\frac{y_1}{y_2} = \frac{x_1}{x_2}$, etc.

If two sets $\{x\}$ and $\{y\}$ are connected by a relation of the form $y = kx^2$ then y is said to be (directly) proportional to the square of x.

In such a case the graph of y against x is a parabola; and the graph of y against x^2 is a straight line through the origin with gradient k.

If y is proportional to x^2, then x is proportional to the square root of y; and

$$\frac{y_2}{y_1} = \left(\frac{x_2}{x_1}\right)^2, \text{ etc.}$$

If two sets $\{x\}$ and $\{y\}$ are connected by a relation of the form $y = \frac{k}{x}$, then y is said to be inversely proportional to x; or directly proportional to the reciprocal of x.

Both methods of expression are written as $y \propto \frac{1}{x}$.

Another way of expressing this relation is $xy = k$.

The graph of y against x is part of a rectangular hyperbola. The graph of y against $\frac{1}{x}$ is a straight line through the origin with gradient k.

If two shapes are geometrically similar, then corresponding lengths are in direct proportion.

Transformations combined

If P is a point or an object, then the image of P under a transformation **A** may be written as P_1, P', or $\mathbf{A}(P)$.

If a transformation **A** followed by a transformation **B** is equivalent to the single transformation **C**, then **C** = **BA**.

(Note therefore that **X** = **YZ** means that **X** is equivalent to **Z** followed by **Y**.)

The inverse of **C** = **BA** is $\mathbf{C}^{-1}$, where

$$\mathbf{C}^{-1} = \mathbf{A}^{-1}\mathbf{B}^{-1}.$$

A rotation of $x°$ about a point P, followed by a rotation of $y°$ about a point Q, is equivalent to a single rotation of $(x + y)°$ about a third point R. (If Q is the same point as P, then so is R.)

A translation **g** followed by a translation **h** is equivalent to the single translation **g** + **h**.

A reflection in a mirror m, followed by a reflection in a parallel mirror n, is equivalent to a single translation perpendicular to the mirrors.

A reflection in a mirror m, followed by a reflection in a mirror n that is not parallel to m, is equivalent to a single rotation about the point where the mirrors intersect. The distance moved, or the angle turned, is twice that between the mirrors.

An enlargement of scale factor x about a centre P, followed by an enlargement of scale factor y about a centre Q, is equivalent to a single enlargement of scale factor xy about a centre R. R lies on PQ.

The combination of a reflection in a mirror m with a translation parallel to m is sometimes considered as a single transformation called a glide reflection.

If this is considered as a single transformation, then it is always possible to map a shape P onto a congruent shape (image) Q by a single transformation. If the shapes are directly congruent this is either a translation or a rotation; if the shapes are oppositely congruent the transformation is a reflection or a glide reflection.

These four transformations are called isometric transformations, since congruency is preserved (i.e. size and shape are invariant).

Exercise B

1 Which of the following pairs of sets are in direct proportion?
For those that are in direct proportion, state the constant of proportionality.

(a)

p	2	5	8	10	12
q	5	10	15	20	25

(b)

x	1	5	8	13	20
y	3	15	24	39	60

(c)

a	4	8	10	15	20
b	10	20	25	37.5	50

(d)

u	30	24	18	10	6
v	15	12	9	5	3

2 The following pairs of sets are in direct proportion. Copy and complete the tables.

(a)

g	3		10	15	30
f		24	40		120

(b)

s			16	12	8	4
t	120	100	80			20

(b)

Q	54	45		27	
V	18		12		6

(d)

y	0.2	0.5	1.0	2.0	
z			0.4		1.0

3 Copy and complete the following tables, subject to the given relations.

(a) L is directly proportional to the square root of the area. (Give values of L correct to the nearest whole number.)

Area	25	64	100	200	
L			50		75

(b) S is inversely proportional to D.

D	4	8	12		20	
S	15			3.75		1

(c) V is directly proportional to the square of the mass.

Mass	3.5	6.0	10	24	40	
V		72			3200	5000

(d) G is inversely proportional to the square of the distance.

Distance	20	50		200	
G	2400		150	24	6

4 For parts (a) and (b) of question 3 draw the appropriate straight-line graphs. Use these graphs to check your answers to parts (a) and (b) of question 3.

5 (a) Figure 6 shows an object F.
Copy the diagram, and on it draw the images **X**(F), **Y**(F), **XY**(F) and **YX**(F); where **X** is reflection in the y-axis, and **Y** is a quarter-turn about the origin.
(b) Describe **XY** and **YX** as single transformations.

6 Repeat question 5 when **X** is an enlargement from the origin with scale factor 2, and **Y** is a translation of $\begin{bmatrix} ^-4 \\ 0 \end{bmatrix}$.

7 Repeat part (a) of question 5 when **X** is a reflection in the line $y = x$, and **Y** is the shear with the x-axis as its base (invariant) line that maps (0, 1) onto (2, 1).

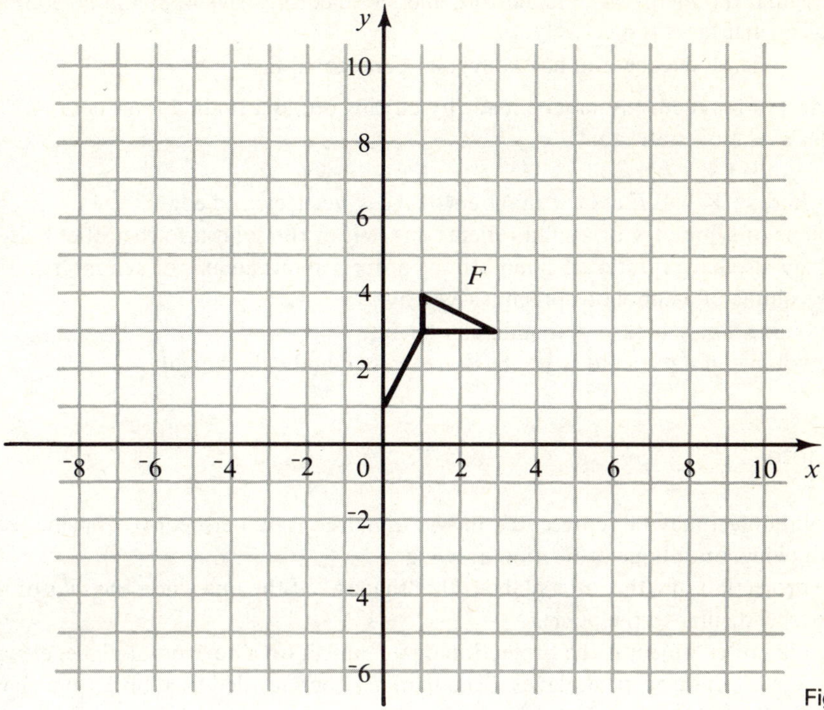

Figure 6

8 Repeat question 5 when **X** is the enlargement from the centre (0, 3) with scale factor 3, and **Y** is the enlargement from the centre (3, 0) with scale factor $\frac{1}{2}$.

4.3 Three-dimensional geometry (Chapters 1, 2 and 3 of *Geometry 3: Three Dimensions*)

Chapter 1

A polyhedron is a solid body, all of whose faces are plane polygons.
Cuboids ('bricks') have six rectangular faces. The faces of a cube are squares.
In a prism any cross-section parallel to the base is congruent to the base. The sides (faces joining the base to the top) are parallelograms. A prism is defined by its base. A prism is 'right' if all the sides are rectangles.
The base of a pyramid is a polygon. The triangular sloping faces meet at the vertex.
A pyramid whose base is a regular polygon is 'right' if all the sloping faces are (congruent) isosceles triangles.
A triangular-based pyramid is called a tetrahedron.
An octahedron has a total of eight faces.

A polyhedron is regular if all the faces are congruent regular polygons, and all the vertices have the same 'shape'.
There are five regular solids.
A cube has 6 square faces.

Regular tetrahedrons, octahedrons, and icosahedrons have 4, 8, and 20 equilateral triangular faces respectively.

A regular dodecahedron has 12 regular pentagonal faces.

Models of polyhedrons may be made by cutting out and folding their nets.

Euler's relation states that

$$F + V = E + 2$$

where F, V, and E are the numbers of faces, vertices, and edges.

A plane of symmetry of a solid reflects one half of the solid into the other half. A solid may also have rotational symmetry of order n about an axis of symmetry.

The volume of a cuboid or prism is given by

volume = base area × perpendicular height.

The volume of a pyramid is $\frac{1}{3}$ × base area × perpendicular height.

Chapter 2

A solid object may be represented in two dimensions by perspective drawing, isometric drawing, or oblique projection drawing.

The projection of a line on a plane is the 'shadow' of the line when the rays of light are perpendicular to the plane.

The plan of an object is the projection of the object on a horizontal plane; elevations are projections on vertical planes. (The plan may be regarded as a 'bird's-eye view' from directly overhead; and the elevations as 'worm's-eye views' from ground level.)

In all these methods of drawing, edges that would be seen if the solid were transparent are described as 'hidden edges' and are represented in the drawings by broken lines.

Chapter 3

The curved surface of a cylinder is a rectangle (think of the label on a tin).

For a cylinder of height h whose base is a circle of radius r:

area of curved surface = $2\pi rh$;

total surface area = $2\pi rh + 2\pi r^2 = 2\pi r(r + h)$;

volume = base area × height = $\pi r^2 h$.

The curved surface of a cone is a sector of a circle whose radius is equal to the slant length (l) of the cone.

For a cone with a height of h and a circular base of radius r:

$l^2 = r^2 + h^2$;

area of curved surface = πrl;

total surface area = $\pi rl + \pi r^2 = \pi r(l + r)$;

volume = $\frac{1}{3}$(base area × height) = $\frac{1}{3}\pi r^2 h$.

A truncated cone is formed when the top of a cone is removed by a plane cut parallel to the base of the cone. The 'subtraction' method should be used for finding the volumes and curved surface areas of truncated cones.

The surface area of a sphere of radius R is $4\pi R^2$; the volume is $\frac{4}{3}\pi R^3$.

The intersection of a plane and a sphere is a circle (on the surface of the sphere). If the plane passes through the centre of the sphere, the circle is called a Great Circle of the sphere.

In all cases the radius of the circle (r), and the distance (d) of the plane from the centre of the sphere, are connected by $r^2 + d^2 = R^2$.

The axis of a right circular cone or cylinder is an axis of symmetry, of infinite order. Any plane containing this axis is a plane of symmetry.

In addition, a cylinder also has a plane of symmetry, half-way between - and parallel to - the base and the top. All lines in this plane through the centre of the circle of intersection are axes of rotational symmetry of order 2.

All planes through the centre of a sphere are planes of symmetry.

All diameters through the centre of a sphere are axes of rotational symmetry.

Exercise C

1 Draw sketches of the following solids.
  (a) A prism whose base is an equilateral triangle.
  (b) A pyramid whose base is a regular pentagon.
  (c) A regular octahedron.
  (d) A cuboid whose sides are in the ratio 1:3:9.
  (In (a) and (b) assume that the prism and pyramid are 'right'.)

2 Sketch possible nets for the four solids described in question 1.

3 Show that Euler's relation is true for the four solids described in question 1.

4 List the symmetries of the four solids described in question 1.

5 Figure 7 shows a symmetrical truncated pyramid whose base $WXYZ$ is a square of side 24 cm and whose top is a square of side 12 cm that is parallel to the base and 8 cm above it.

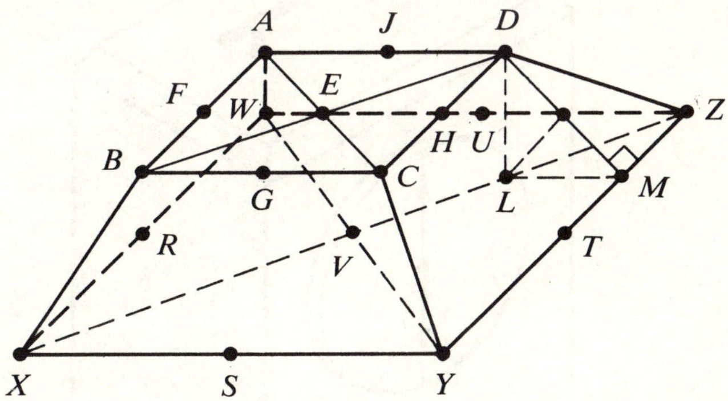

Figure 7

  (a) Describe the symmetry of this solid.
  (b) Calculate the length of DM, and hence draw an accurate net of the solid, using a scale of 1 cm to represent 4 cm.
  (c) Calculate the volume and the surface area of the full-size truncated pyramid.

6 A regular octahedron has edges of length 20 cm.
Calculate the volume and surface area of this octahedron.

7 Draw an isometric drawing of the truncated pyramid described in question 5.

8 Figure 8 shows the plan and elevations of a garage.
(a) Draw an isometric view of the garage with the point V nearest the viewer.
(b) Draw an oblique projection view of the garage looking straight at the doors.

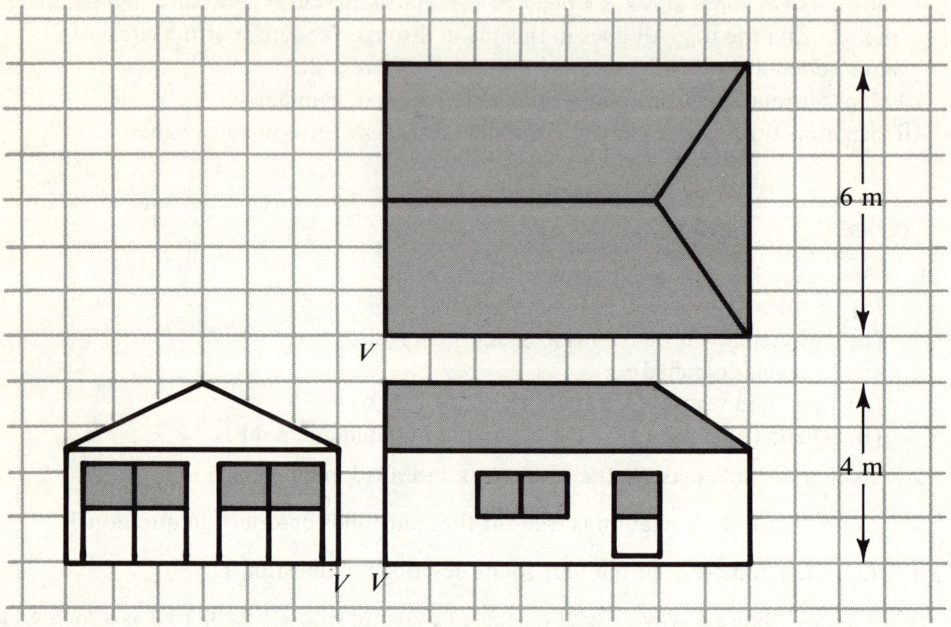

Figure 8

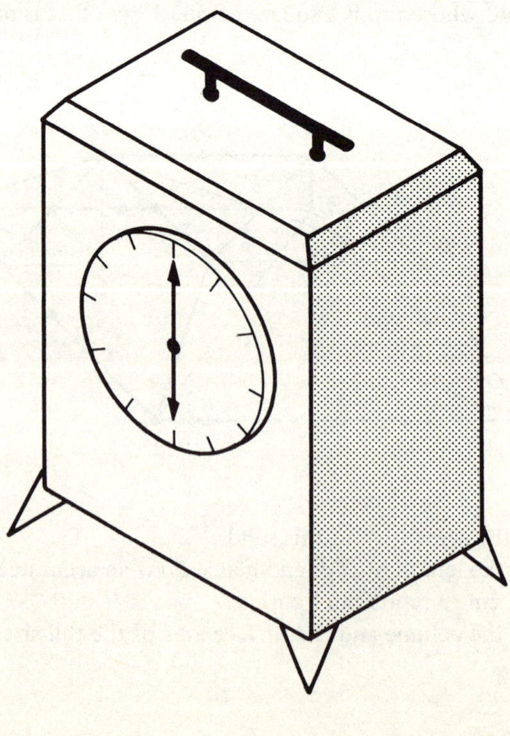

Figure 9

9 Draw the plan and elevations of the carriage clock shown in Figure 9.

10 Calculate the surface areas and the volumes of the following.
(a) A cylinder of height 12 cm, whose base is a circle of **diameter** 10 cm.
(b) A cone of height 12 cm, whose base is a circle of **radius** 10 cm.
(c) A sphere of **diameter** 14 cm.

11 Draw the plans and elevations of the three solids described in question 10.

12 The top and bottom of a truncated 'right' cone are parallel circles, of radii 6 cm and 9 cm respectively, that are 4 cm apart.
(a) Draw an isometric view of this solid.
(b) Calculate the volume and the total surface area of this solid.

13 (a) A cylindrical glass jar has a circular base, of diameter 10 cm, and a volume of 500 ml. Calculate the height of the jar.
(b) Another cylindrical jar of the same volume (500 ml) has a height of 10 cm. Calculate the diameter of its base.

14 Figure 10 shows a small capsule made from a cylinder and two hemispheres. The 'height' of the **cylinder** is twice the radius of the circular 'base'.

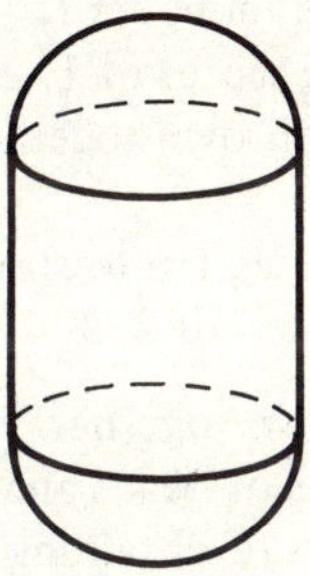

Figure 10

(a) If the radius of the 'base' is 3 mm, calculate the volume of the capsule.
(b) If the volume of the capsule is 1300 mm^3, find the radius of the 'base', correct to two significant figures.

4.4 Probability (Chapter 4 of *Probability and Statistics*)

If an element is to be chosen 'at random' from a population, then the method used must be such that each member of the population has an equal chance of being chosen.

For an ordinary pack of playing cards

Let $P = \{\text{picture cards}\}$. Then $n(P) = 12$.
Let $H = \{\text{cards that are hearts}\}$. Then $n(H) = 13$.
Since $n(P \cap H) = 3$, $n(P \cup H) = 22$, and $n(\mathcal{E}) = 52$; then

$$\text{prob}\ (P \text{ and } H) = \frac{n(P \cap H)}{n(\mathcal{E})} = \frac{3}{52}$$

(i.e. the probability of choosing the jack or the queen or the king of hearts is $\frac{3}{52}$);

$$\text{prob}\ (P \text{ or } H) = \frac{n(P \cup H)}{n(\mathcal{E})} = \frac{22}{52}$$

(i.e. the probability of choosing either a picture card or a heart is $\frac{22}{52}$).

For a series of events with associated outcomes $A_1, A_2, A_3, \ldots$ for which the individual probabilities are $p(1), p(2), p(3), \ldots$, then the probability of the outcome $A_1A_2A_3\ldots$ (occuring in that order) is $p(1) \times p(2) \times p(3) \times \ldots$.

If four cards are chosen from a pack, the probability that they are all aces is $\frac{4}{52} \times \frac{3}{51} \times \frac{2}{50} \times \frac{1}{49}$ (about 0.000 004).

(The second event, for example, is choosing an ace from a pack that now contains 51 cards of which 3 are aces.)

Combined events and their outcomes can be illustrated by tree diagrams and by possibility space diagrams.

A possibility space diagram is useful when only two events are combined, but each has a number of possible outcomes (for example, the possible scores when two dice are thrown). If more than two events are involved, then a tree diagram should be used.

Exercise D

1 (a) An unbiassed cubical die has the numbers 1, 2, 1, 3, 2, 2 on its faces. Write down (as fractions) the probabilities of obtaining scores of 1, 2, and 3 when this die is thrown once.

(b) A second such die has the numbers 1, 1, 2, 3, 1, 2 on its faces. Write down the probabilities of obtaining scores of 1, 2, and 3 with this die.

(c) When these two dice are thrown together, the 'total score' is the sum of the separate scores.

Draw a possibility space diagram to show the possible 'total scores', and find the probabilities of 'total scores' of 2, 3, 4, 5, and 6.

2 Four unbiassed coins are thrown together.

(a) List the five combinations of heads and tails that are possible.

(b) Calculate the probabilities of obtaining each of these combinations.

(c) The four coins are thrown 400 times. About how many of these throws would you expect to be a combination of two heads and two tails?

3 Records from a certain seaside resort show that in the last fifty years the weather on 1 August was 'fine' 27 times, 'dull' 11 times, and 'wet' 12 times.

(a) What is the probability that it will be 'fine' on 1 August next year?

(b) How many times will you expect it to be 'wet' on 1 August in the next eight years?

4 A bag contains ten marbles of which three are red and the remainder are blue. If two marbles are taken out at random, what is the probability that

(a) they are both red;

(b) they are of different colour?

5 You are dealt three cards from an ordinary pack of 52 playing cards.
Calculate (as decimals correct to five places) the probabilities of the following.

(a) Three aces.

(b) Three cards of the same 'value' (i.e. 'three of a kind').

(c) A jack, a queen, and a king, in that order.

6 You are dealt three cards from an ordinary pack of 52 playing cards.

(a) What is the probability that the first card is a picture card (jack, queen or king)?

(b) If the first card is a picture card, what is the probability that the second card is a **different** picture card? (For example, if the first card is a jack, then the next is a queen or king.)
(c) What is the probability that the first two cards are different picture cards (i.e. jack and queen, or jack and king, or queen and king, in either order)?
(d) What is the probability that the three cards are a jack, a queen, and a king (not necessarily in that order)?

7 A 'mystery' coach tour starts out from A along the road AB. (See Figure 11.) At each junction the driver is twice as likely to turn left as he is to turn right. (He does not turn back at any junction.)

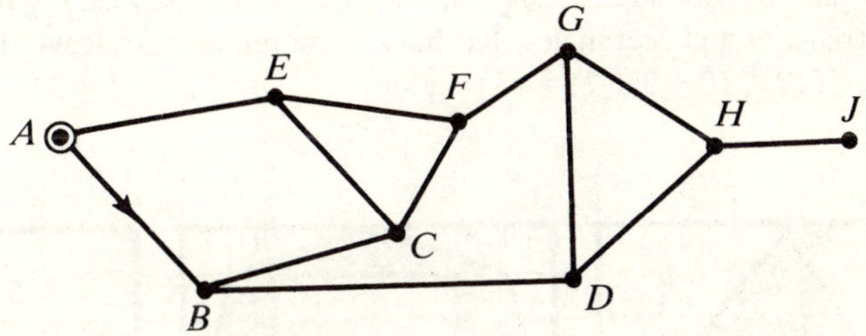

Figure 11

(a) Draw a tree diagram to show the outcomes at the first three junctions of the tour.
(b) What is the probability that, after turning left or right at three junctions, the coach is back at A; is at F; is at G?

8 In a four-leg relay race, the team manager reckons that the probability that his team will be in the lead after the first leg is 0.5. After that he reckons that if his team is in the lead at the end of any leg, then the probability that they will retain the lead is 0.7; but if they are not in the lead at the end of any leg, then the probability that they will regain the lead by the end of the next leg is 0.4.

Draw a tree diagram to find the probabilities (correct to two decimal places) that
(a) the team will be in the lead throughout the race;
(b) the team will win the race.

Answers

Exercise A

1 See Figure A, where ticks are drawn in those squares considered to be 'in'. (Do not worry if you do not agree with all the borderline cases.)
(a) 20 squares (b) 29 squares (c) 48 squares
(The star (a) is a square with four quadrants removed. The 'true' area is 21.5 squares. (c) is an ellipse whose 'true' area is 47 squares.)

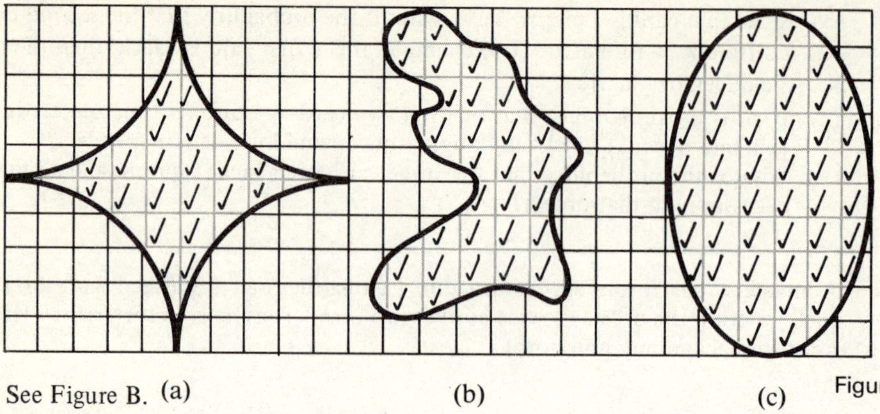

Figure A

2 See Figure B.
In each part the outside rectangle has an area of 72 squares. Figure B shows the areas of the triangles and rectangles that have to be removed to leave the shaded regions.
(a) $72 - (12 + 10 + 3 + 2) = 45$ (squares) (b) $72 - 41 = 31$ (c) $72 - 42 = 30$

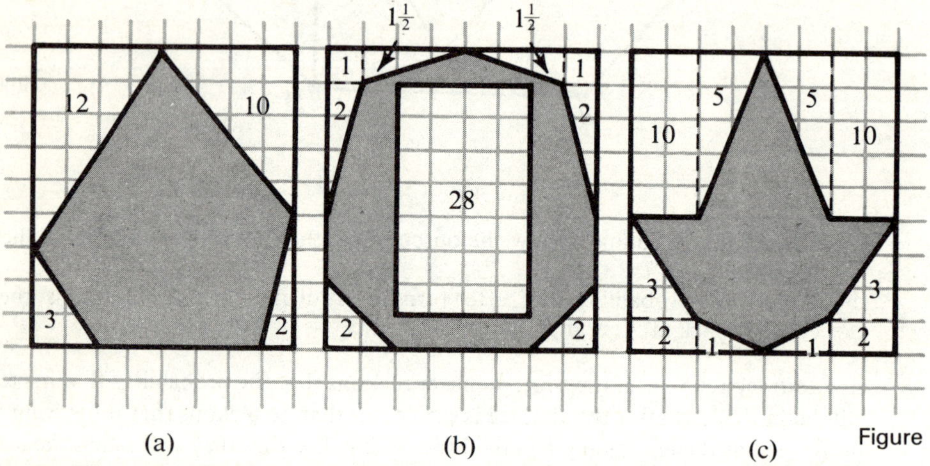

Figure B

3 See Figure C.
Since a square is also a rhombus, both shapes are rhombuses.
(a) Area = $0.5 \times 8 \times 8$ cm^2 = 32 cm^2. Length of side = $4\sqrt{2}$ cm = 5.7 cm (2 s.f.)
(b) Area = $0.5 \times 10 \times 24$ cm^2 = 120 cm^2.
The length of one side (using Pythagoras' theorem) = $\sqrt{(5^2 + 12^2)}$ cm = 13 cm.
(The area of a rhombus is half the product of the diagonals.)

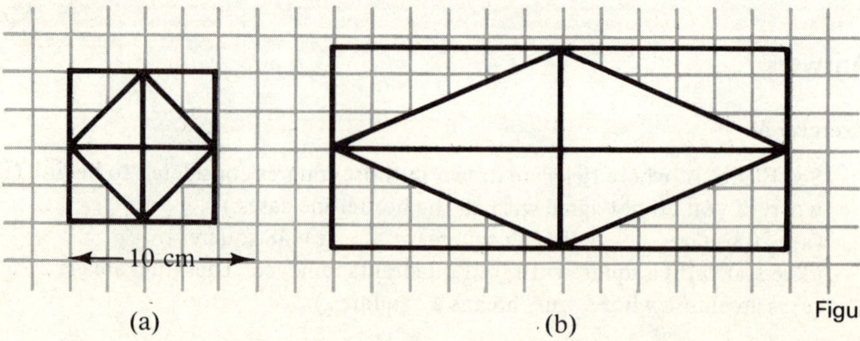

Figure C

4 All these shapes have a height of 6 (units).

(a) $0.5 \times 8 \times 6 = 24$ (squares) (b) $0.5 \times 5 \times 6 = 15$ (c) $0.5 \times 5 \times 6 = 15$

(d) $8 \times 6 = 48$ (e) $0.5 \times (8 + 13) \times 6 = 63$ (f) $5 \times 6 = 30$

5 (a) The shape is a trapezium. Area = $0.5 \times (4 + 9) \times 9$ squares = 58.5 squares. Each square represents 1 cm/s for 4 seconds, i.e. 4 cm. Hence the area under the graph shows a distance travelled of 58.5×4 cm = 234 cm.

(b) By counting squares, the area under the graph is approximately 65 squares. Each square represents 5 km/h for half a minute, i.e. a distance of $\frac{1}{24}$ km. Hence the distance travelled is approximately $65 \times \frac{1}{24}$ km, or about 2.7 km.

(c) By counting squares, or dividing the area into six trapeziums, the area under the curve is approximately 41 squares. Each square represents an area of 5 cm^2 multiplied by a height of 0.5 cm, i.e. a volume of 2.5 cm^3. Hence the total volume represented is 41×2.5 cm^3 = 100 cm^3 (2 s.f.). (The graph in fact shows the cross-sectional areas of a cone of radius 4 cm and height 6 cm. The true volume of such a cone is 101 cm^3.)

(d) The area under the graph is approximately 80 squares. Each square represents 10 m^3/s for half-an-hour, i.e. a volume of 10×1800 m^3, or 18 000 m^3. The total volume of water taken from the reservoir is about $80 \times 18\,000$ m^3, or 1.4×10^6 m^3.

6 (a)

Radius (cm)	32	5.67	0.92
Circumference (cm)	201	35.6	5.78
Area (cm^2)	3220	101	2.66

(b)

Diameter	200 m	0.6 cm
Circumference	628 m	1.88 cm
Area	31 400 m^2	0.283 cm^2

(c) 8.91 cm 0.140 m

(d) 19.5 cm 0.252 m

7 See Figure D.
A circle of radius 6 cm has a circumference of 37.7 cm, and an area of 113 cm^2.

Figure D

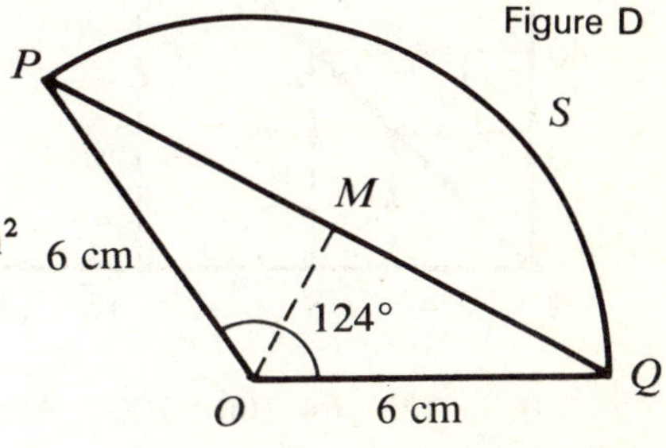

(a) $\frac{124}{360} \times 37.7$ cm = 13.0 cm

(b) $2 \times 6 \times \sin 62° = 10.6$ cm

(c) $\frac{124}{360} \times 113$ cm^2 = 38.9 cm^2

(d) $OM = 6 \times \cos 62° = 2.82$ cm;
area of triangle $OPQ = OM \times PM = 14.9$ cm^2

(e) $(38.9 - 14.9)$ cm^2 = 24.0 cm^2

8 (a) $f = 90$, $g = 18$, $h = 72$

(b) $j = k = 66$, $l = 180 - 66 = 114$

(c) $m = 25$, $n = 90 - 25 = 65$, $p = m = 25$, $q = p = 25$, $r = p + q = 50$

(d) reflex angle $AOB = 360° - 144° = 216°$, $s = \frac{216}{2} = 108$, $t = \frac{180 - 144}{2} = 18$

(e) $u = 180 - 57 = 123$, $v = 82$

(f) $x = \frac{360}{5} = 72$, $y = \frac{180 - 72}{2} = 54$, $z = \frac{72}{2} = 36$

Exercise B

1 (a) These sets are not proportional. (For example, 2:5 is not equal to 5:10.)
(b) These sets are proportional. The constant of proportionality is 3.
(c) These sets are proportional. The constant of proportionality is 2.5.
(d) These sets are proportional. The constant of proportionality is 0.5.

2 (a)

g	3	6	10	15	30
f	12	24	40	60	120

The constant of proportionality is 4.

(b)

s	24	20	16	12	8	4
t	120	100	80	60	40	20

The constant of proportionality is 5.

(c)

Q	54	45	36	27	18
V	18	15	12	9	6

The constant of proportionality is 1/3.

(d)

y	0.2	0.5	1.0	2.0	2.5
z	0.08	0.20	0.40	0.80	1.0

The constant of proportionality is 0.4.

3 (a) Since $\sqrt{100} = 10$, $L = 5\sqrt{(\text{area})}$.

Area	25	64	100	200	225
L	25	40	50	71	75

(b) From the first pair of values, $D \times S = 60$.

D	4	8	12	16	20	60
S	15	7.5	5	3.75	3	1

(c) Since $6^2 = 36$, $V = 2 \times (\text{mass})^2$.

Mass	3.5	6	10	24	40	50
V	24.5	72	200	1152	3200	5000

(d) From the first pair of values, $G \times d^2 = 960\,000$.

Distance	20	50	80	200	400
G	2400	384	150	24	6

4 See Figure E.

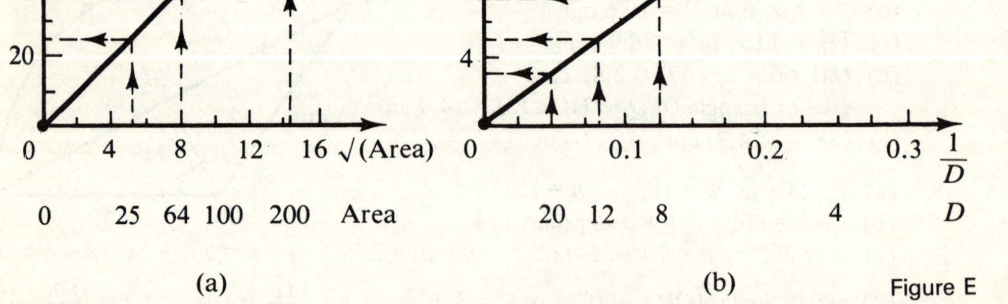

Figure E

5 (a) See Figure F.
(b) **XY** is reflection in the line $y = x$; **YX** is reflection in the line $x + y = 0$.

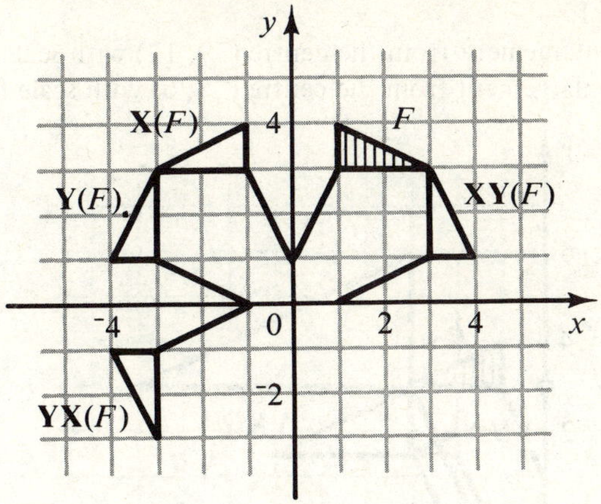

Figure F

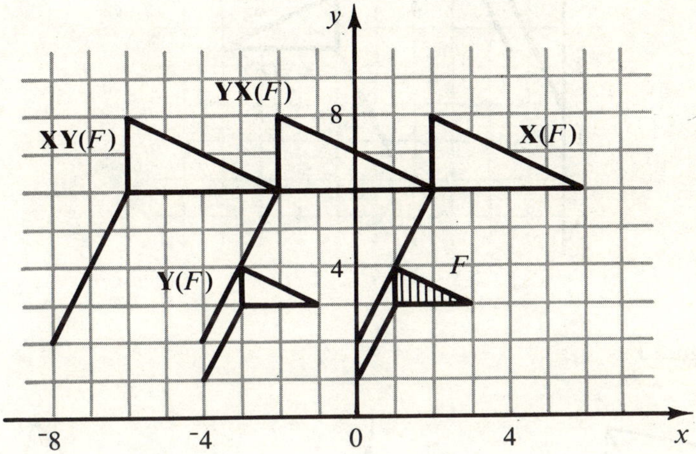

Figure G

6 (a) See Figure G.

(b) **XY** is an enlargement from the centre (8, 0) with scale factor 2;
YX is an enlargement from the centre (4, 0) with scale factor 2.

7 See Figure H.

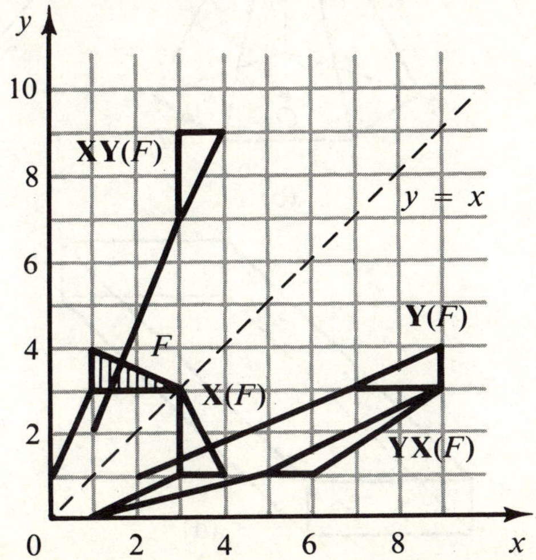

Figure H

8 (a) See Figure I.
(b) **XY** is an enlargement from the centre ($^-9$, 12) with scale factor 1.5;
YX is an enlargement from the centre ($^-3$, 6) with scale factor 1.5.

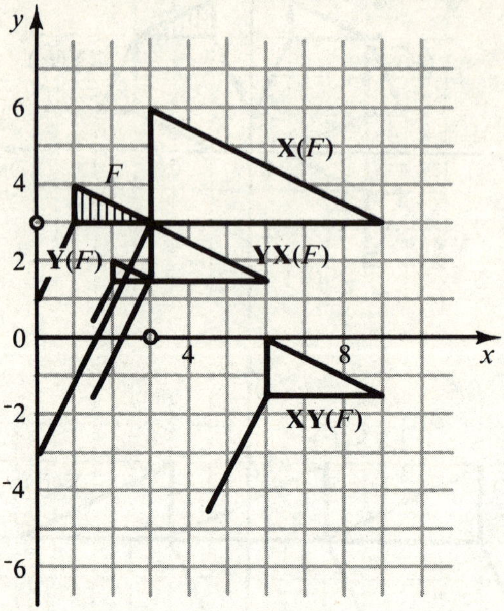

Figure I

Exercise C

1 See Figure J.

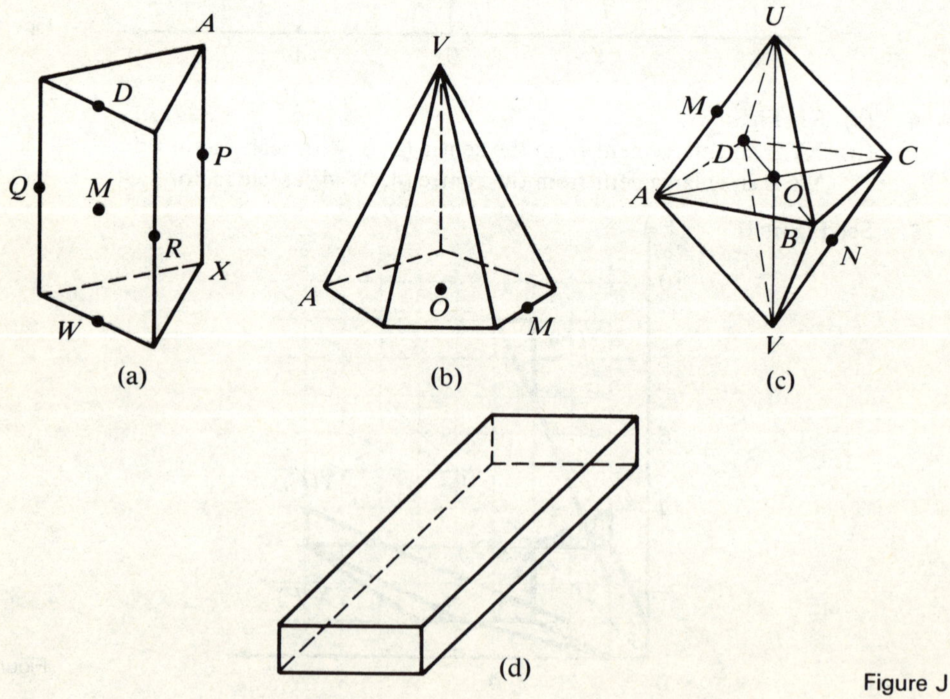

Figure J

2 Figure K shows one possible net for each object; but note that there are several other possible nets for each part.

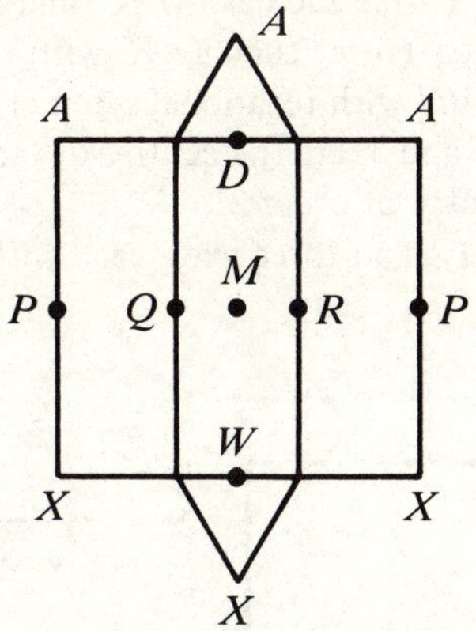

(a)

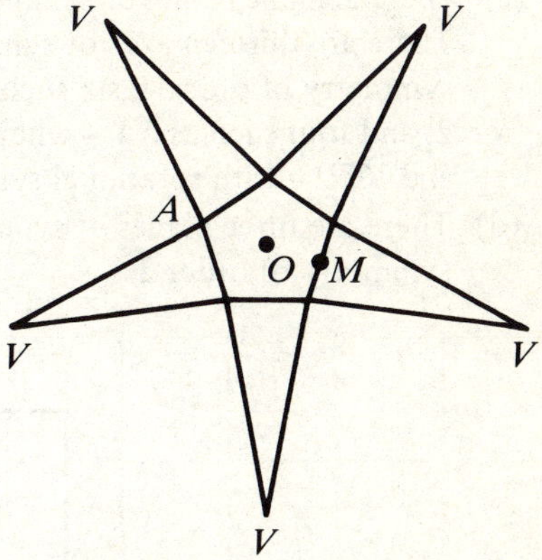

(b)

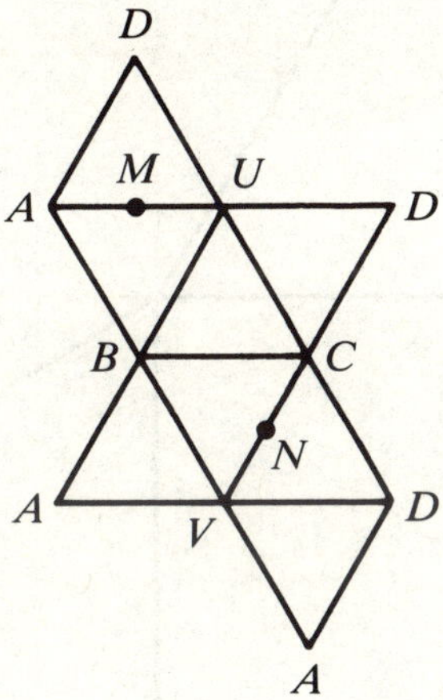

(c)

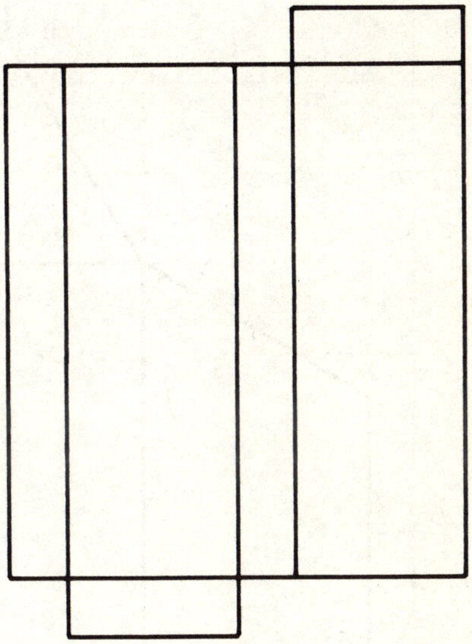

(d)

Figure K

3

Object	F	V	E	$F + V$	$E + 2$
Prism	5	6	9	11	11
Pyramid	6	6	10	12	12
Octahedron	8	6	12	14	14
Cuboid	6	8	12	14	14

4 See Figures J and K.

(a) There are four planes of symmetry (one horizontal plane *PQR*, and three vertical planes such as *ADWX*), and four axes of symmetry (one vertical axis with rotational symmetry of order 3, and three horizontal axes such as *PM* with rotational symmetry of order 2).

(b) There are five vertical planes of symmetry such as *VAM*.
There is one vertical axis of symmetry *VO* with rotational symmetry of order 5.

(c) There are nine planes of symmetry (three such as *UAVC*, and six such as *BMDN*).
There are thirteen axes of symmetry (three such as *AC* with rotational symmetry of order 4, six such as *MN* with rotational symmetry of order 2, and four such as *XY* - where *X* and *Y* are the centres of faces *UAB* and *VCD* - with rotational symmetry of order 3.

(d) There are three planes of symmetry; and three axes, each with rotational symmetry of order 2.

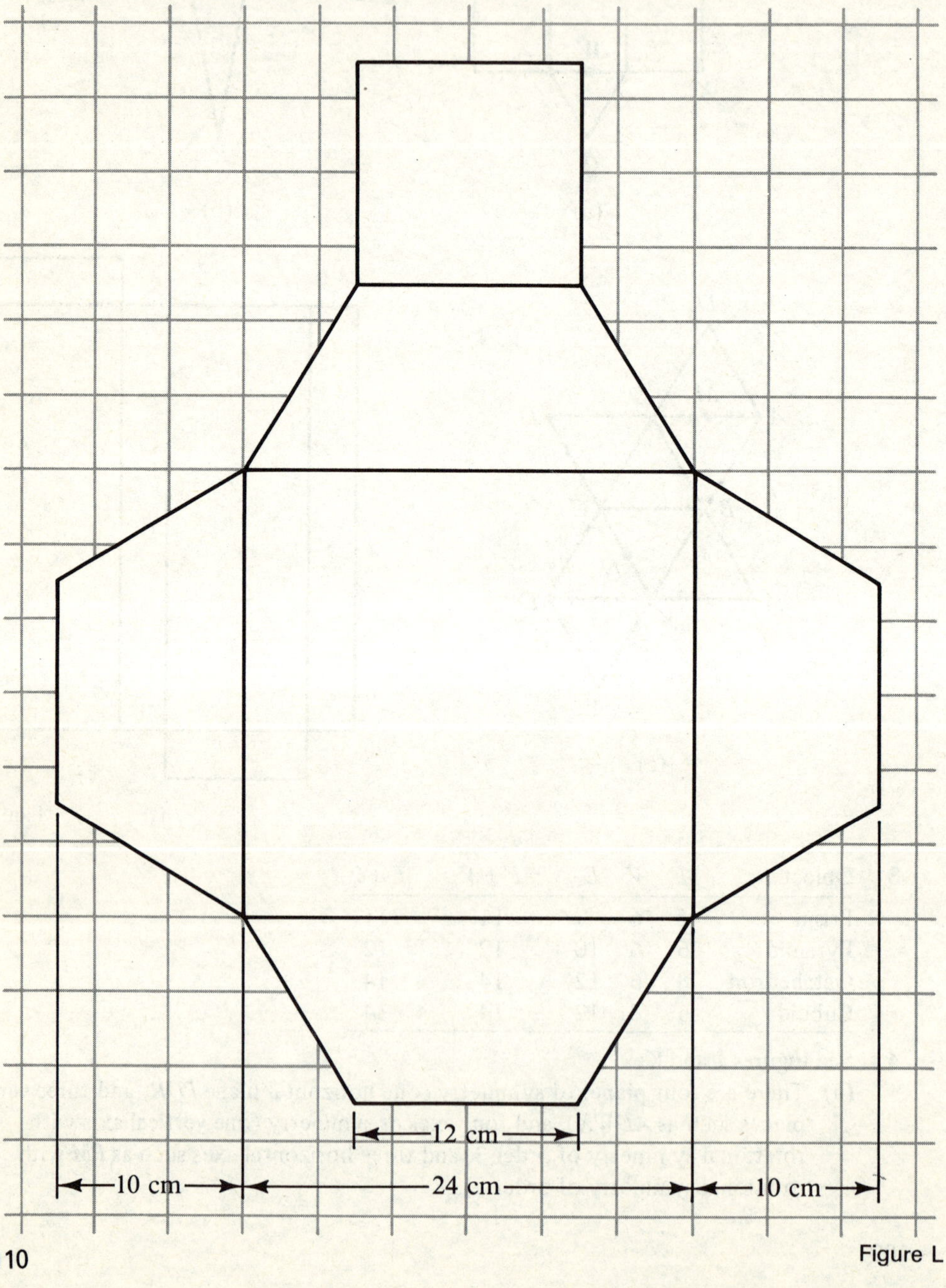

Figure L

5 (a) The object has the same symmetry as the 'original' pyramid, namely four planes of symmetry (*AWYC, BXZD, FRTH,* and *GSUJ*), and one axis of symmetry *EV*, with rotational symmetry of order 4.

(b) In triangle *DLM*, $DL = 8$ cm, and $LM = 6$ cm (half of $WZ - AD$). Hence $DM = 10$ cm. The net is shown in Figure L.

(c) The sides of the square *ABCD* are half the length of those of square *WXYZ*. The 'original' pyramid (*OWXYZ* say) would therefore have been twice the height of the pyramid *OABCD*, and eight times its volume. The volume of the truncated pyramid is therefore seven times the volume of *OABCD*; i.e. $7 \times \frac{1}{3} \times 12 \times 12 \times 8)$ cm^3, = 2688 cm^3.

Surface area of truncated pyramid = large square + small square + 4 trapeziums
= $(24 \times 24 + 12 \times 12 + 4 \times 18 \times 10)$ cm^2,
= 1440 cm^2.

(For the trapezium, the height is 10 cm; the average width is $(12 + 24)/2$ cm = 18 cm.)

6 See Figure J (c).
$OU = OV = OA = \ldots = 10\sqrt{2}$ cm. $BM = 10\sqrt{3}$ cm.
Volume of octahedron = 2 × volume of tetrahedron *UABCD*
= $(2 \times \frac{1}{3} \times 20 \times 20 \times 10\sqrt{2})$ cm^3
= 3770 cm^3 (correct to three significant figures).

Surface area = 8 × area of triangle *UAB*
= $8 \times (\frac{1}{2} \times 20 \times 10\sqrt{3})$ cm^2
= 1390 cm^2 (correct to three significant figures).

7 See Figure M.

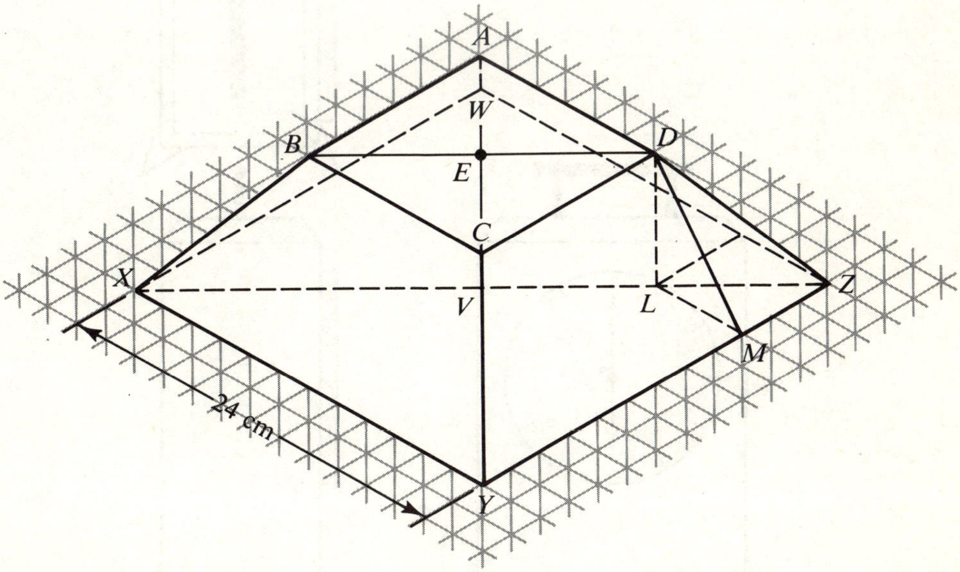

Figure M

8 See Figure N.

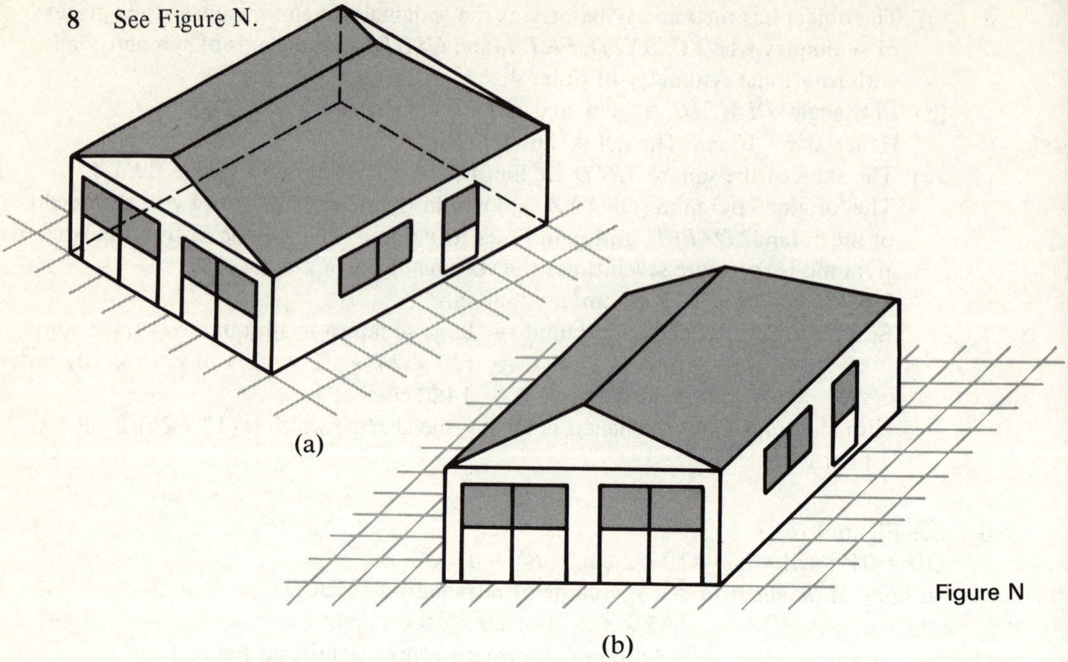

Figure N

9 See Figure O.

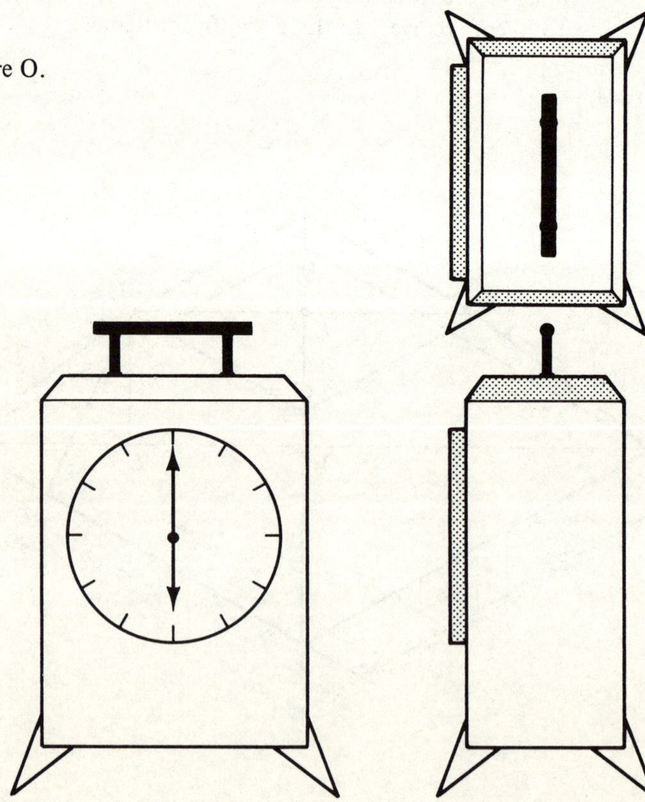

Figure O

10 See Figure P. The numerical answers below are correct to three significant figures.

(a) Total surface area $= 2 \times \pi \times 5(5 + 12)\ \text{cm}^2 = 170\pi\ \text{cm}^2 = 534\ \text{cm}^2$.
Volume $= \pi \times 5 \times 5 \times 12\ \text{cm}^3 = 300\pi\ \text{cm}^3 = 942\ \text{cm}^3$.

(b) Slant length $= \sqrt{(10^2 + 12^2)}\ \text{cm} = \sqrt{244}\ \text{cm} = 15.6\ \text{cm}$.
Total surface area $= \pi \times 10 \times (10 + 15.6\ldots)\ \text{cm}^2 = 256\ldots\pi\ \text{cm}^2 = 805\ \text{cm}^2$.
Volume $= \frac{1}{3} \times \pi \times 10 \times 10 \times 12\ \text{cm}^3 = 400\pi\ \text{cm}^3 = 1260\ \text{cm}^3$.

(c) Radius of sphere $= 7$ cm.
Surface area $= 4 \times \pi \times 7 \times 7\ \text{cm}^2 = 196\pi\ \text{cm}^2 = 616\ \text{cm}^2$.
Volume $= \frac{4}{3} \times \pi \times 7 \times 7 \times 7\ \text{cm}^3 = 1440\ \text{cm}^3$.

11 See Figure P.

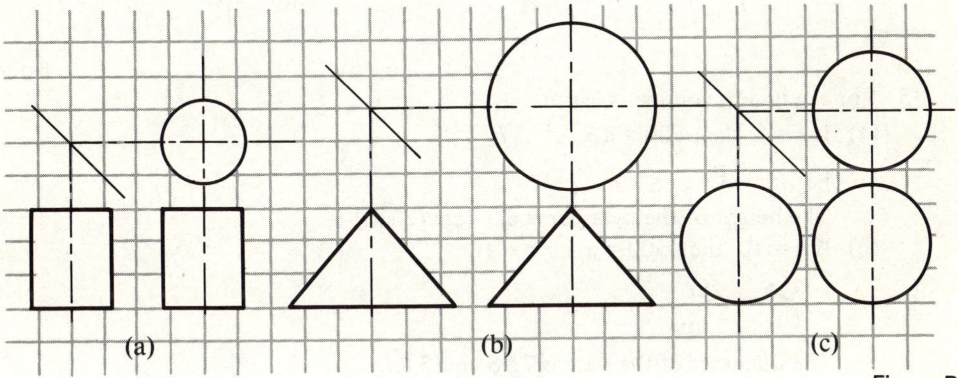

Figure P

12 (a) See Figure Q.

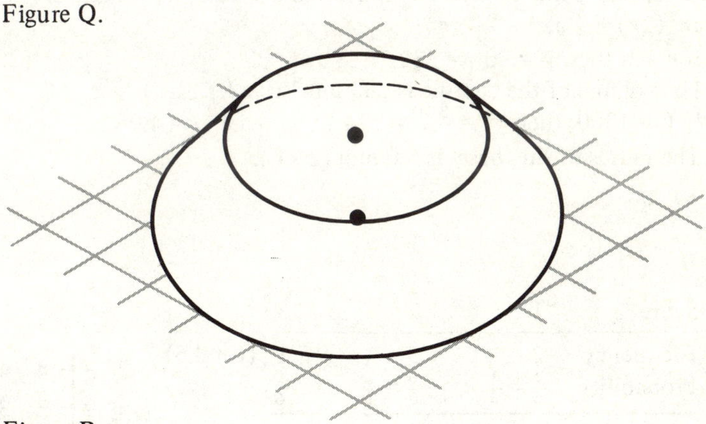

Figure Q

(b) See Figure R.
Cone I will have a height of 12 cm, a base radius of 9 cm, and a slant length of 15 cm.
For cone I: volume $= \frac{1}{3} \times \pi \times 9 \times 9 \times 12\ \text{cm}^3 = 324\pi\ \text{cm}^3$;
curved surface area $= \pi \times 9 \times 15\ \text{cm}^2 = 135\pi\ \text{cm}^2$.

Height of cone II : height of cone I $= 2 : 3$;
hence surface area of cone II : surface area of cone I $= 4 : 9$.
Curved surface area of III $= \frac{5}{9} \times 135\pi\ \text{cm}^2 = 75\pi\ \text{cm}^2$;
total surface area of III $= (\pi \times 9 \times 9 + \pi \times 6 \times 6 + 75\pi)\ \text{cm}^2 = 192\pi\ \text{cm}^2$
$= 603\ \text{cm}^2$.

Volume of cone II : volume of cone I = 8 : 27;
hence volume of cone III = $\frac{19}{27} \times 324\pi$ cm^3 = 716 cm^3

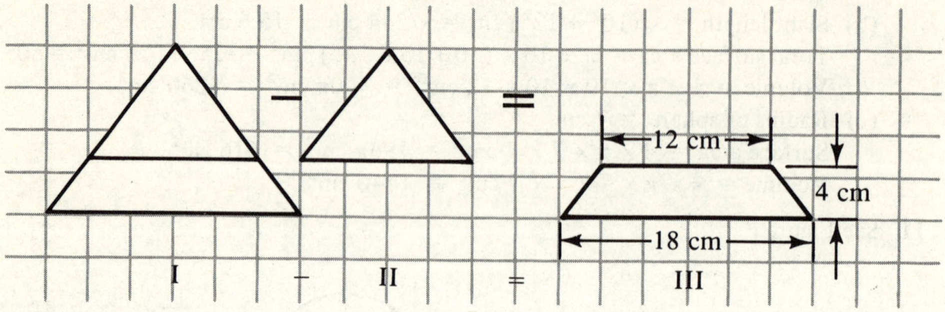

Figure R

13 For a cylinder, volume = $\pi r^2 h$.

(a) If $r = 5$, then $500 = \pi \times 5^2 \times h$

i.e. $h = \frac{20}{\pi} = 6.366\ldots$

The height of the cylinder is 6.37 cm (3 s.f.)

(b) If $h = 10$, then $500 = \pi \times r^2 \times 10$

i.e. $r^2 = \frac{50}{\pi}$

$r = 3.989\ldots$

The diameter of the base is 7.98 cm (3 s.f.).

14 As the capsule is made from a cylinder and a sphere, its volume is
$V = \pi r^2(2r) + \frac{4}{3}\pi r^3 = \frac{10}{3}\pi r^3$

(a) If $r = 3$, then $V = 90\pi = 282.7\ldots$

The volume of the capsule is 283 mm^3 (3 s.f.).

(b) If $V = 1300$, then $r^3 = \frac{390}{\pi} = 124.1\ldots$ i.e. $r = 4.98\ldots$

The radius of the 'base' is 5.0 mm (2 s.f.).

Exercise D

1 (a)

Score	1	2	3	
Frequency	2	3	1	(total 6)
Probability	$\frac{2}{6} = \frac{1}{3}$	$\frac{3}{6} = \frac{1}{2}$	$\frac{1}{6}$	

(b)

Score	1	2	3
Probability	$\frac{1}{2}$	$\frac{1}{3}$	$\frac{1}{6}$

(c) See Figure S.

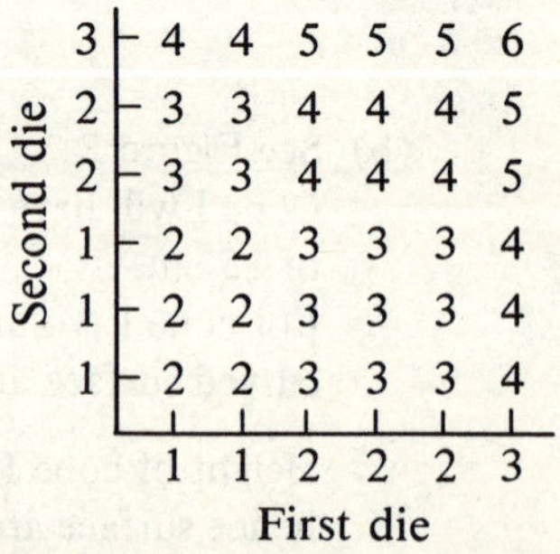

Total score	2	3	4	5	6
Probability	$\frac{6}{36}$	$\frac{13}{36}$	$\frac{11}{36}$	$\frac{5}{36}$	$\frac{1}{36}$

Figure S

2 (a) 4 heads, 3 heads and 1 tail, 2 heads and 2 tails, 1 head and 3 tails, 4 tails
(b) The ‘equally likely’ possibilities are HHHH, HHHT, HHTH, HTHH, THHH, HHTT, HTHT, HTTH, THHT, THTH, TTHH, HTTT, THTT, TTHT, TTTH, TTTT.

Combination	4H	3H + 1T	2H + 2T	1H + 3T	4T
Probability	$\frac{1}{16}$	$\frac{4}{16} = \frac{1}{4}$	$\frac{6}{16} = \frac{3}{8}$	$\frac{4}{16} = \frac{1}{4}$	$\frac{1}{16}$

(c) The expected number of 2H + 2T $= \frac{3}{8} \times 400 = 150$.

3 (a) The probability that 1 August will be fine $= \frac{27}{50}$ (0.54).
(b) The probability that 1 August will be wet $= \frac{12}{50}$ (0.24).
Therefore in eight years 1 August is likely to be wet 8×0.24 times; i.e. approximately twice.

4 (a) The probability that they are both red $= \frac{3}{10} \times \frac{2}{9} = \frac{1}{15}$.
(b) The probability that they are both blue $= \frac{7}{10} \times \frac{6}{9} = \frac{7}{15}$.
Hence the probability that the marbles are of different colour is $1 - (\frac{1}{15} + \frac{7}{15}) = \frac{7}{15}$.

5 (a) $\frac{4}{52} \times \frac{3}{51} \times \frac{2}{50} = \frac{1}{5525} = 0.000\,18$
(b) $13 \times$ (a) $= \frac{1}{425} = 0.002\,35$
(c) $\frac{4}{52} \times \frac{4}{51} \times \frac{4}{50} = \frac{8}{16575} = 0.000\,48$

6 (a) $\frac{12}{52} = \frac{3}{13}$ (0.230 77)
(b) $\frac{8}{51}$ (0.156 86)
(c) $\frac{3}{13} \times \frac{8}{51} = \frac{8}{221}$ (0.036 20)
(d) $\frac{8}{221} \times \frac{4}{50} = \frac{16}{5525}$ (0.002 90)

7 (a) See Figure T.

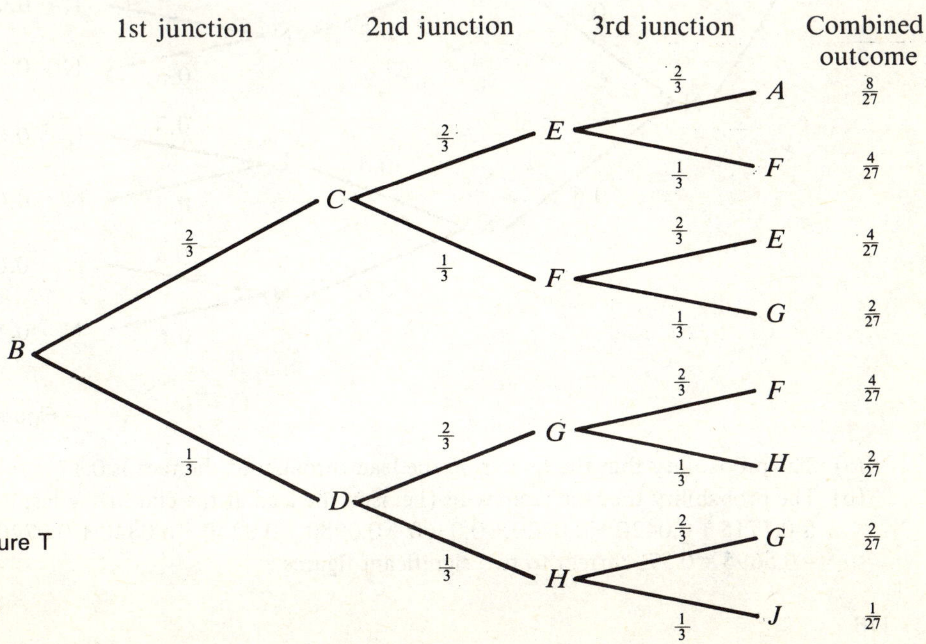

Figure T

(b) Prob (coach at A) $= \frac{2}{3} \times \frac{2}{3} \times \frac{2}{3} = \frac{8}{27}$ (0.296 . . .)
Prob (coach at F) $= \frac{2}{3} \times \frac{2}{3} \times \frac{1}{3} + \frac{1}{3} \times \frac{2}{3} \times \frac{2}{3} = \frac{8}{27}$ (0.296 . .)
Prob (coach at G) $= \frac{2}{3} \times \frac{1}{3} \times \frac{1}{3} + \frac{1}{3} \times \frac{1}{3} \times \frac{2}{3} = \frac{4}{27}$ (0.148 . .)

8 See Figure U.
(L = team is in the lead, N = team is not in the lead, at the end of a leg.)

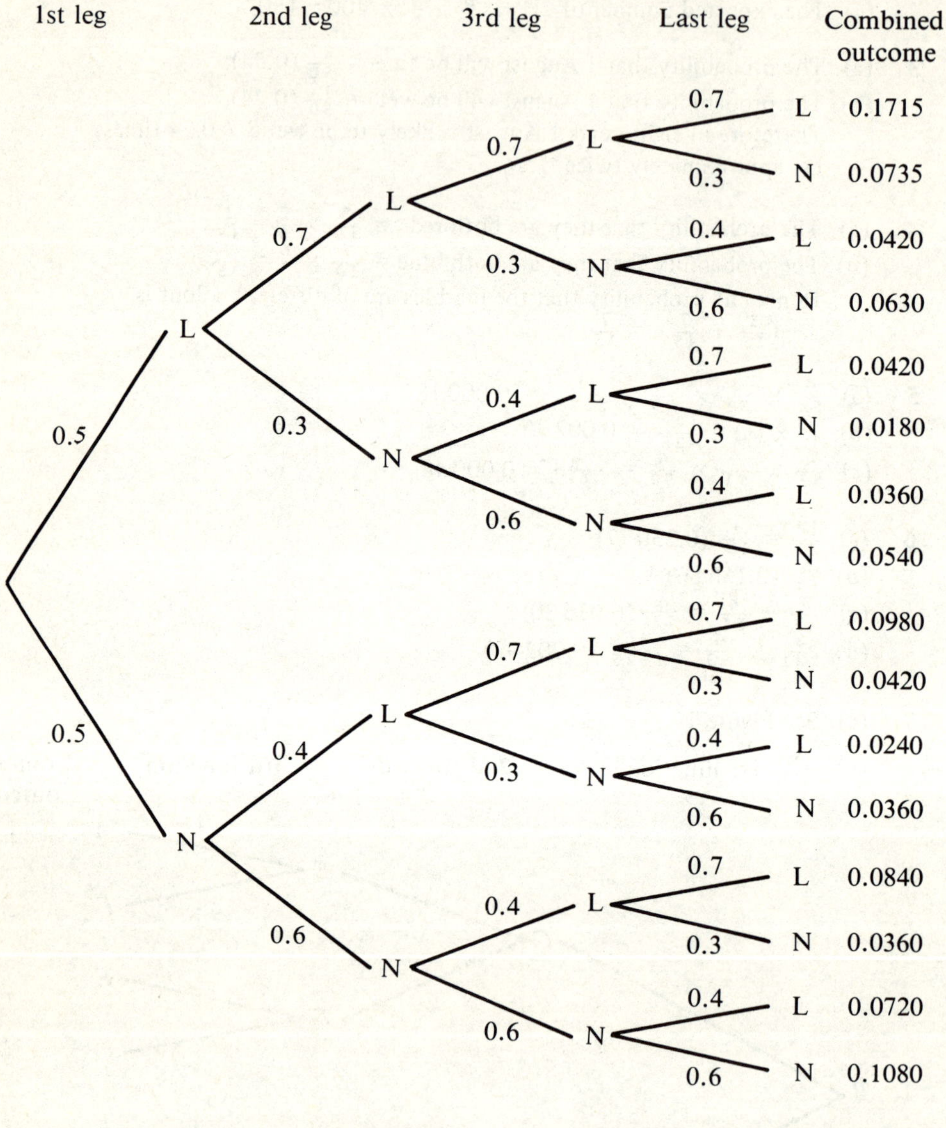

Figure U

(a) The probability that the team is in the lead throughout the race is 0.1715.
(b) The probability that the team wins (i.e. is in the lead at the end of the last leg) is 0.1715 + 0.0420 + 0.0420 + 0.0360 + 0.0980 + 0.0240 + 0.0840 + 0.0720 = 0.5695 = 0.57, correct to two significant figures.

Consolidation 5

This chapter covers Units 43 to 48 of the course.
These units are to be found in the following books:
Algebra 2: Equations, Formulas and Graphs (Chapter 4);
Further Algebra and Computation (Chapter 4);
Further Matrices and Transformations (Chapters 4 and 5);
Geometry 3: Three Dimensions (Chapters 4 and 5).

5.1 Linear programming (Chapter 4 of *Algebra 2: Equations, Formulas and Graphs*)

A mathematical model is a set of conditions (often equations or inequalities) used to represent or formulate a problem.

Linear programming is used when the conditions are given by linear inequalities.

If only two variables are involved then a set of solutions can be found graphically by plotting the inequalities.
It does not matter how many inequalities there are.

In graphical solutions it is better to 'shade out' the unwanted (i.e. 'not possible') regions.
Any region that remains unshaded after this has been done represents the solution set.

The boundary of many linear inequalities is a line whose equation is of the form
$ax + by = c$ where a, b and c are all positive numbers.
This line cuts the y-axis at the point $(0, Y)$, where $Y = c/b$, and the x-axis at the point $(X, 0)$, where $X = c/a$.
(If either of X or Y is not an integer it is usually more accurate in graphical work to find another point on the boundary line whose coordinates are integers.)

For given values of a and b the lines

$$ax + by = k$$

form a set of parallel lines for different values of k. If $k = 0$ the line goes through the origin; as k increases, the line moves to the right. This idea is used to 'maximise' or 'minimise' an expression within a solution set (or region).

Exercise A

1 (a) Draw x- and y-axes for values of x and y from 0 to 10.
On your diagram draw the straight lines with the following equations.
$x = 4$; $x + y = 8$; $x + 3y = 9$; $2x + y = 10$; $y = 4$; $y = 2x$

(b) On another diagram show (by shading the **unwanted** regions) the region defined by the following.
$x \leqslant 4$; $x + 3y \geqslant 9$; $y < 2x$

(c) On a third diagram show the region defined by the following.
$x + y \leqslant 8$; $2x + y \geqslant 10$; $0 < y < 4$

2 (a) From Figure 1 write down the equations of the lines OA, BD, PQ and CP.

(b) Write down the inequalities that define the **unshaded** region.

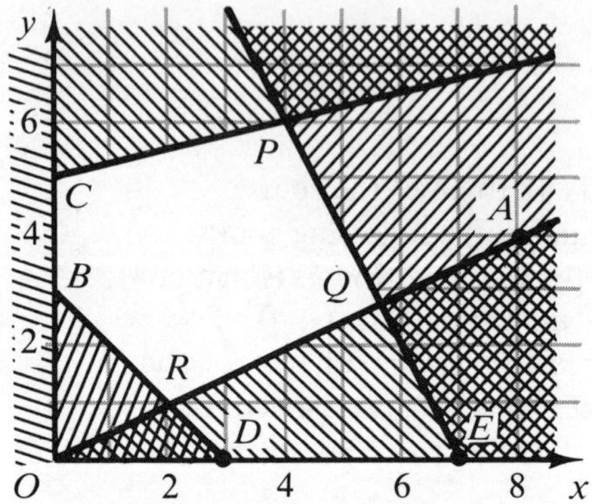

Figure 1

3 (a) A ferry is carrying x cars and y coaches. Write down a statement about the number of vehicles on the ferry.

(b) Each car carries 4 passengers, and each coach carries 52 passengers. Write down a statement about the largest number of passengers that can be carried in the cars and coaches.

(c) Draw x- and y-axes for values of x from 0 to 36, and values of y from 0 to 12. On these axes draw and label the straight line that corresponds to the statement 'There is a total of 11 vehicles on the ferry.'
Write down some possible combinations of x and y that satisfy this statement.

(d) On the same axes draw the straight line that corresponds to the statement 'When all the vehicles are full the number of passengers being carried is 188.'

(e) From your graph read off the combination of x and y (the ordered pair (x, y)) that satisfies both the statements (conditions) stated in (c) and (d).

4 (a) Find the maximum and minimum values of the expression $3x + 5y$ in the unshaded region (including the boundaries) shown in Figure 2.

(b) Repeat part (a) for the expression $2y - x$.

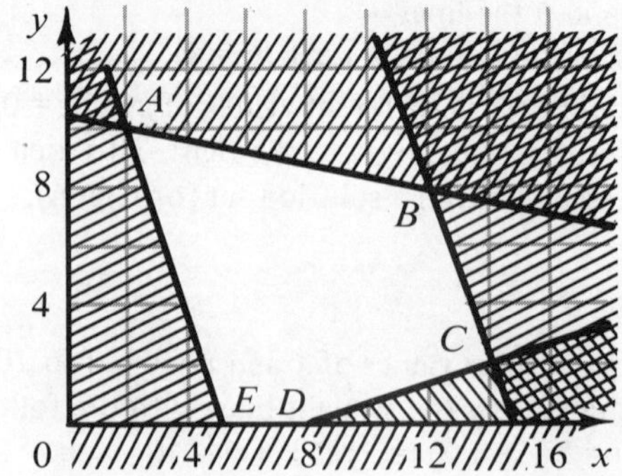

Figure 2

5 A gardener is asked to plant daffodils and tulips in a flower-bed whose area is 1 m^2. For a reasonable display, daffodils should be planted at the rate of 140 bulbs per square metre, and tulips at the rate of 70 bulbs per square metre.

(a) What areas can be planted with the following numbers of daffodils?
420, 140, 70, x

(b) What areas can be planted with the following numbers of tulips?
420, 140, 70, y

(c) Write down the equation in x and y that states that if an area of 1 m^2 is planted with x daffodil bulbs and y tulip bulbs, a 'reasonable' display will be produced.

(d) A further requirement is that neither flower shall occupy more than 60% of the area of the flower-bed.
Write down two inequalities (one involving x and the other involving y) that express these conditions.

(e) The gardener has £10 to spend on bulbs. Daffodil bulbs cost 8p each, and tulip bulbs cost 12p each.
Express this information as an inequality in x and y.

(f) Show all these results on a graph. Which combination of daffodils and tulips uses the smallest number of bulbs?

6 Within the region defined by
$x \geqslant 0$; $y \geqslant 0$; $2x + y \leqslant 8$; $2x + 5y \leqslant 20$
find the maximum and minimum values of
(a) $x + 3y$, (b) $2x + 3y$, (c) $3x - y$.

7 A rectangle has sides of lengths x cm and y cm.
The perimeter of the rectangle must not exceed 50 cm, and the area of the rectangle must be at least 96 cm^2.

(a) Express these conditions as inequalities in x and y.

(b) Show these inequalities graphically, and hence find the largest possible **integral** value of x.

5.2 Growth and decay (Chapter 4 of *Further Algebra and Computation*)

A function $f(x)$ is exponential if $\dfrac{f(x+1)}{f(x)} = a$, where a is a (positive) constant, for all values of x.

If $a > 1$ then $f(x)$ increases as x increases. The constant a is sometimes called the 'growth factor'.

If $a < 1$ then $f(x)$ decreases as x increases. In this case the constant a is sometimes called the 'decay factor'.

If $f(x) = k$ when $x = 0$, an exponential function may be written in the form
$f : x \to ka^x$.

The growth of something (population, area, money, etc) is exponential if the rate of growth is directly proportional to its present size.

For example, if the number of books in use increases at a constant rate of 6%, the ratio

$$\frac{\text{number of books in use in a year's time}}{\text{number of books in use now}} = 1.06; \text{ which is constant.}$$

Hence the growth in the number of books is exponential, and the numbers of books at the beginning and end of a period of time are related by the formula

$$n = N \times (1.06)^t$$

where N was the number of books 'at the beginning' and n is the number of books t years later.

To find the time taken for a population to undergo a required change (for example, to double itself), use a calculator, if necessary, to evaluate successive values of $f(x)$ until the required result is obtained.

To find an initial value, work backwards. (For example; if the number of books is 10 000, then the number of books five years ago (assuming the growth rate has been constant at 6%) was

$$\frac{10\,000}{(1.06)^5} = \frac{10\,000}{1.338...} = 7470 \text{ (3 s.f.)).}$$

Simple interest: $I = \frac{PTR}{100}$ where P is the principal (original sum); T is the time; and $R\%$ is the rate of interest.

(The time element in R must be in the same units as T. For example, to find the interest after three months, the rate must be expressed as a 'percentage per month'.)

Compound interest: If the interest is compounded at regular intervals (i.e. added on to the original sum, so that the original sum **and** the interest earn interest) then the growth is (approximately) exponential.

The total amount (A) after t years, at a rate of $r\%$ per annum (year) compounded annually, is given by the formula

$$A = P\left(1 + \frac{r}{100}\right)^t.$$

If the interest is compounded more frequently, this formula needs adjusting.

For example, if interest at a rate of $r\%$ per annum is compounded monthly, the formula becomes

$$A = P\left(1 + \frac{r}{12 \times 100}\right)^{12t}.$$

Exercise B

1 (a) Copy and complete the following table for the function $p = 3^t$.

t	0	1	2	3	4
p	1				81

(b) Draw the graph of $p = 3^t$, for values of t from 0 to 4.

(c) From your graph estimate the value of p when $t = 3.5$. Use a calculator to verify your results.

(d) From your graph estimate the value of t when $p = 20$.

2 Sketch the graphs of the following functions for values of x from $^-2$ to $^+2$.

(a) $y = 5 \times 5^x$ (b) $y = 10 \times 3^{-x}$ (c) $y = {}^-2 \times 1.05^x$ (d) $y = 0.8^x$

3 For each part of Figure 3 deduce the equation of the given graph.

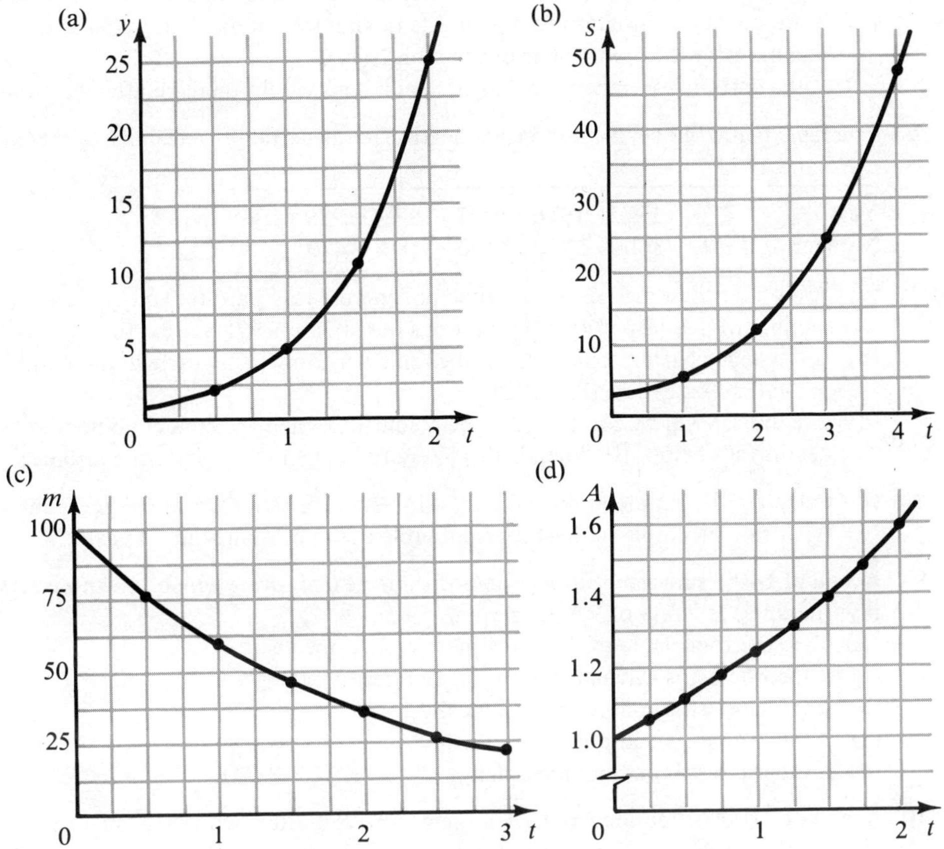

Figure 3

4 In 1980 a country's output of tin was 12 000 tonnes; and the annual rate of increase of output was 4%.
   (a) Assuming that the rate of increase of output was constant for the previous three years, calculate the output in 1977 (correct to three significant figures).
   (b) Calculate the estimated output in 1984 if the rate of increase remains constant.
   (c) Estimate the output in 1984 if the rate of increase of output increases by 1% each year.

5 Show your results for question 4 on a graph.

6 The number of dandelions in a field on the last day of the month for a period of six months was as follows.

Month	1	2	3	4	5	6
Number of dandelions	67	101	152	228	342	512

   (a) For months 2 to 6 calculate the increase in the number of dandelions during the month, and express this increase as a percentage of the number of dandelions at the end of the previous month.

(b) How many dandelions were there in the field at the beginning of the first month?
(c) Write down the equation that connects the number of dandelions (d) at the end of a month with the number of the month (m).
(d) If the pattern continued, how many dandelions would there be after 12 months?

7 The table below shows the number of deaths from a certain tropical disease between 1975 and 1981.

Year	1975	1976	1977	1978	1979	1980
Number of deaths	3600	2160	1300	780	470	280

(a) Show that these figures follow an exponential decay pattern, and express the number of deaths per year (D) in terms of t, taking 1975 as year 0.
(b) If the decay pattern continues in the same way, in which year will the number of deaths first be less than 100?
(c) The disease will be considered to be eradicated when the annual number of deaths falls below 10. When is this likely to happen if the pattern continues?

8 (a) Calculate the simple interest on £750 invested for five years at 6% per annum.
(b) What rate of simple interest would double a sum of money in 12 years?

9 A sum of £400 is invested for a period of three years (during which time no interest is withdrawn) at a rate of 9% per annum.
Calculate the total value of the investment after three years
(a) if the interest is calculated on a simple interest basis;
(b) if the interest is compounded annually;
(c) if the interest is compounded monthly;
(d) if the interest is compounded daily.

10 A sum of £1000 is required to have a value of £1250 after two years.
Calculate the annual rate of interest necessary if the interest is
(a) worked out on a simple interest basis;
(b) compounded annually;
(c) compounded monthly.

11 How long will it take for a sum of money to double in value if the annual rate of interest is 6%, and the interest is
(a) worked out on a simple interest basis;
(b) compounded annually;
(c) compounded monthly.

12 Repeat question 11 for an annual rate of interest of 12%.

5.3 Matrices and topology (Chapters 4 and 5 of *Further Matrices and Transformations*)

Chapter 4

The vectors $\mathbf{i} = \begin{bmatrix} 1 \\ 0 \end{bmatrix}$ and $\mathbf{j} = \begin{bmatrix} 0 \\ 1 \end{bmatrix}$ are called the base or unit vectors (for cartesian axes).
The position vector of any point in a plane can be written in terms of $\mathbf{i}$ and $\mathbf{j}$.
(For example; the position vector of $P(3, 4)$ is $\mathbf{p} = 3\mathbf{i} + 4\mathbf{j}$.)
The vectors $\mathbf{i}$ and $\mathbf{j}$ are the position vectors of the vertices $I(1, 0)$ and $J(0, 1)$ of the unit square $OIUJ$.

Under an 'affine' transformation, all the squares of a piece of graph paper are transformed into (congruent) parallelograms.

An affine transformation may be represented by a 2×2 matrix, provided the origin is one of the invariant points of the transformation.

Conversely, every non-singular 2×2 matrix represents an affine transformation under which the origin is invariant.

If a transformation can be represented by a 2×2 matrix **M**, then the two columns of **M** give the images of the position vectors **i** and **j**. (This enables us to picture the image of the unit square, and hence obtain some idea of the type of transformation.)

Conversely, if the image of the unit square is known (or can be deduced), then the matrix for the transformation can be written down.

The matrix for the inverse of a transformation is the inverse of the matrix for the original transformation.

Bold capital letters, such as **M**, **T**, etc., are used either for transformations, or for the matrices representing these transformations.

If **T**, **X** and **Y** are three transformations (or their matrices), the statement **T** = **XY** means that **T** is the result of (i.e. is equivalent to) **Y** followed by **X**.

If $\mathbf{T} = \mathbf{XY}$, then $\mathbf{T}^{-1} = \mathbf{Y}^{-1}\mathbf{X}^{-1}$.

Two simultaneous linear equations may be written in the form $\mathbf{Ar} = \mathbf{b}$, where **r** is the vector $\begin{bmatrix} x \\ y \end{bmatrix}$.

If **A** is non-singular (i.e. the determinant of **A** is not zero), then there is a unique solution given by $\mathbf{r} = \mathbf{A}^{-1}\mathbf{b}$.

If **A** is singular, then there is either an infinite number of solutions (one equation is, in fact, just a multiple of the other equation) or no solution.

Geometrically, a linear equation is represented by a straight line. The 'ordinary' solution corresponds to the intersection of two lines. 'No solution' represents a pair of parallel lines.

Chapter 5

A topological transformation allows twisting and stretching; but not tearing or joining.

Some properties that are invariant under a topological transformation are:

the order of arrangement of points on a line;

the number of lines meeting at a point;

the number, and sequence, of lines surrounding an area.

Length, size of angle, direction, and area are some properties that are not invariant, and so cannot be measured from a topological map.

Two figures are topologically equivalent if one can be transformed into the other by a topological transformation.

If two networks are topologically equivalent they have the same (route) matrix; and vice versa.

A simple closed curve is topologically equivalent to a circle.

A node is a point (vertex, 'town'). The order of a node is the number of lines (routes or roads) leading to or from it.

It is not possible to draw a network with an odd number of odd nodes.

A figure is traversable if it can be drawn with one movement of a pencil, without lifting the pencil off the paper, or going over any line twice.

A traversable figure has either no odd nodes, or just two odd nodes.

An arc is a line (road or route) joining two nodes.

The area bounded by one or more arcs (forming a simple closed curve) is a region. The area outside a network is counted as one of the network's regions.

For a closed network on a plane, Euler's relation states that $N - A + R = 2$, where N, A and R are the numbers of nodes, arcs and regions.

Squaring a one-stage route matrix gives the two-stage route matrix; etc.

For a given network, various incidence matrices are possible. Three of these are

R – incidence of nodes on arcs;
S – incidence of arcs on regions;
T – incidence of nodes on regions.

Various results connect incidence matrices: for example, **RS** = 2**T**.

Exercise C

1 Write down the position vectors, in terms of the unit vectors **i** and **j**, for the following points.

(a) $P(4,1)$ (b) $Q(2,{}^-3)$ (c) $R(0,{}^-5)$ (d) $S({}^-6,{}^-6)$ (e) $T({}^-4,4)$

2 Two base vectors **g** and **h** are defined by

$$\mathbf{g} = \begin{bmatrix} 2 \\ 1 \end{bmatrix} \quad \text{and } \mathbf{h} = \begin{bmatrix} 0 \\ {}^-1 \end{bmatrix}.$$

Express the position vectors of the points P, Q, R, S and T defined in question 1 in terms of **g** and **h**.

3 Sketch the images of the unit square $OIUJ$ (labelling I', J' and U') under the transformations with the following matrices.

(a) $\begin{bmatrix} 1 & 0 \\ 0 & {}^-3 \end{bmatrix}$ (b) $\begin{bmatrix} {}^-1 & 2 \\ {}^-2 & 3 \end{bmatrix}$ (c) $\begin{bmatrix} 0 & 2 \\ 3 & 0 \end{bmatrix}$ (d) $\begin{bmatrix} {}^-3 & {}^-4 \\ 4 & {}^-3 \end{bmatrix}$

4 Each part of Figure 4 shows the image of the rectangle $O(0,0)$ $A(4,0)$ $B(4,2)$ $C(0,2)$ under a transformation **T**.

For each part

(i) deduce the image of the unit square;
(ii) write down the matrix for the transformation;
(iii) describe the transformation as simply as possible.

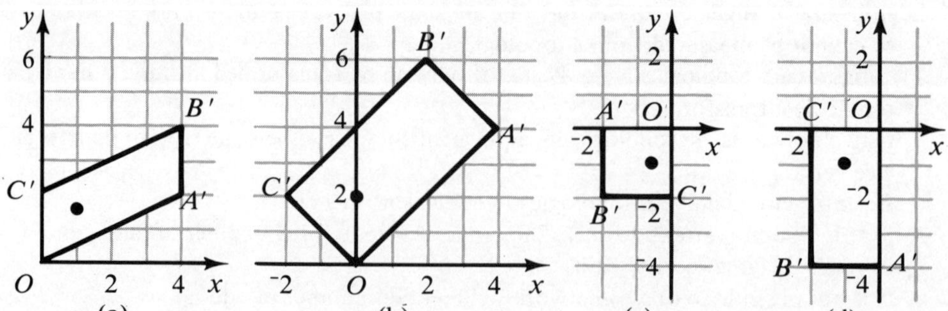

Figure 4

5 For each transformation defined in question 3,

(i) write down and evaluate the determinant of the matrix for the transformation;

(ii) state the area factor of the transformation;

(iii) describe, as simply as possible, the transformation.

6 Draw and label sketches to show the images of the unit square *OIUJ* under the following transformations.

(a) An enlargement from the origin with scale factor $^-4$.

(b) A two-way stretch from the x- and y-axes with scale factors $^-3$ and $\frac{1}{2}$ respectively.

(c) A shear with base (invariant) line $x + y = 0$ under which the image of $(1,1)$ is the point $(5,^-3)$.

(d) An enlargement from the origin with scale factor 3, followed by a quarter turn about the origin.

7 Write down the matrices for the transformations described in question 6.

8 Figure 5 shows an object F.
Make one copy of Figure 5, and on it show the final images of F under a transformation **X** followed by a transformation **Y**, and describe the equivalent single transformation, when

(a) **X** is a quarter-turn about the point $(2, 0)$ and **Y** is a translation of $\begin{bmatrix} 2 \\ -2 \end{bmatrix}$;

(b) **X** is a reflection in the line $x = 2$, and **Y** is a half-turn about the point $(2,0)$;

(c) **X** is a reflection in the line $y = {}^-1$ and **Y** is a reflection in the line $x = {}^-2$.

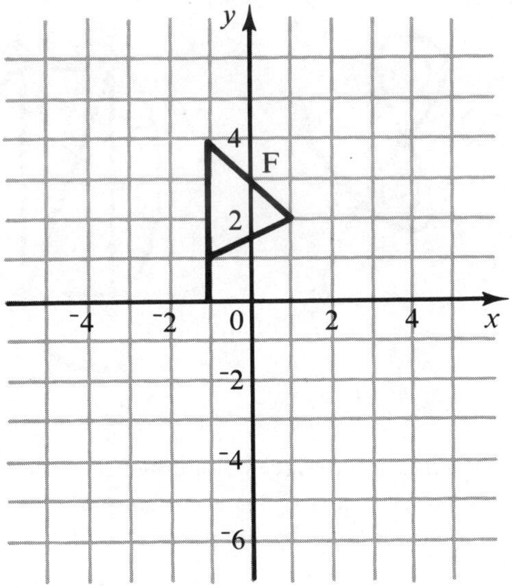

Figure 5

9 Use matrix methods to find (or comment on) the solutions to the following pairs of simultaneous equations.

(a) $2x - y = 3$, $4x + 5y = {}^-15$ (b) $4y = x + 4$, $3y = x$ (c) $^-3x + 5y = 6$, $15y - 9x = {}^-18$

10 List the parts of Figure 6 in three sets so that within each set the members are topologically equivalent to each other.

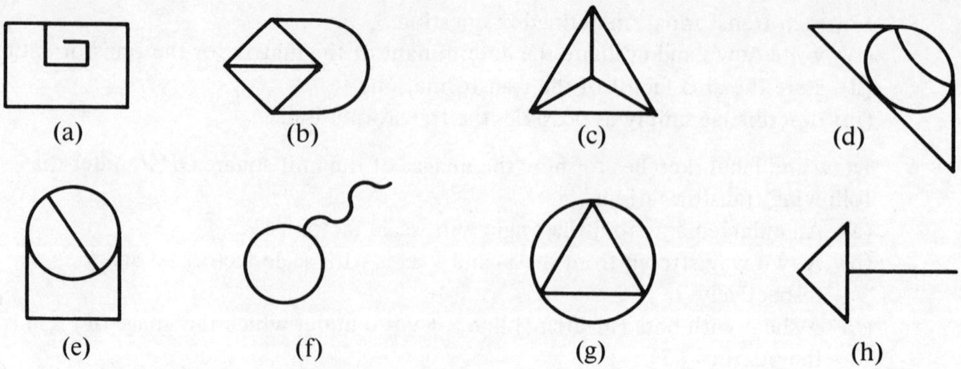

Figure 6

11 Draw where possible
(a) a network with three nodes, six arcs, and five regions;
(b) a network with one node, two arcs, and three regions;
(c) a network whose directed-route matrix is

$$\begin{bmatrix} 2 & 1 & 0 \\ 0 & 0 & 3 \\ 0 & 2 & 1 \end{bmatrix}.$$

12 For each of the networks shown in Figure 7,
(i) show that Euler's relation is satisfied;
(ii) write down the direct route matrix **M**;
(iii) evaluate the two-stage route matrix $\mathbf{M}^2$.

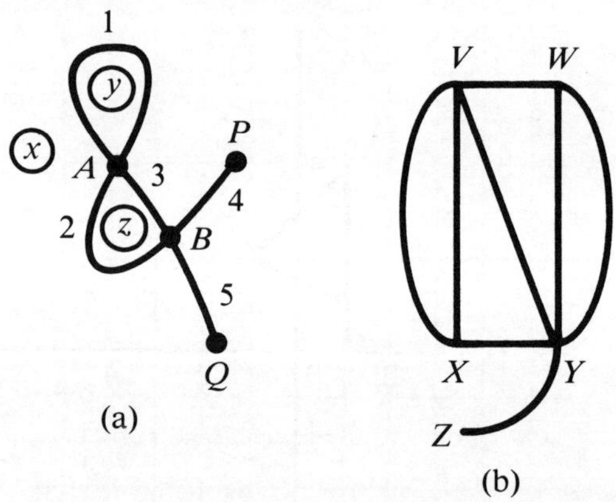

Figure 7

13 For the network shown in Figure 7(a) write down the incidence matrices for nodes on regions (**T**) and regions on arcs (**V**), and evaluate the product **TV**.
What information (if any) is given by the product **TV**?

5.4 Three-dimensional geometry (Chapters 4 and 5 of *Geometry 3: Three Dimensions*)

Chapter 4

The intersection of a plane and a sphere is a circle. If the plane passes through the centre of the sphere, the circle is a Great Circle.

The two points at the ends of a diameter of a sphere are said to be diametrically opposite to each other.

If J and K are two points on the surface of a sphere (centre O) that are not diametrically opposite, there is only one Great Circle through J and K: that given by the intersection of the sphere with the plane OJK.

The shortest route between J and K on the surface of the sphere is the minor arc of the Great Circle through J and K.

The Earth may be regarded as a sphere. It has a radius of approximately 6370 km and a circumference of 40 000 km.

The diameter N (North Pole) to S (South Pole) is the Polar Axis.

Circles of longitude are Great Circles that pass through N and S. Each such circle is composed of two meridians: semi-circles joining N to S.

The meridian passing through the Observatory at Greenwich is the Greenwich Meridian. All other meridians are described as being θ° E or W of Greenwich, where θ° is the angle between the planes containing the Greenwich Meridian and the other meridian.

The Equator is a 'horizontal' Great Circle on the Earth. It therefore has a length (circumference) of 40 000 km. It divides the surface of the Earth into the Northern and Southern Hemispheres.

Circles of latitude are circles on the surface of the Earth that are parallel to the Equator. They are defined as being θ° N or S of the Equator.

Figure 8 shows the 40° N circle of latitude.

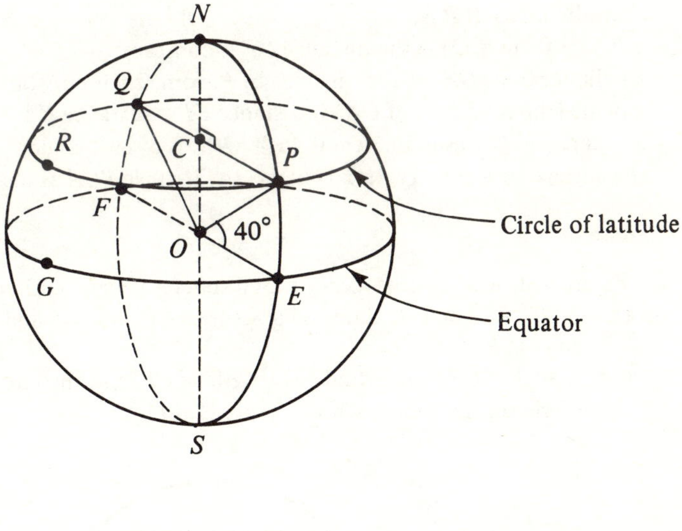

Figure 8

The position of a place on the surface of the Earth is determined by its latitude and longitude (in that order) given as degrees. Where greater accuracy is required, a degree is divided into 60 minutes. $(1^\circ = 60')$

A nautical mile (1 n.m.) is the length of the arc of a Great Circle that subtends an angle of 1 minute at the centre of the Earth. (Hence 1° along a Great Circle is a distance of 60 n.m., and the circumference of the Earth is 360×60 n.m. = 21 600 n.m.)

A speed of 1 knot is a speed of 1 nautical mile per hour.

Distances along a Great Circle are calculated from the angle 'traversed'.

For example: from $P(40^\circ$ N, 15° W) to $Q(12^\circ$ S, 15° W)

'traverses' $40^\circ + 12^\circ = 52^\circ$, a distance of 52×60 n.m.

Distances along a circle of latitude are calculated similarly, but using a scale factor of $\cos\theta^\circ$, where θ° is the latitude of the circle.

Chapter 5

The projection of a point P onto a plane is the point Q such that PQ is perpendicular to the plane. (It may be thought of as the shadow of P when the rays of light are perpendicular to the plane.)

The projection of a line onto a plane may be thought of as the shadow of the line in a similar way.

The angle between a line and a plane is the acute angle between the line and its projection on the plane.

Two planes intersect in a straight line. If the line is w, and V is a point on w, then the angle between the two planes is the angle SVT; where VS and VT are lines, one in each plane, perpendicular to w.

In three dimensions the position of a point may be defined by coordinates x, y, z.

The equation $ax + by + cz = d$ (where a, b, c and d are constants, possibly zero) represents a plane in three dimensions.

If O and A are fixed points, and P is a variable (moveable) point, in three dimensions, then the locus of P is:

a sphere (centre O) if the distance OP is constant;
a cylinder (axis OA) if the distance of P from OA is constant;
a plane (the mediator of OA) if distance OP = distance PA;
a sphere (on OA as diameter) if angle OPA is a right-angle;
the surface of a cone (vertex O, axis OA) if angle POA is constant.

Exercise D

1 Figure 9 shows the cross-section of a sphere of radius 12 cm.

(a) If OC = 8 cm, calculate the lengths of CP and NP, and the sizes of angles EOP and ONP.

(b) If angle $EOP = 52^\circ$, find the length of CP, and the circumference of the Small Circle on the sphere whose centre is at C.

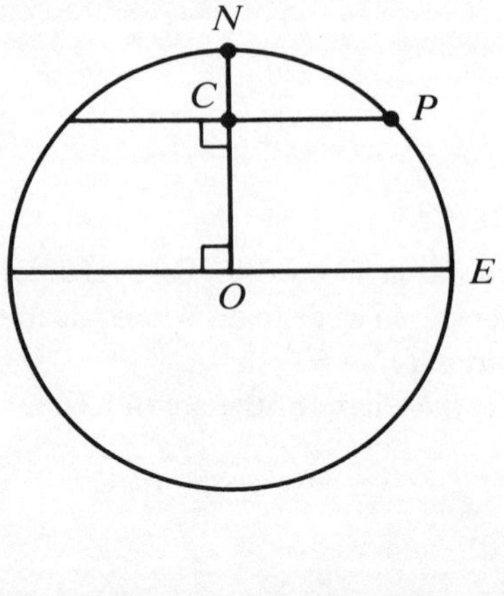

Figure 9

2 State the latitude and longitude of the points on the surface of the Earth diametrically opposite to the following points.
(a) $P(12° \text{ N}, 45° \text{ E})$ (b) $Q(32° \text{ S}, 0°)$ (c) $R(88° \text{ S}, 112° \text{ W})$

3 Calculate the shortest distances on the surface of the Earth between:
(a) $F(25° \text{ N}, 66° \text{ E})$ and $G(38° \text{ S}, 66° \text{ E})$;
(b) $F(25° \text{ N}, 66° \text{ E})$ and $H(38° \text{ S}, 114° \text{ W})$;
(c) $P(0°, 99° \text{ W})$ and $Q(0°, 99° \text{ E})$.

4 Calculate the shorter distances **along the circles of latitude** between the following pairs of places.
(a) $L(45° \text{ S}, 32° \text{ W})$ and $M(45° \text{ S}, 132° \text{ W})$
(b) $U(80° \text{ N}, 25° \text{ E})$ and $V(80° \text{ N}, 155° \text{ W})$

5 For the last part of question 4 (distance from U to V) would it have been shorter to go over the North Pole?

6 Figure 10 shows a satellite S directly over the North Pole N, and two other satellites S_1 and S_2, at the same height above the Earth as S, and due south of S, so positioned that direct 'visual' contact along the lines SS_1 and S_1S_2 is just possible.
(a) Calculate SN, the height of S above the North Pole, if a 'ring' of twelve such satellites is just able to circle the Earth.
(b) If $SN = 2640$ km calculate the angle SOS, and hence find how many satellites at this height will be needed to circle the Earth.

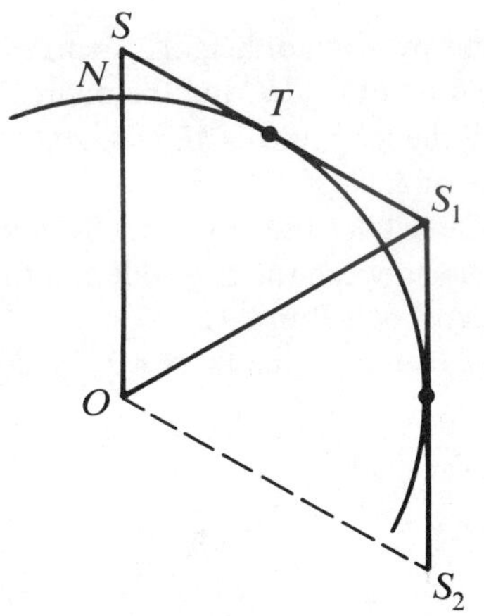

Figure 10

7 The satellite S_1 of question 6(a) circles the Earth so that the stationary satellite S is always just in visual contact.
(a) Describe the position of the centre of the circle along which S_1 travels, and calculate the radius and circumference of this circle.
(b) Calculate (correct to two significant figures) the speed, relative to the Earth, of the satellite S_1, if it circles the Earth once every 90 minutes.

8 Figure 11 shows a cube of side 2 units. The point P is the centre of the face $CDUE$, and the point Q is the centre of the base $OAFB$.

Write down the projections of the point D and of the line CF on the following planes.

OAFB, *OAEC*, *ABDE*, *OCUF*, *AEUF*

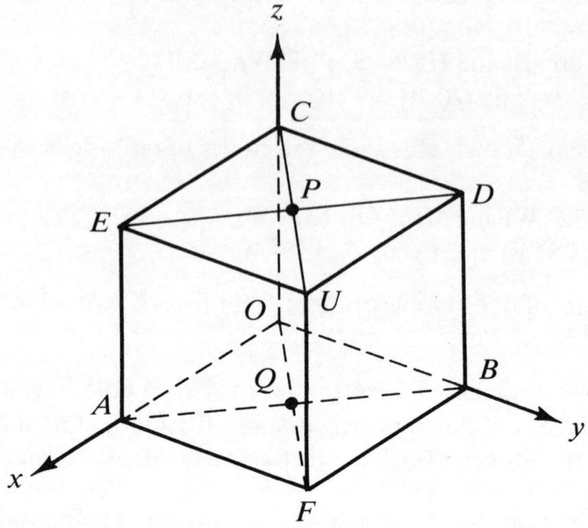

Figure 11

9 From Figure 11 write down

(a) the coordinates of the points *A, C, D, P, Q* and *U*;

(b) the equations of the planes *OAEC, OCUF, BDUF, ABDE* and *ACDF*.

10 Figure 12 shows a right pyramid of height 12 cm, whose base is a square of side 10 cm. The point *M* is the mid-point of *AB*, and the point *P* is the projection of *A* on *BV*.

(a) State or calculate the lengths of *AM, OM, AO, AV* and *MV*.

(b) Calculate the size of angle *ABV*.

(c) Calculate the angle between the planes *ABV* and *ABCD*.

(d) Calculate the angle between the edge *AV* and the base *ABCD*.

(e) Calculate the lengths of *AP* and *AC*.

(f) Calculate the angle between the faces *ABV* and *CBV*.

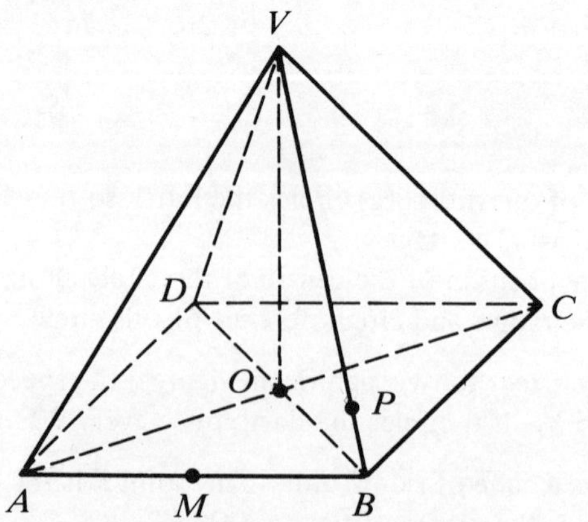

Figure 12

Exercise A

1 See Figure A.

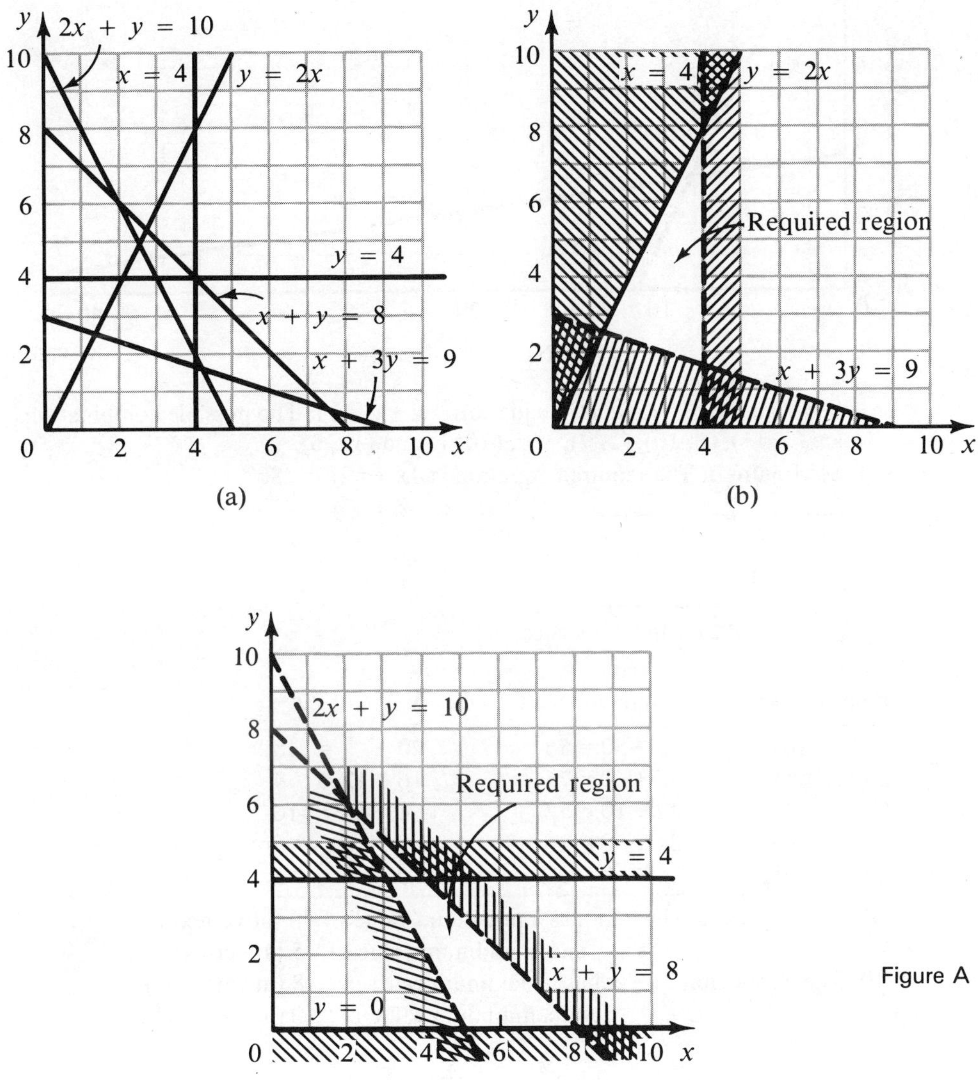

Figure A

2 (a) OA is $y = \frac{1}{2}x$ (or $2y = x$)
BD is $x + y = 3$
PQ (i.e. PE) is $2x + y = 14$
CP is $y = \frac{1}{4}x + 5$ (or $4y = x + 20$, or $x = 4(y - 5)$, etc.)

(b) Using the boundary lines BC, CP, PQ, QR and RB respectively, the unshaded region is
$x > 0$; $4y < x + 20$; $2x + y < 14$; $2y > x$; $x + y > 3$

3 (a) 'The number of vehicles on the ferry is $x + y$.'
(or 'There are $x + y$ vehicles on the ferry', etc.)
(b) 'The maximum number of passengers on the ferry is $4x + 52y$', etc.

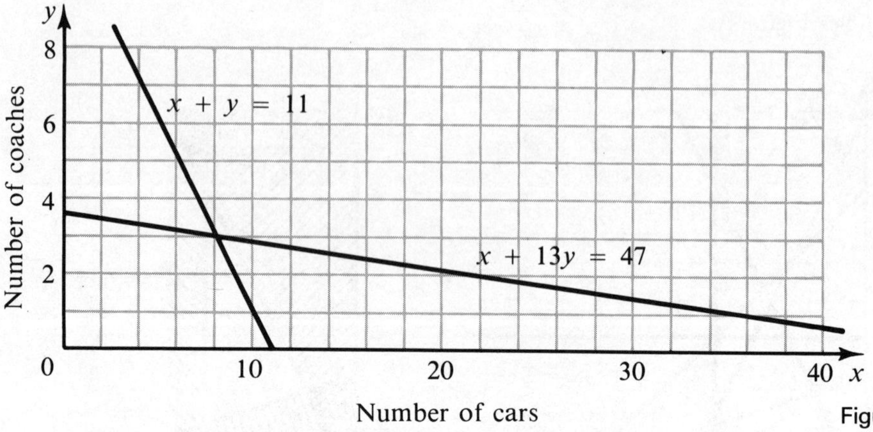

Figure B

(c) See Figure B. The required equation is $x + y = 11$. The possible combinations are (0, 11), (1, 10), (2, 9), . . . , (10, 1) and (11, 0).
(d) See Figure B. The required equation is $4x + 52y = 188$
or $x + 13y = 47$

x	34	21	8
y	1	2	3

(e) (8, 3) i.e. 8 cars and 3 coaches

4

Point (x, y)	Value of $3x + 5y$	Value of $2y - x$
A (2, 10)	$6 + 50 = 56$	$20 - 2 = 18$
B (12, 8)	$36 + 40 = 76$	$16 - 12 = 4$
C (14, 2)	$42 + 10 = 52$	$4 - 14 = {}^{-}10$
D (8, 0)	$24 + 0 = 24$	$0 - 8 = {}^{-}8$
E (5, 0)	$15 + 0 = 15$	$0 - 5 = {}^{-}5$

(a) The expression $3x + 5y$ has a maximum value of 76 (at vertex B), and a minimum value of 15 (at vertex E).
(b) The expression $2y - x$ has a maximum value of 18 (at vertex A), and a minimum value of $^{-}10$ (at vertex C).

5

(a) 3 m^2; 1 m^2; 0.5 m^2; $\frac{x}{140}$ m^2

(b) 6 m^2; 2 m^2; 1 m^2; $\frac{y}{70}$ m^2

(c) $\frac{x}{140} + \frac{y}{70} = 1$ (or $x + 2y = 140$)

(d) $\frac{x}{140} \leqslant \frac{3}{5}$ (or $x \leqslant 84$) and $\frac{y}{70} \leqslant \frac{3}{5}$ (or $y \leqslant 42$)

(e) $8x + 12y \leqslant 1000$ (or $2x + 3y \leqslant 250$)

(f) See Figure C.

$x + 2y = 140$

x	40	60	80	100
y	50	40	30	20

$2x + 3y = 250$

x	50	80	110
y	50	30	10

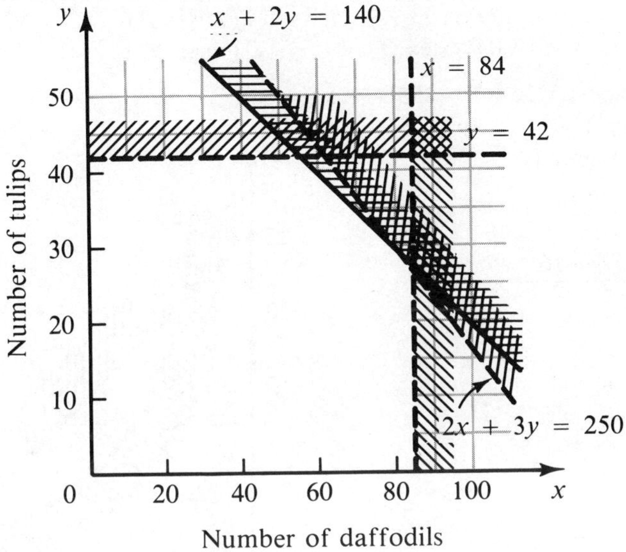

Figure C

Possible combinations must satisfy $x + 2y = 140$; $y \leqslant 42$; $x \leqslant 80$, i.e. (56, 42), (58, 41), (60, 40), . . . (78, 31), (80, 30).
$(x + y)$ is a minimum for (56, 42).
The minimum number of bulbs is $56 + 42 = 98$.

6 Figure D shows the given region.

$2x + y = 8$

x	2	3	4
y	4	2	0

$2x + 5y = 20$

x	0	2.5	5
y	4	3	2

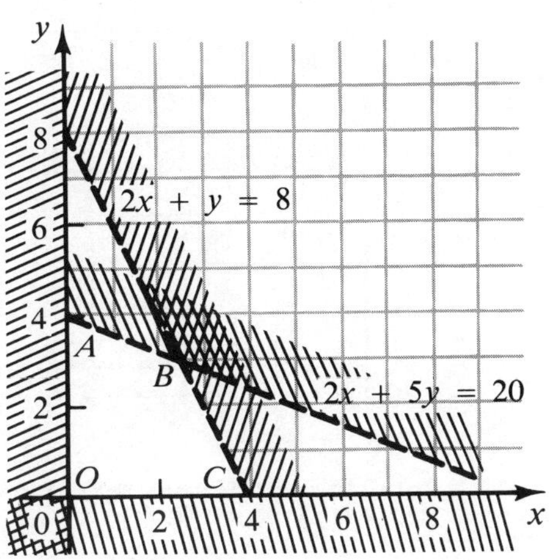

Figure D

Vertex (x, y)	Value of $x + 3y$	Value of $2x + 3y$	Value of $3x - y$
O (0, 0)	0	0	0
A (0, 4)	12	12	$^-4$
B (2.5, 3)	11.5	14	4.5
C (4, 0)	4	8	12
Maximum	12 (vertex A)	14 (vertex B)	12 (vertex C)
Minimum	0 (vertex O)	0 (vertex O)	$^-4$ (vertex A)

7 (a) Perimeter: $2x + 2y \leqslant 50$ (i.e. $x + y \leqslant 25$)
Area: $xy \geqslant 96$

(b) See Figure E.

$xy = 96$

x	4	6	8	10
y	24	16	12	9.6

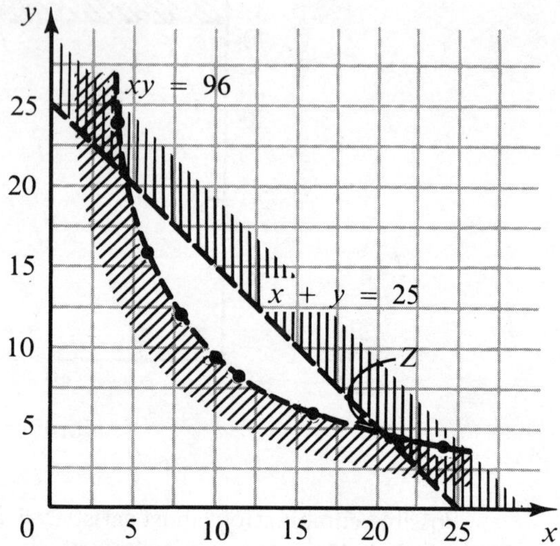

Figure E

The largest integral value for x is 20, shown at Z in Figure E.

Exercise B

1 (a)

t	0	1	2	3	4
p	1	3	9	27	81

(b) See Figure F.

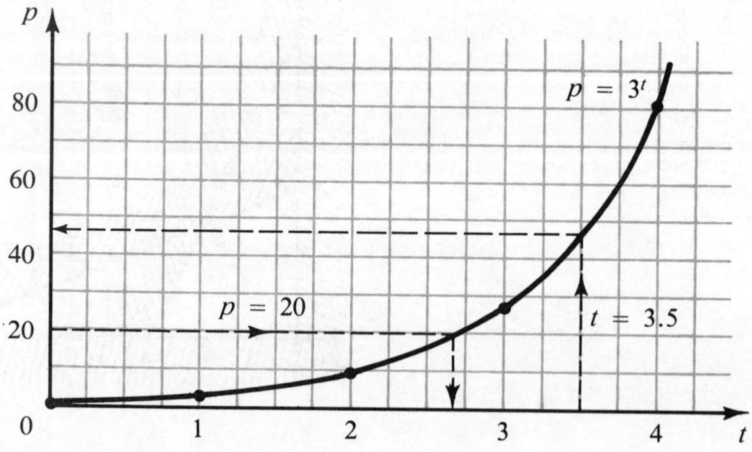

Figure F

(c) When $t = 3.5$ the value of p is approximately 50.
(Since $3^{3.5}$ is the square root of 3^7, $p = \sqrt{(2187)} = 47$ (to 2 s.f.).)

(d) When $p = 20$, the value of t is approximately 2.7. (By calculation, $t = 2.73\ldots$)

2 See Figure G.

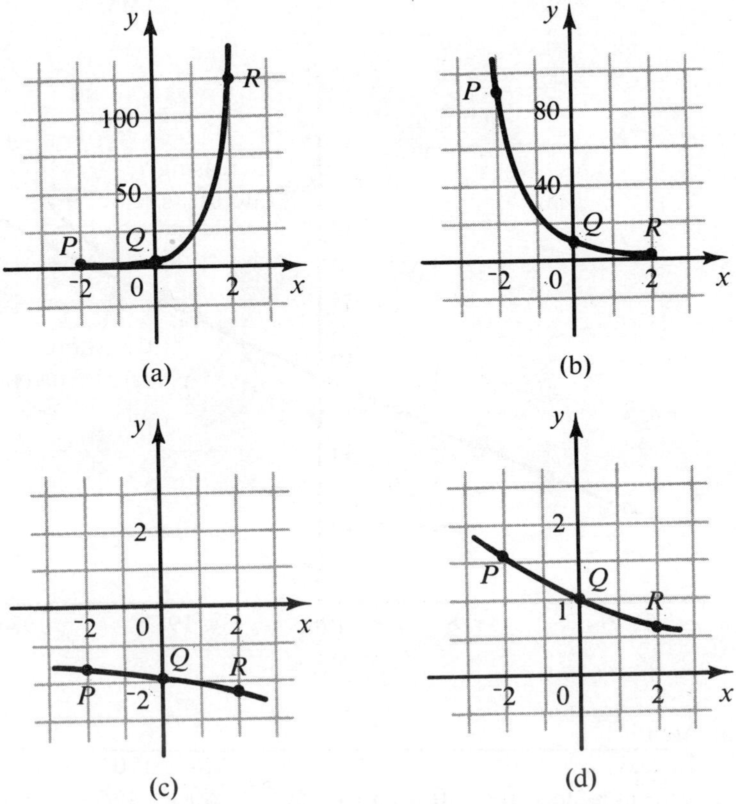

Figure G

	(a) $y = 5 \times 5^x$	(b) $y = 10 \times 3^{-x}$	(c) $y = {}^-2 \times 1.05^x$	(d) $y = 0.8^x$
P	(⁻2, 0.2)	(⁻2, 90)	(⁻2, ⁻1.81)	(⁻2, 1.56)
Q	(0, 5)	(0, 10)	(0, ⁻2)	(0, 1)
R	(2, 125)	(2, 1.1)	(2, ⁻2.21)	(2, 0.64)

3 All the graphs show an exponential function of the form $t \to k \times a^t$. The value of k is given by the y-coordinate of the point where the graph crosses the y-axis. The value of a is best found by reading off the value of y when $t = 1$.
(For example, in (b) $k = 3$; and when $t = 1$, $s = 6$; i.e. $ka = 6$; hence $a = 2$.)
(a) $y = 5^t$ (b) $s = 3 \times 2^t$ (c) $m = 100 \times (0.6)^t$ (d) $A = (1.25)^t$

4 For a constant rate of increase of 4%, the output in the year $1980 + t$ will be $12\,000 \times (1.04)^t$ tonnes.

(a) Putting $t = {}^-3$, the output in 1977 should have been
$12\,000 \times (1.04)^{-3} = 10\,700$ tonnes.

(b) Putting $t = {}^+4$, the estimate for the output in 1984 is
$12\,000 \times (1.04)^4 = 14\,000$ tonnes.

(c) The estimated output for 1981 is 12 000 × 1.04 tonnes;
the estimated output for 1982 is 12 000 × 1.04 × 1.05 tonnes;
the estimated output for 1984 is 12 000 × 1.04 × 1.05 × 1.06 × 1.07 tonnes, or about 14 900 tonnes.

5 See Figure H.

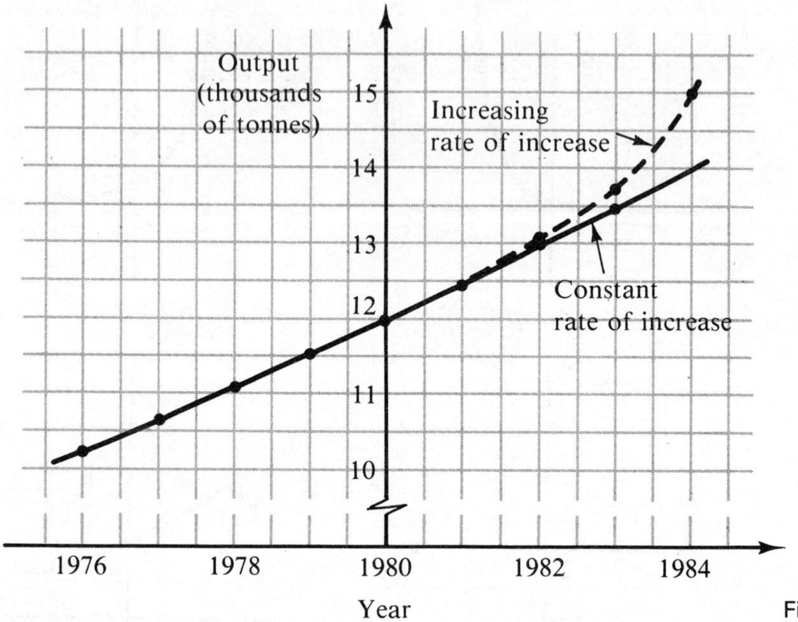

Figure H

6 (a)

Month	2	3	4	5	6
Increase	34	51	76	114	170
Percentage increase	50.7	50.4	50	50	49.7

(b) The number of dandelions is increasing by 50% each month, and so the number at the end of the first month is 150% of the number at the beginning of the month. Hence the number at the beginning of month 1 is $\frac{2}{3} \times 67$, or approximately 45.

(c) $d = 45 \times (1.5)^m$

(d) Putting $m = 12$, $d = 45 \times (1.5)^{12} = 45 \times 130$ (approx.) = 5850.

7 (a)

Year	1976	1977	1978	1979	1980
Decrease on previous year	1440	860	520	310	190
Decrease as a percentage of previous year's total	40	40	40	40	40

In year t (1975 = year 0) the number of deaths (D) is given by $D = 3600 \times (0.60)^t$. On this pattern the number of deaths in future years will be as follows.

Year	1981	1982	1983	1984	1985	1986	1987
Number of deaths	170	100	60	36	22	13	7.8

(b) In 1982 the number of deaths will be about 100. Hence in 1983 the number of deaths will be below 100 for the first time.

(c) The annual number of deaths should be less than 10 (for the first time) in 1987.

8 (a) Simple interest = £(750 × 0.06 × 5) = £225.

(b) The interest on an original sum of £A after 12 years at r% is $\dfrac{£(A \times r \times 12)}{100}$.

If the original sum has doubled, then interest = original amount:

i.e. $\dfrac{(A \times r \times 12)}{100} = A,$

hence $r = 8\frac{1}{3}$ (%).

9 (a) Interest = £400 × 0.09 × 3 = £108. Total value after three years is £508.

(b) Total amount after three years is £400 × $(1.09)^3$ = £518.01.

(c) The interest is compounded monthly at the rate of 0.75% per month. Total amount after 36 months is £400 × $(1.0075)^{36}$ = £523.46.

(d) Interest is compounded daily at a rate of $\dfrac{9}{365}$ % per day for 3 × 365 days.

Total amount is £400 × $\left(1 + \dfrac{9}{36\,500}\right)^{1095}$ = £523.97.

10 (a) Interest is £250 after two years on an original amount of £1000.

The rate of interest is $\dfrac{100 \times £250}{£1000 \times 2}$ % = 12.5%.

(b) Hence

$$\left(1 + \frac{r}{100}\right)^2 = 1.25$$

$$1 + \frac{r}{100} = \sqrt{(1.25)} = 1.118$$

$$r = 11.8\ (\%)$$

(c) $£1250 = £1000 \times \left(1 + \dfrac{r}{1200}\right)^{24}$

$$1 + \frac{r}{1200} = (1.25)^{1/24} = 1.009\,34$$

$$r = 1200 \times 0.009\,34 = 11.2\%$$

11 (a) Interest is the same as the original sum. Hence rate × time = 100.

The time required is $\dfrac{100}{\text{rate}} = \dfrac{100}{6} = 16\frac{2}{3}$ years.

(b) The total amount is twice the original amount (£P).

Hence £$2P$ = £P × $\left(1 + \dfrac{6}{100}\right)^t$,

which gives $(1.06)^t = 2$, or $t = 11.9$ (years).

(c) If t is still the time in years, we now have £$2P$ = £P × $\left(1 + \dfrac{6}{1200}\right)^{12t}$

which gives $(1.005)^{12t} = 2$, or $t = 11.6$ (years).

12 Working in a similar way to question 11 gives

(a) time = $\dfrac{100}{\text{rate}} = 8\frac{1}{3}$ years;

(b) $(1.12)^t = 2$, which gives $t = 6.1$ years;

(c) $(1.01)^{12t} = 2$, which gives $t = 5.8$ years.

Exercise C

1 (a) $4\mathbf{i} + 1\mathbf{j}$ or just $4\mathbf{i} + \mathbf{j}$ (b) $2\mathbf{i} + {}^-3\mathbf{j}$ or $2\mathbf{i} - 3\mathbf{j}$
(c) $0\mathbf{i} + ({}^-5)\mathbf{j}$ or ${}^-5\mathbf{j}$ (d) ${}^-6\mathbf{i} - 6\mathbf{j}$ or ${}^-6(\mathbf{i} + \mathbf{j})$
(e) ${}^-4\mathbf{i} + 4\mathbf{j}$ or $4(\mathbf{j} - \mathbf{i})$

2 Figure I shows **gh**-axes superimposed on the normal **ij**- (or *xy*-) axes.
(a) $2\mathbf{g} + \mathbf{h}$ (b) $\mathbf{g} + 4\mathbf{h}$ (c) $5\mathbf{h}$ (d) ${}^-3\mathbf{g} + 3\mathbf{h}$ (e) ${}^-2\mathbf{g} - 6\mathbf{h}$

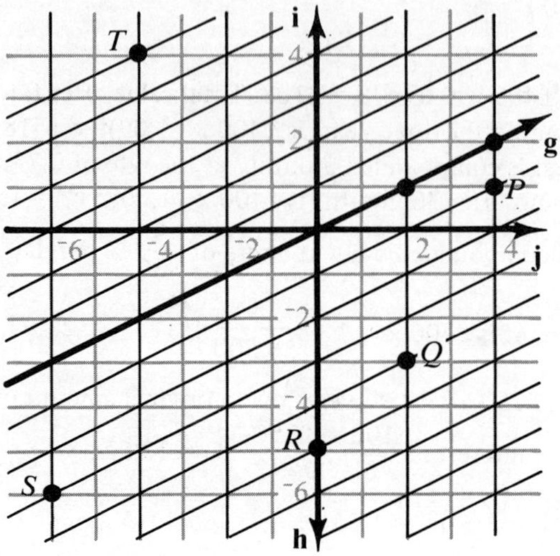

Figure I

3 See Figure J.

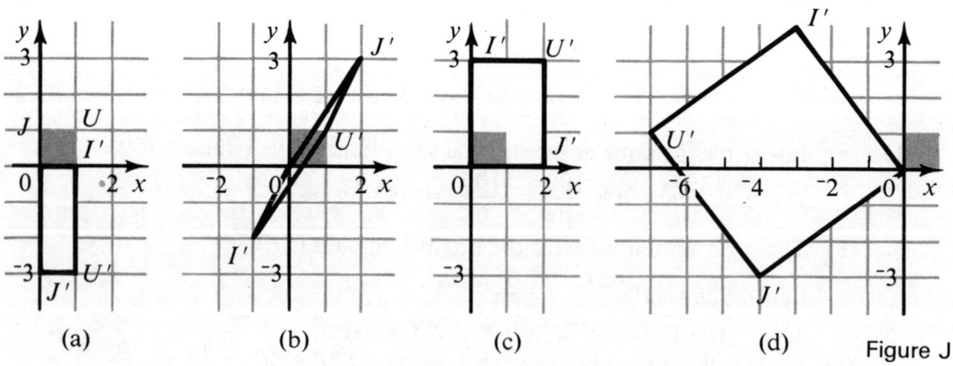

Figure J

4

Images of	(0, 0)	(1, 0)	(1, 1)	(0, 1)
(a)	(0, 0)	(1, 0.5)	(1, 1.5)	(0, 1)
(b)	(0, 0)	(1, 1)	(0, 2)	(⁻1, 1)
(c)	(0, 0)	(⁻0.5, 0)	(⁻0.5, ⁻1)	(0, ⁻1)
(d)	(0, 0)	(0, ⁻1)	(⁻1, ⁻1)	(⁻1, 0)

	Matrix	Transformations
(a)	$\begin{bmatrix} 1 & 0 \\ 0.5 & 1 \end{bmatrix}$	Shear with base line $x = 0$ that maps (1, 1) onto (1, 1.5).
(b)	$\begin{bmatrix} 1 & ^-1 \\ 1 & 1 \end{bmatrix}$	Rotation through 45° combined with an enlargement with scale factor $\sqrt{2}$.
(c)	$\begin{bmatrix} ^-0.5 & 0 \\ 0 & ^-1 \end{bmatrix}$	Two-way stretch from $x = 0$ and $y = 0$ with stretch factors $^-0.5$ and $^-1$.
(d)	$\begin{bmatrix} 0 & ^-1 \\ ^-1 & 0 \end{bmatrix}$	Reflection in the line $x + y = 0$.

5

	Determinant	Area factor	Transformation
(a)	$1 \times {}^-3 - 0 \times 0 = {}^-3$	$^-3$	One-way stretch from the line $y = 0$ with stretch factor $^-3$.
(b)	$^-1 \times 3 - 2 \times {}^-2 = 1$	1	Shear, with base line $y = x$, such that the image of (0, 1) is (2, 3).
(c)	$0 \times 0 - 2 \times 3 = {}^-6$	$^-6$	Reflection in $y = x$, followed by a two-way stretch from the x- and y-axes with stretch factors of 3 and 2.
(d)	$^-3 \times {}^-3 - {}^-4 \times 4 = 25$	25	An enlargement, scale factor 5, combined with a rotation of 127° about the origin.

6 See Figure K.

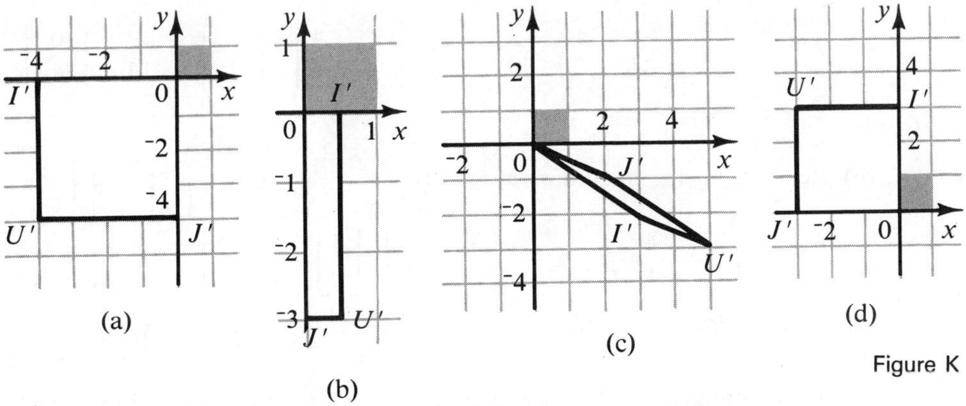

Figure K

7 The columns of the matrix for a transformation are the position vectors of the images of the vertices $I(1, 0)$ and $J(0, 1)$ of the unit square. See Figure K.

(a) $\begin{bmatrix} ^-4 & 0 \\ 0 & ^-4 \end{bmatrix}$ (b) $\begin{bmatrix} 0.5 & 0 \\ 0 & ^-3 \end{bmatrix}$ (c) $\begin{bmatrix} 3 & 2 \\ ^-2 & ^-1 \end{bmatrix}$ (d) $\begin{bmatrix} 0 & ^-3 \\ 3 & 0 \end{bmatrix}$

8 See Figure L.

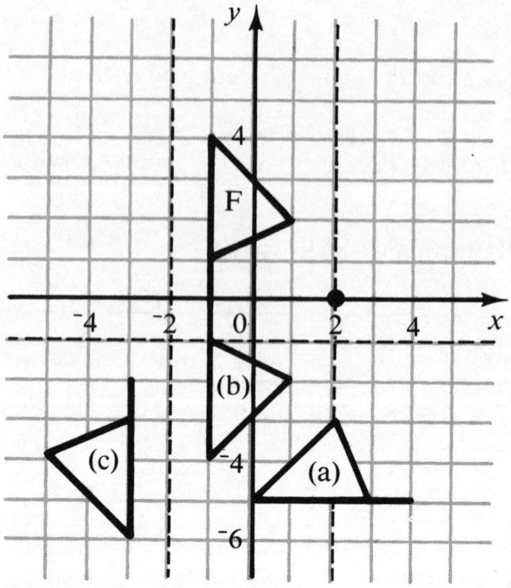

Figure L

(a) A quarter-turn about the point (4, 0)
(b) Reflection in the line $y = 0$ (the x-axis)
(c) A half-turn about the point $(^-2, {}^-1)$

9 Express each pair of equations in the matrix form $\mathbf{Ax} = \mathbf{b}$.
The solution is then given by $\mathbf{x} = \mathbf{A}^{-1}\mathbf{b}$ – unless the determinant of $\mathbf{A}$ is 0.

(a) $\mathbf{A} = \begin{bmatrix} 2 & ^-1 \\ 4 & 5 \end{bmatrix}$ Determinant of $\mathbf{A} = 2 \times 5 - (^-1) \times 4 = 14$

$\mathbf{A}^{-1} = \frac{1}{14}\begin{bmatrix} 5 & 1 \\ ^-4 & 2 \end{bmatrix}$; $\mathbf{x} = \frac{1}{14}\begin{bmatrix} 5 & 1 \\ ^-4 & 2 \end{bmatrix}\begin{bmatrix} 3 \\ ^-15 \end{bmatrix} = \frac{1}{14}\begin{bmatrix} 0 \\ ^-42 \end{bmatrix}$

$x = 0$
$y = {}^-3$

(b) Re-arranging the equations as $^-x + 4y = 4$, $^-x + 3y = 0$ gives $\mathbf{A} = \begin{bmatrix} ^-1 & 4 \\ ^-1 & 3 \end{bmatrix}$.

$\mathbf{A}^{-1} = \begin{bmatrix} 3 & ^-4 \\ 1 & ^-1 \end{bmatrix}$; $\mathbf{x} = \begin{bmatrix} 3 & ^-4 \\ 1 & ^-1 \end{bmatrix}\begin{bmatrix} 4 \\ 0 \end{bmatrix} = \begin{bmatrix} 12 \\ 4 \end{bmatrix}$ $x = 12$, $y = 4$

(c) Re-arranging the second equation as $^-9x + 15y = {}^-18$ gives $\mathbf{A} = \begin{bmatrix} ^-3 & 5 \\ ^-9 & 15 \end{bmatrix}$.

The determinant of **A** is zero, and hence there is not a unique solution; and since the second equation is not a multiple of the first, there is no solution.

10 (i) {(a), (f), (h)} (ii) {(b), (c), (e)} (iii) {(d), (g)}

11 See Figure M. (There are many possibilities for (a).)

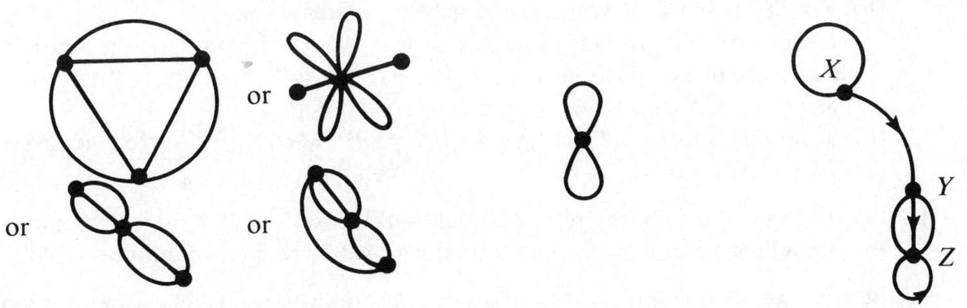

(a) (b) (c)

Figure M

12 Euler's relation is satisfied if nodes − arcs + regions = 2.

(a) (i) 4 nodes, 5 arcs, 3 regions

(ii) $\mathbf{M} = \begin{bmatrix} 2 & 2 & 0 & 0 \\ 2 & 0 & 1 & 1 \\ 0 & 1 & 0 & 0 \\ 0 & 1 & 0 & 0 \end{bmatrix}$

(iii) $\mathbf{M}^2 = \begin{bmatrix} 8 & 4 & 2 & 2 \\ 4 & 6 & 0 & 0 \\ 2 & 0 & 1 & 1 \\ 2 & 0 & 1 & 1 \end{bmatrix}$

(b) (i) 5 nodes, 8 arcs, 5 regions

(ii) $\mathbf{M} = \begin{bmatrix} 0 & 1 & 2 & 1 & 0 \\ 1 & 0 & 0 & 2 & 0 \\ 2 & 0 & 0 & 1 & 0 \\ 1 & 2 & 1 & 0 & 1 \\ 0 & 0 & 0 & 1 & 0 \end{bmatrix}$

(iii) $\mathbf{M}^2 = \begin{bmatrix} 6 & 2 & 1 & 4 & 1 \\ 2 & 5 & 4 & 1 & 2 \\ 1 & 4 & 5 & 2 & 1 \\ 4 & 1 & 2 & 7 & 0 \\ 1 & 2 & 1 & 0 & 1 \end{bmatrix}$

13

$\mathbf{T} = \begin{array}{c} \\ A \\ B \\ P \\ Q \end{array}\begin{array}{c} \begin{array}{ccc} x & y & z \end{array} \\ \begin{bmatrix} 2 & 1 & 1 \\ 3 & 0 & 1 \\ 1 & 0 & 0 \\ 1 & 0 & 0 \end{bmatrix} \end{array}$ $\quad \mathbf{V} = \begin{array}{c} \\ x \\ y \\ z \end{array}\begin{array}{c} \begin{array}{ccccc} 1 & 2 & 3 & 4 & 5 \end{array} \\ \begin{bmatrix} 1 & 1 & 1 & 2 & 2 \\ 1 & 0 & 0 & 0 & 0 \\ 0 & 1 & 1 & 0 & 0 \end{bmatrix} \end{array}$ $\quad \mathbf{TV} = \begin{array}{c} \\ A \\ B \\ P \\ Q \end{array}\begin{array}{c} \begin{array}{ccccc} 1 & 2 & 3 & 4 & 5 \end{array} \\ \begin{bmatrix} 3 & 3 & 3 & 4 & 4 \\ 3 & 4 & 4 & 6 & 6 \\ 1 & 1 & 1 & 2 & 2 \\ 1 & 1 & 1 & 2 & 2 \end{bmatrix} \end{array}$

The product **TV** states the number of ways of going from a particular node onto a particular arc via the adjacent regions.

Exercise D

1 (a) $CP^2 = OP^2 - OC^2 = (144 - 64)\text{ cm}^2 = 80\text{ cm}^2$. $CP = 8.94$ cm
$NP^2 = CP^2 + CN^2 = (80 + 16)\text{ cm}^2 = 96\text{ cm}^2$. $NP = 9.80$ cm

(or: $\cos PON = \frac{8}{12}$; angle $PON = 48.2°$; $PN = 2 \times 12 \times \sin 24.1°$)
Angle $EOP = 90° -$ angle $NOP = 41.8°$
Angle $ONP = \frac{1}{2}(180° -$ angle $NOP) = 69.1°$

(b) Angle CPO = angle EOP; $CP = OP \times \cos CPO = 12 \times \cos 52°$ cm = 7.39 cm
Circumference of Small Circle = $2 \times \pi \times 7.39$ cm = 46.4 cm.

2 (a) (12°S, 135°W) (b) (32°N, 180°) (c) (88°N, 68°E)

3 (a) Travelling along the 66° E meridian across the equator, the angle at the centre of the Earth is $(25 + 38)° = 63°$;
and so the distance travelled = 63×60 nautical miles = 3780 n.m.

(b) The 66° E and 114° W meridians make up a Great Circle;
the shorter route from F along this circle is over the equator and the South Pole.
The angle turned through is $25^\circ + (180-38)^\circ = 167^\circ$,
and so the distance is 167×60 n.m. = 10 020 n.m.

(c) Travelling west from P an angle of $(180-99)^\circ + (180-99)^\circ = 162^\circ$ is covered;
i.e. a distance of 162×60 n.m. = 9720 n.m.

4 (a) 100° along the 45° S circle of latitude = $100 \cos 45^\circ \times 60$ n.m. = 4240 n.m.

(b) Travelling either east or west, 180° along the 80° N circle of latitude = 1880 n.m.

5 Between any two points on the surface of a sphere the Great Circle distance is shorter than any non-Great Circle distance. In this instance the Great Circle distance is 20×60 n.m. = 1200 n.m. (less than two-thirds of the circle of latitude distance).

6 (a) If 12 satellites form a ring, then angle $SOS_1 = (360/12)^\circ = 30^\circ$, and angle $SOT = 15^\circ$.

Hence $OS \times \cos 15^\circ = OT$;

$$OS = \frac{OT}{\cos 15^\circ} = 6595 \text{ km};$$

and $SN = (6595 - 6370)$ km = 225 km (approx.).

(b) If $SN = 2640$ km, then $OS = 9010$ km.

$$\cos SOT = \frac{OT}{OS} = \frac{6370}{9010};$$

angle $SOT = 45^\circ$

At this height, four satellites will be needed to circle the earth.

7 (a) The centre of the circle is the point Q on ON such that S_1QO is a right-angle.
Radius = $S_1O \times \sin S_1OQ = SO \times \sin 30^\circ = (6595 \times \sin 30^\circ)$ km = 3300 km.
Circumference = $(2 \times \pi \times 3300)$ km = 20 700 km (3 s.f.)

(b) The speed, relative to the Earth, is (20 700/1.5) km/h = 13 800 km/h;
or 14 000 km/h (2 s.f.).

8

Plane	$OAFB$	$OAEC$	$ABDE$	$OCUF$	$AEUF$
Projection of D	B	C	D	P	U
Projection of CF	OF	CA	PQ	CF	EF

9 $A(2, 0, 0)$, $C(0, 0, 2)$, $D(0, 2, 2)$, $P(1, 1, 2)$, $Q(1, 1, 0)$, $U(2, 2, 2)$

(a)	Plane	$OAEC$	$OCUF$	$BDUF$	$ABDE$	$ACDF$
(b)	Equation	$y = 0$	$y = x$	$y = 2$	$x + y = 2$	$x + z = 2$

10 (a) $AM = OM = 5$ cm, $AO = \sqrt{50}$ (or $5\sqrt{2}$) cm = 7.07 cm
($ABCD$ is a square of side 10 cm.)
$AV^2 = AO^2 + OV^2 = (50 + 144)$ cm^2 = 194 cm^2; $AV = 13.9$ cm
The length of MV can be found from either triangle AMV or triangle OMV.
Triangle OMV will give a more accurate answer as we know OV 'exactly'.
Applying Pythagoras' theorem to this triangle gives $MV = 13$ cm.

(b) Angle ABV = angle BAV = angle MAV;
$\tan MAV = MV/AM = 13/5 = 2.6$; angle ABV (angle MAV) = 69.0°

(c) The required angle is OMV. Tan $OMV = 12/5 = 2.4$; angle $OMV = 67.4^\circ$

(d) The required angle is OAV. Tan $OAV = 12/7.07 = 1.70$; angle $OAV = 59.5^\circ$

(e) $AP = AB \times \sin ABV = 10 \times \sin 69.0^\circ$ cm $= 9.34$ cm.
$AC = 2 \times AO = 14.1$ cm.

(f) The required angle is APC.
By symmetry, $AP = CP$, and so angle $APC = 2 \times$ angle APO.
Angle AOP is a right-angle, and so $\sin APO = AO/AP = 7.07/9.34$.
Hence angle $APO = 49.2^\circ$, and the angle between the faces ABV and CBV is 98.4°.